"Intelligence" vs. Common Sense

US and Israeli Intelligence Services and the "Not-So-Deep" State

BY AVINOAM SAPIR

"Intelligence" vs. Common Sense:
US and Israeli Intelligence Services
and the "Not-So-Deep" State
By Avinoam Sapir

Published by the Laboratory For Scientific Interrogation
P.O.Box 17286
Phoenix, Arizona, USA
Email: info@LSISCAN.com
www.LSISCAN.com

Printed in Israel

ISBN: 978-965-572-784-5

"...if the people of the land take a man from among them, and set him for their watchman… if the watchman see the sword come, and blow not the horn, and the people be not warned, and the sword do come, and take any person from among them... his blood will I require at the watchman's hand." (Ezekiel 33:2,6)

This book is dedicated to Yoel Ben-Porat
and all those who "sounded the horn".

About the author – Avinoam Sapir

Avinoam Sapir served in the Israeli Military Intelligence Unit 8200 (SIGINT).   He holds a B.A. in both Psychology and Criminology, and an M.A. in Criminology. His M.A. thesis was on "Interrogation in Jewish Law".

Mr Sapir worked as a polygraph examiner in the Israeli Police Department, and as a polygraph examiner in the private sector.

During the past few decades, Mr Sapir has conducted training in interviewing for various government agencies in Israel, the US, Canada, and several other countries around the world.

He developed the SCAN technique by conducting extensive research into verbal communication, looking into the linguistic behavior used by people in communication. SCAN (Scientific Content Analysis) analyzes a text or statement strictly according to the words used. The SCAN technique is currently being used in many police departments and other government agencies in many countries.

Mr Sapir's first book, "Linguistic Archeology", analyzes the text of the book of Genesis, as a demonstration of the use of SCAN in analyzing an ancient text. The book was published in Hebrew in Israel with the title "What Does the Bible Conceal?"

Mr Sapir and his wife have 3 children and several grandchildren. They divide their time between the US and Israel.

-

Intelligence or Information – Definition

In the Hebrew language, every word has a three-letter root, from which various derivatives create different words with closely-related meanings.

One of the derivatives of the root meaning "to know" is "mo-di-in", which stands for both "Information" (at the airport or central bus station) or "Intelligence" as in "Military Intelligence".

It is interesting to note that there is a saying in the US that "military intelligence" is an oxymoron, or in Hebrew "a contradiction within itself". There is a saying in Israel that "where military starts, logic ends".

Language-wise, it is a point to realize that the framers of the Israeli military did not want to call the Intelligence as such (e.g. with a derivative of the root for "wisdom"), but preferred to find a derivative of the word "information". After all, the "intelligence" provides information.

Table of Contents

Introduction

This book analyzes the memoirs published by high-ranking Intelligence personnel from the US and Israel. It includes a lot of information that even the writers of the memoirs did not realize they were revealing. The analysis uses the SCAN technique (Scientific Content Analysis) which I developed while teaching classes on interviewing and interrogation. (I have described the main principles of SCAN in an appendix, for anyone who is not yet familiar with the technique.)

Books by nature are classified by Intelligence as "open sources", just like interviews in newspapers or magazines. After all, once a book has been published, it is accessible by all. It is not a "secret". Moreover, the writer cannot retract it. It is in print.

One might think that the SCAN rule of "Everyone wants to give every information to everyone" would not apply to members of the Intelligence Community (i.e. personnel of intelligence agencies), since they come from a culture of keeping secrets. Personally, when I started to analyze (not just to "read") these books, I didn't expect to find so much information. The assumption would be that a person who is so trusted to keep secrets, might not be as open to revealing information as the average person in society. But the fact is that a book can and does expose a lot.

At times, people ask me during my class if one can really analyze a book. After all, we should not disregard the fact that a "book editor" is involved in the production of a book, and in some memoirs the name of a co-author is mentioned openly on the cover.

Moreover, as Michael Hayden, former Director of both NSA and CIA, mentions in his book – anything he writes needs to go through a process of approval by the government, to make sure that as a former government employee, he does not expose any secrets. And his books did go through that process. So why do his books still expose so much secret information?

It came to a point where I realized that the books were exposing information that could quite likely endanger US national security, as the books **imply** the methods and techniques used by the intelligence services to conduct their job. At this point, I decided not to include that type of information in this book. It is not my intention to publicize hazardous information. I still have the responsibility to keep secrets, unlike the writers of the above-mentioned memoirs.

But perhaps they didn't even realize what they were doing. After all, another SCAN rule states that "the subject is dead, the statement is alive." This means that it doesn't matter what the person **wanted** to say. What matters is only what the person **actually said**.

As I discuss it in my class, once a person starts talking or writing, within a few sentences the person loses control over the text. In a way, we can say that the person "does not write the text". The text writes itself.

The objective in this book is to present the information to the reader about US politics and US society, and to let the reader realize for himself/herself what is going on at the moment.   The hot topic today is the allegation that there was Russian interference in the 2016 elections, and possibly even collusion between the Russian effort and the Trump campaign.

The reader will also encounter several characteristics that are unique to American society, and a comparison to Israeli society. These points come across very easily in the text.

Let the text speak for itself!

Presidential Elections of 2016

James Clapper says in his book that once he heard of the elections results, "I was surprised…" (JC 1). He also adds that "…*Everyone* was shocked, including Mr. Trump…" (JC 1-2). If this not enough, Clapper returns to the same point towards the end of his book, saying, "…On Election Day, November 8, no one really believed Mr. Trump had a chance…" (JC 356). Michael Hayden, in his book, adds, "After all, foreign capitals were as surprised **as most of us** at the election's outcome." (MH2 – 134)

Clapper and foreign capitals were not the only ones to be surprised. President Obama was in shock as well. Ben Rhodes, in his memoir "The World as It Is, A Memoir of the Obama White House", brings us the following conversation that President Obama had with him after the election.

> "What if we were wrong?" Obama said…
>
> "Wrong about what?" I asked.
>
> For days, we had been trying to deconstruct what had happened in the recent election. Obama had complained **he couldn't believe that the election was lost**…"

Clapper explains his surprise as due to the fact that the intelligence "…capabilities were oriented outward toward the threat and largely incapable of looking inward, even if we wanted to." (JC – 3). He repeats the same point towards the end of his book, saying, "…our professional attention as intelligence officers was always turned outward to understanding the world and helping policy makers work to make it safer." (JC 289).

But this is not the only reason explaining why the intelligence experts did not read the US correctly. Hayden in his book talks about his "internationalist mind" (MH2 119). He explains it by saying, "American intelligence professionals, through a process of self-selection and acculturation, much like their diplomatic counterparts, trend overwhelmingly internationalist." (MH2 21)

Hayden even mentions a term being used in the intelligence "culture" – "OCONUS (outside the continental United States)" relating to people who "…live a good portion of their adult lives" outside the US.

Hayden says, "My personal experience was **longer than most**… …some thirty-nine years, much of it lived abroad on Guam, in Korea (twice), Germany, and even in Communist Bulgaria." (MH2 - 21-22)

Back to Clapper

What was the basis of Clapper's assumptions, that brought him to be in shock by the results of the elections? Clapper explains it by saying, "**According to polls**, he [meaning Trump] was far behind Clinton before the release of the *Access Hollywood* tape **and had since fallen further still**" (JC 354).

The bottom line is that Clapper based himself upon the polls.

Reliability of US Polls

In the Israeli military, when an officer is rating anyone under him, the form calls for the officer's commander to rate the same officer. Is he strict, or is he lenient? After all, if a very strict officer rates a soldier as "medium", it might mean that a very lenient officer might rate that same soldier very highly.

So, how should we rate the polls in the US? Are they reliable? And if they are, to what degree? Even the pollsters tell us that the polls have a margin of error. But does this margin enable us to reach a conclusion?

Tuvia Tenenbom, a journalist in Germany, was contracted by the newspaper Der Spiegel to travel around the United States and interview people who were sitting at small-town diners, to get their views of the US. In his book, which was also published in the US in English as "Lies People Tell", Tenenbom shares with his readers his experiences going all over the US from east to west, going into diners in small towns, as well as the inner city (Chicago). He talked with law-abiding citizens and with residents of drug-infested neighborhoods.

The main finding in his field research was that whenever he started a conversation with someone, at first the person would give him the regular "mantra" that is so often mentioned in the news media, of brotherhood and love between people, talking about civil rights, etc. But each time, and with no exception, once he told the person (or persons, in case of couples) that he was a journalist from Germany, and he wanted to know what they really think, the person(s) opened up and told him their true opinions.

The bottom line coming out of this field research, which covered the US from east to west and north to south, is that people do not feel free to share with strangers their true opinions and feelings about what is going on in their mind. In other words - they lie.

The only question is: what is the percentage of people who feel obligated to lie to a stranger about their true political views? If Tenenbom's results reflect the overall trend in American society (and this is a major "IF"), then no poll in the US can be accepted as reliable, due to the percentage of people who lie. And even if Tenenbom is wrong, and not **everyone** is lying, we would still have to say that a large percentage do lie. Is it 10%? 15%? or even 20%?

Back to Clapper

When Clappers says, "**According to polls**, he [Trump] was far behind Clinton before the release of the *Access Hollywood* tape **and had since fallen further still**" (JC 354), Clapper as an "intelligence officer" should **not** have reached the conclusion that this is reality. He should have reminded himself that it is only "according to the polls..."

This means that it is just one source of information, and the results should be accepted only after being corroborated by another source of information; and even then only after the two sources had been rated for reliability.

And when Clapper says that after the "Access Hollywood tape" Trump "had since fallen further" in the polls, in retrospect we must realize that once Trump behaved and talked more and more contradictory to the politically-correct environment (e.g., as in the "Access Hollywood" tape, or when he criticized the Gold Star family that had criticized him), that people had simply started to lie even more. After all, how can they defend someone who talks about women in such a way? How can they defend someone who goes against a family who lost their son in battle, even if they criticized him? The people who wanted to vote for Trump due to his policies, in spite of his personality and style, had to go "under cover" and simply lie about their opinion.

Back to lying in the polls

I can share with the reader that when I read the last poll a few days before the elections, the poll that stated that Trump is trailing Clinton by 4%, I told myself that this is a great opportunity to find out if Tenenbom is right. If his results are accurate, Clinton is going to lose with this 4% margin. In order to win, Clinton - the epitome of the politically correct environment - had to be at least 20% above Trump to offset the "lying component" of the polls. And Tenenbom was right; as a result, I was not shocked as Clapper was.

Another mistake of Clapper

Clapper was mistaken, not only by basing himself upon the polls. There is another mistake that Clapper made, and since he was a veteran "intelligence officer", it is amazing that he made such a mistake. Clapper himself outlines to his readers his own mistake.

In another place in his book, not relating to the US, Clapper coined a new term: "unpredictable instability". This is a situation that brought "…pain, war, and suffering to the world…" (JC 357). This coined term relates to the fact that economical conditions (poverty and unemployment) along with lack of opportunities bring "instability". These are the conditions that brought the "Arab Spring" to the Middle East.

[As a personal note I am not that sure that economy brings war to the world. I know it is quite accepted by the news media and academia, but the fact is that there are many poor countries in the world that do not attack the US, and they do not rebel against their autocratic regimes.]

But according to Clapper this "unpredictable instability" explains a lot of what is going on in the world. And if so, why didn't he connect the dots? In fact, he does say the following:

"…the same electorate that had been showing signs of political and social instability for years…" (JC 350), and "…people whose jobs had evaporated in the recession…" could not relate to "…progressive ideas about valuing diversity in race, gender, sexual orientation, and religious expression…" (JC 326)

Clapper goes on to say that "…Donald Trump understood this anger as well as anyone in American politics…" If we have any doubt where this anger was directed, Clapper explains, "that no one incited this anger more than Barack Obama… …he was seen… as smug, overly educated liberal… cerebral… When in April 2011 President Obama was heard on tape talking about people who 'cling to guns and religion,' rural America heard that as mocking them behind their backs." (JC 326-327).

President Obama himself campaigned strongly against Donald Trump, even though the one who was running for office was Hillary Clinton. Clapper says that President Obama was the main factor that helped Donald Trump to be elected in "rural America", and by people who "cling to guns and religion".

In fact, there were polls that showed that 80% of the population believed that the country was going the wrong way. In other words, when the poll didn't discuss "people" but discussed "policies", the vast majority of the population felt that something was wrong. In reporting the various polls stating the same, it was said that respondents couldn't put their finger on what was wrong, but they still felt that the country was going the wrong way.

So why does Clapper start and end his book by professing shock on Donald Trump's success, if he himself brings us the reasons for such success?

Conclusion

We are witnessing a veteran high-ranking intelligence officer who has the data in front of him; but even with his knowledge of the right and correct data, he reached a wrong conclusion, that brought him to be surprised by the results of the election.

In his favor, we can say that he is not geared to look "inward" but "outward". But the fact is that he produced a very detailed analysis showing that the US suffered from the same phrase he coined:

"unpredictable instability". Maybe he should have called it "predictable instability".

Is this the only mistake that was reached by US intelligence officers?

CIA Report on Israeli Intelligence Community

Introduction

When the Iranians raided the American embassy in Teheran and took the US personnel there as hostages, they also took possession of many documents, some of them secret and even top secret. The Iranian regime, aiming to embarrass the US, decided to publish these documents. Among these documents there was one that was classified as "secret" and included a survey by the CIA of the Israeli Intelligence Community.

There was one journalist in Israel, focusing on intelligence matters, who took upon himself to translate this document into Hebrew. The translator and editor of the Hebrew version commented: "…the author uses professional words from the intelligence world and idioms commonly used in CIA documents…" Still, the translator puts the reader on alert that he cannot vouch for the accuracy of the report: "…and if we accept the assumption of several intelligence experts that the report is authentic and not a work of fraud and forgery, it enables us to see the structure of the [Israeli intelligence] community with all its organizations."

The Report

There are several fundamental mistakes in this report, and here the mistakes will be outlined:

First, the report starts by saying that the Israeli Intelligence Community is organized under the umbrella of the "The Committee of the Heads of the Services".

Although such a committee does exist, it is incorrect to say that this committee is a structure under which all the services are organized. This is more of an American way of looking at things, than an actual way that things are done in Israel.

The committee mentioned in this report would be more of a venue for the heads of the services to meet and to "sit around the camp fire" (an Israeli expression of soldiers sitting together passing time). The committee does not yield any authority or power over the entire community.

This does not mean that the services do not work in unison. They do. Especially in the anti-terrorism activities, there are reports that the military works in harmony with the General Security Services. And whenever there is a need for an operation in a hostile environment, like the operation in which Israel raided the city of Beirut in Lebanon to reach the heads of terror who had killed the eleven Israeli athletes in the Olympics in Germany, the military and the Mossad operated together.

But to come and say that the services operate under some Chief coordinating their operation would be a mistake. Maybe the CIA should have read the book written by Zbigniew Brzeszinski, who was National Security Adviser to President Carter, and who accurately compared the Israeli delegation at Camp David with the American delegation.

"Although Israel enjoyed the advantage of having the clearest and most precise goals, it suffered from having the **least cohesive** negotiating team. They were, in a word, **prima donnas**… … bickering Israeli team" (Pages 237-238).

On the other hand, "The American delegation was remarkably united… … and a well-orchestrated, **tactically effective** but **strategically somewhat ambivalent** American side." (Page 239)

In other words, the US has a "Commander in Chief", while Israel does not. Although the Americans tend to look at the Israeli Prime Minister as equivalent to the US President, they tend to neglect the fact that the Israeli government is always a coalition government, created by combination of several parties. The prime minister is the head of the largest party, but he is not in charge of the ministries that are headed by his coalition partners. The Prime Minister has the authority to fire a minister, but if he/she would exercise this right, the party of the fired minister would leave the coalition, and the prime minister might not be prime minister anymore.

Till 1973 the law in Israel did not specify who is the "commander of chief" of the military. After the 1973 war, the Knesset (Parliament) legislated that the government as a whole is the "commander of chief". This means that a committee of 23 people is conducting the war. It didn't take long to realize that this is not a solution, and today there is a small "cabinet" of eight ministers authorized by the government to be the "commander in chief". Later on, they even went to arrange for a "mini-cabinet" of 3 people.

Zbigniew Brzeszinski was very right in his observation of Israeli ministers as being "prima donnas". The same applies to the entire Israeli Intelligence Community, and to the entire Israeli society.

There is a well-known joke from the time of the early state, in which the Israeli President (who is a figurehead, similar in this respect to the queen in England) met the US President. The US President told his Israeli counterpart that it is not easy to be a president of 250 million people. The Israeli President replied that his American counterpart has an easy job. He, the Israeli President, must deal with 3 million presidents.

What do we know of the Committee of Heads of Services?

The former Chief of the General Security Service (GSS), Carmi Gilon (who was removed from his job after the murder of Prime Minister Rabin) gives us a description in his book of the work of this committee. (Note: the GSS is also known by its Hebrew acronym as Shabak or Shin-Beth.)

According to him, the committee is convened once a month at the office of the Chief of the Mossad., although the Chief of the Mossad cannot dictate the agenda, which is decided by all participants. The Chief of the Mossad does not even have the authority to remove an item from the agenda.

As a matter of fact, the Chief of the GSS even disputes the priority of the Chief of the Mossad. According to him, the Chief of the Military Intelligence should chair the meetings since by law he is the "National Assessor".

There are no votes in the meetings, and if there is a dispute between the chiefs of the different services, this dispute is brought before the Prime Minister. And in fact, the three chiefs do not need to approach the prime minister with this dispute, since the military secretary of the prime minister is present in all of these meetings, as an observer. Due to the informal atmosphere ruling in Israel, this observer can participate in the discussions and express his opinions.

The Chief of the GSS comments that these meetings are not necessary for anyone in the field in any particular service to call his equivalent-in-rank counterpart in another service and discuss a certain point together. Only when there is no agreement, that issue will be brought to the Chiefs in their meetings.

In summary, Zbigniew Brzeszinski was right in his observation of the Israeli high echelons as being "prima donnas". There is no way that one service would be in charge of another. Not even in this committee. And to look upon this committee, that convenes once a month, as if it is in charge of the Israeli Intelligence Community, would be a gross misrepresentation.

The second mistake

It is understood that a report written by the CIA will perceive the Israeli equivalent of the CIA (the overseas intelligence service) as the most important service, and as such the report would list the Mossad first.

Both James Clapper, who served as Director of National Intelligence, and Michael Hayden, who served as Director of NSA and then CIA, list the US intelligence services in their books, and they perceive the CIA, the NSA, and the NRO (satellites) as the major organizations. They list the military intelligence services as being much lower in importance.

This is not the case in Israel. Since Israel is a very small country, and has been threatened since its establishment by Arab countries who declared that their goal is to annihilate the country (although nowadays this is changing somewhat), the military intelligence is the dominant service in the community. It is in charge of presenting the national intelligence assessment, and is in charge of producing the warning for any upcoming war.

Moreover, although the CIA report accurately states that the Chief of Intelligence is under the Chief of Staff of the military, it would be a gross mistake to think of this officer as only a general in the military.

The Israeli Chief of Military Intelligence sits in the weekly government sessions (every Sunday), to provide the government ministers with updated intelligence. The military chief of intelligence meets the prime minister periodically, and several reports written by former chiefs testify to this. In some cases they have even advised the Prime Minister with options of how to respond. The same Chief is also an advisor to the parliament, and he appears in the sessions of the Foreign Affairs and Defense Committee of the Parliament, reporting to the members on the intelligence picture.

The Chief of Military Intelligence is a 2-star general. (The highest rank in the Israeli military – the Chief of Staff – is a 3-star general.) This Chief of Intelligence is so dominant, that in fact he has a one-star general under him to head the Intelligence branch, running the daily operation. After all, it would not be easy for the Chief of Intelligence to meet the Prime Minister, the government, and the parliament, and still have the time to run the operation.

The bottom line is that the Mossad is not the dominant intelligence service in Israel. Although the Mossad, structurally, is directly under the Prime Minister, its military counterpart is much more dominant internally.

After the 1973 war the commission of inquiry, investigating the failures of intelligence, recommended that the Mossad would establish its own assessment branch, to produce its own assessment of the threats against the state. But in fact, the military intelligence is still the "big guy in the neighborhood".

The mistake of the CIA report (assuming this knowledge was not updated since 1979), is that the CIA personnel meet their counterparts from the Mossad. Naturally, they will perceive their Mossad counterparts to be the most important. However, if they do not meet the Military Chief of Intelligence, they have a major gap in knowledge regarding the Israeli Intelligence Community.

The bottom line is that the CIA report tends to view Israel through American eyes. It is natural that they would do so, but then their view is biased and factually wrong.

When I first read this report after it was published in Israel in the early eighties, I told myself – if this is what the Americans know about an **ally** – a democratic country, a very open society, with national secrets spilled into the news media almost every other day, what would they know about the **enemy**?

The Mossad Today

It was reported in the news that on the anniversary of the establishment of the Mossad, Prime Minister Benjamin Netanyahu attended the ceremony. In his congratulatory speech he encouraged the Mossad to move from being a "regional" player, to become a "global" player.

If one might think that Israel would use its cyber power to spy on European and other politicians, then one is mistaken. One only needs to listen to the Prime Minister, who added in another speech he gave, that the information collected globally by the Mossad is a "currency" that Israel can use to establish relations with other countries.

And since the Intelligence in Israel does not define itself in the American way of keeping the country "safe and free", but to provide a "warning" against an upcoming or planned attack, it has been reported in the news that Israel has already prevented an attack on an **Australian** aircraft. Israel already prevented an attack in **France** against an Iranian dissident, an attack that was planned by an Iranian diplomat who was arrested in Germany. Israel also prevented an attack in the **Netherlands**. I wonder if Israel would be able to prevent an attack on the US.

In fact, throughout the years the EU has been very much for the "Palestinians"[1]. The EU is funding the Arabs residing in Judea and Samaria (also known as "the West Bank"), money that cannot be seen on the ground. However, in over a year, there has been a total silence by the EU in criticizing Israel. After all, it would be difficult for European diplomats to talk against the country that prevents terrorism in their own countries. This is what the Prime Minister referred to as "currency" in exchange for relations.

Being important globally is not likely to make the Mossad more important **in Israel**. The fact is that the Military Intelligence is still in charge of providing the warning of an attack against Israel. And since Zbigniew Brzeszinski was right in defining the Israelis as "prima donnas", it is very unlikely that the Chief of Military Intelligence will yield power to the Mossad.

Safe and Free? Really?

"Intelligence collection is… … about gaining information otherwise unavailable that would help keep Americans **safe and free**." (Michael Hayden in MH1 - 415); "…intercepting communications that contain information that would help keep Americans **free and safe**…" (Michael Hayden in MH1 - 10)

Is It Really Safe and Free?

There have been many incidents in which the US Intelligence Community "got it wrong", with major implications to American society. Let's go chronologically.

When discussing the WMD issue in Iraq, in his book "Playing to the Edge", Michael Hayden tells us that he was contacted by "an NSA historian" who alerted him that the issue of non-existence of WMD in Iraq resembled an event that took place many years earlier.

The Gulf of Tonkin Event

Hayden says, "SIGINT misread North Vietnamese reporting on their continuing recovery operations from the first night as a second attack and issued a CRITIC (a kind of global warning)." (MH1 - 51)

The "mistake" escalated when NSA picked up "North Vietnamese shore-based communications" reporting on US navy activity as "further evidence that a second attack was under way."

These two mistakes brought the US Congress to deliver the "Gulf of Tonkin Resolution" which escalated the US involvement in Vietnam to become the Vietnam War.

Hayden says that "NSA stuck to its story that a second attack had occurred". He also says that "It's unclear if the agency's subsequent investigation was careless, misguided, or just consciously ignored evidence. But it is clear that the August 4 reporting was wrong." (MH1 -52).

Hayden counts the following options: "careless, misguided, or just **consciously ignored evidence**." But "consciously ignored evidence" is a very nice name for a "cover-up".

In many detached words, Hayden says that a mistake by NSA brought the US into Vietnam, a mistake that had huge implications on US society, not to mention the tens of thousands killed, and hundreds of thousands wounded, both physically and psychologically.

Hayden ends his report by saying, "Tonkin and Iraq's WMD were sobering lessons."

Sobering lessons? Let's move fast forward in time and let's see the Iraq situation

Iraq WMD

James Clapper reports that General Norman Schwarzkopf, the commander of US Central Command, in briefing the Pentagon on Saddam Hussein amassing his military on the border of Kuwait, assessed "that there were a lot of reasons for Saddam Hussein to bluff... He concluded that the chances of Iraq invading Kuwait were 'slim.'" (JC 58)

Although General Schwarzkopf was not from the Intelligence Community, we should still register this as the first mistake in this area.

Clapper says regarding NIMA (the Satellite Imagery Agency): "We set to work, analyzing imagery to eventually identify, with varying degrees of confidence, more than 950 sites where we **assessed** there might be WMDs or a WMD connection." (JC 97)

Using this information, Clapper "participat[ed] as part of the review process that would certify the National Intelligence Estimate on Iraq's Continuing Programs for Weapons of Mass Destruction **as a consensus view of the IC**." (JC 97).

So we see an "assessment" and a "consensus view of the IC" (Intelligence Community), two terms that will star later in other mistakes of the IC.

Clapper himself explains the mistaken "assessment" and the mistaken "consensus view of the IC" by saying, "…we'd made some **assumptions** we shouldn't have, though the **circumstantial** prewar **evidence** seemed compelling, and admitted that I was still baffled that no WMD sites had been discovered." (JC 98)

Clapper sums up the non-existent Iraqi WMD by saying that US intelligence was "…connecting dots **that weren't really there**, which helped to lead us into Iraq." (JC 154-155)

But the non-existent Iraqi WMD was not only a mistake of imagery. Hayden says that "…CIA's misjudgments about weapons of mass destruction in Iraq had become part of its history." (MH1 - 179) He goes on to say that "The national estimate on the Iraqi nuclear program had been wrong, but beyond wrong it had also given **a false sense of confidence**. We had since learned to share not just what we **believed**, but also our **doubts**." (MH1 - 262)

Did they really learn to "share not just what we **believed**, but also our **doubts**"?

Summary of Language

To our accumulation of two terms – "assessment" and "consensus view of IC" – we can now add a few more terms: "assumptions", "circumstantial evidence", "false sense of confidence", "belief", and "doubts".

9/11

Hayden says, "…We were surprised on September 9/11. People wanted to know why." (MH1-153). Let's see if we can find out why "they" were surprised, and more importantly, if they should have been surprised.

FBI

Senator Bob Graham, in his book on the findings of the Senate investigations regarding the events that led to the 9/11 attack, lists 12 mistakes done by the FBI. If even one of these mistakes would have been avoided, the 9/11 attack would have been prevented.

Minnesota

One well-known mistake involves a report sent by an FBI agent in Minnesota to the FBI headquarters, reporting about the one who approached a flying school stating that he wants to learn how to take off, but since he is in a rush, he didn't want to learn how to land. The report arrived at the FBI Headquarters and was ignored. Later on, the Minnesota FBI agent was interviewed, and was very upset that all her efforts had been ignored.

Phoenix

Minnesota was not the only "mistake". The 9/11 Commission Report brings us another mistake.

"An FBI agent in the Phoenix field office sent a memo to FBI headquarters and to two agents on international terrorism squads in the New York Field Office, advising of the 'possibility of a coordinated effort by Usama Bin Ladin' to send students to the United States to attend civil aviation schools. The agent based his theory on the 'inordinate number of individuals of investigative interest' attending such schools in Arizona." (9/11 272)

The report continues to discuss the FBI Phoenix agent who also sent "…four recommendations to FBI headquarters: to compile a list of civil aviation schools, establish liaison with those schools, discuss his theories about Bin Ladin with the intelligence community, and seek authority to obtain visa information on persons applying to flight schools." (9/11 272)

What happened with his recommendations? The Commission does not keep it secret – "His recommendations were not acted on." (9/11 272)

Summary

Two reports came from two different FBI offices, one in Minneapolis and one in Phoenix, addressing the same issue – signals that there is an attempt to learn flying, by people who are suspected of having some hidden agenda for doing it.

Moreover, The 9/11 Commission Report tells us the Minneapolis FBI agent "…quickly learned that Moussaoui possessed jihadist beliefs." (9/11 273)

Why did two FBI offices function as if each one of them is in a vacuum?

The 9/11 Commission Report tells the public the reason. The director of the FBI, who would remain in office until June 2001, "…believed that the FBI's work should be done primarily by the field offices. To emphasize this view he cut headquarters staff and **decentralized operations**. The special agents in charge gained power, influence, and **independence**." (9/11 76)

The Commission also stated, "…in this **decentralized system**… …everyone in the Directorate of Operations presumed that it was the job of headquarters to support the field, rather than **manage field activities**." (9/11 89)

Actually, the 9/11 Commission Report is saying that the US did not have one FBI agency, but in practice 56 FBI offices, and each one of them gained "gained power, influence, and independence."

If this is not enough to conclude that we are facing a major systemic failure, the Commission tells us that, "…**the FBI had little appreciation for the role of analysis**. Analysts continued to be used primarily in a tactical fashion—providing support for existing cases. Compounding the problem was the FBI's tradition of hiring analysts from within instead of recruiting individuals with the relevant educational background and expertise." (9/11 77)

In a way, the Commission is wrong. We are not talking here about "analysis" or "assessing information". We are talking here of "collecting information". In other words, looking at the FBI as one unit, and not 56 offices. If the FBI would have acted as one cohesive agency, and not as 56 independent entities, then each field office should have sent its information to headquarters with a copy to all other field agencies.

In addition, there should have been one center in the FBI Headquarters in DC to get all the information from the field offices, to review the information, to connect the dots, and to reach the conclusion that there is a group of people spread over the US, some in Arizona, and some in

Minnesota, who have the same plan. Maybe even in some other states, as some of the hijackers were in California.

If there were to be such a unit in FBI headquarters, the FBI wouldn't have the need to get any information from other intelligence services (such as NSA) to be able to prevent the 9/11 attack. In other words, the final conclusion of the Commission that the US needed a "Director of National Intelligence" to coordinate the intelligence coming from different intelligence services, was quite likely promoted by the intelligence services themselves, and in this case, the FBI, to cover up their **systemic failure** due to a wrong vision of how an agency should operate. The way they operated was gross negligence due to mismanagement within the agency itself.

The lack of coordination within the FBI is emphasized by the Commission saying: "The acting director of the FBI did not learn of his Bureau's… arrest of an Islamic extremist taking flight training until September 11. (9/11 352)

Then one should ask a simple common-sense question: if so, why the need for a Director of the Agency?

Minnesota and Arizona were two "mistakes" (which can be described as "criminal negligence"), but the Senator listed several other "mistakes". Each one of them could have prevented the 9/11 attack.

Richard Helms, Director of CIA under Presidents Johnson and Nixon, in his book "A Look over My Shoulder" says, "The need for headquarters **to establish a central authority** through which all collection requirements were to be funneled and assigned a priority was one of the first postwar lessons I learned in Berlin." (61). Helms says that this lack of "central authority" was the reason for the Japanese surprise attack on Pearl Harbor in December 1941.

"…in the weeks before December 7, 1941, the United States had collected enough information to have shown that the Japanese were planning an attack that might most plausibly fall upon Pearl Harbor. Because there was no **central office** responsible for collecting and evaluating information, these bits and pieces of intelligence were strewn among codebreakers, the Department of State, War Department, Navy Department, and the White House. Coherent analysis and dissemination was impossible." (66)

The idea of "central authority" and/or "central office" was a lesson from 1941. Why did the Director of FBI before 9/11 decide on his own to go against this lesson?

The failure to prevent the 9/11 attack was not the only "mistake" by the FBI, although the most devastating one. There were other similar "mistakes" (i.e. ignoring information about upcoming attacks) by the FBI in other cases: e.g. ignoring a report about a Russian spy in the US Navy, ignoring a report of two Jihadists from Chechnya, who later attacked the Boston Marathon, and more… But let's stay on course dealing with 9/11.

Israel and US response to an attack

After the Yom Kippur war in 1973 in which 2,500 soldiers were killed and more were wounded, a commission of inquiry recommended to fire the Chief of Staff and three high-ranking officers in the Military Intelligence. In the US, after the 9/11 attack in which close to 3,000 were killed, the President decided to give the FBI the sole authority in the US to fight terrorism.

9/11 and NSA

In his book "Playing to the Edge", Hayden brings to the reader the fact that Senator Richard Shelby of Alabama asked the NSA regarding two "intercepts" that were made one day before the 9/11 attack (on 9/10). One "intercept" contained: "The match is about to begin", and the other: "Tomorrow is zero hour". Senator Shelby asked a simple question: why were these two important "intercepts" not processed, translated, and reported until September 12, one day after the attack? In other words, the Senator wanted NSA Director Hayden to explain why the NSA had functioned as a simple "history department", reporting these two "intercepts" a day after the attack, and not in real time, when in real time they would have provided a "warning" before the attack.

Hayden's explanation is a major eye opener: "I explained that NSA **rarely listens to a conversation while it is taking place**. Intercepts are collected, stored, and sorted, and then a linguist works his or her way through the queue." (MH1 - 45)

NSA does not function in real time. "Rarely". The way they relate to intercepts is that they "…are collected, stored, and sorted, and then a linguist works his or her way through the queue."

It took me over one day to realize the full impact of what the Director of NSA was saying. NSA does not see itself as first line in providing a "warning" of an upcoming attack on the US.

At this point of time, it is fitting to quote from a book written by a former Chief of the Mossad, Meir Amit. In his book "Head On", Amit wrote:

"The information has value not only by the reliability of the information, **but also if it arrives on time** and is distributed to the right address. **Information which arrives late has questionable value, like yesterday's newspaper**." (262)

The book "Mr. Intelligence" – a biography of Aharon Yariv, the longest serving Israeli Chief of Military Intelligence – brings us what happens when there is a delay in relaying the information from the source to the field: "The warning indeed came on the 27th of July, Sunday, at 08:50. But what happened was that there was a delay of 5 minutes in relaying the warning to the Air Force. **These are a critical five minutes**… This is a failure of warning, and again it comes from problems in reporting, and not from lack of information!" (435)

The book is telling us that even a delay of 5 minutes might be "critical". Not to mention 2 days.

Back to NSA and Hayden

Hayden defends his leadership by stating that he is presiding over the "department of history", and not providing an advance warning against an imminent attack.

One can easily say that NSA has a global reach, and they have stations everywhere, and they are not capable of processing each "intercept" in real time. However, this is NOT a valid claim at all.

NSA is the largest intelligence agency of the US, with close to 100,000 employees. Instead of tapping the phone of Europeans leaders, devoting manpower and resources to do so, leaders that do not impose any threat to the US, the NSA should have set priorities. If the threat to the US at the time came mainly, if not only, from Al-Qaeda, it would have been very easy for the NSA to recruit enough people to monitor 24/7/365 ALL "intercepts" of all Al-Qaeda members, from the top to the bottom, and to do so in real time. This is called providing a "warning".

Hayden himself says in his book that when they started a program to monitor all the phone metadata in the US, they recruited thousands of people to work on that program. Hayden adds, "We hired several thousand people in the four years after 9/11…" (MH1 - 135)

Moreover, in talking about the CIA, Hayden says, "We still **didn't have auditable accounts (no one in the IC did)** nor could we really tote up the real cost of manpower…" (MH1 - 287). So money was not the issue. It was the wrong set of priorities.

Not processing information in a timely manner is not the only "mistake" the NSA made. The 9/11 Commission Report lists another one.

"In late 1999, the National Security Agency (NSA) analyzed communications associated with a man named Khalid, a man named Nawaf, and a man named Salem. Working-level officials in the intelligence community knew little more than this. But they correctly concluded that 'Nawaf' and 'Khalid' might be part of 'an operational cadre' and that 'something nefarious might be afoot.'" (9/11 353)

What did NSA do with this information? Even though NSA figured that these two – "Nawaf" and "Khalid" – might be "part of 'an operational cadre'", the Commission says that "The NSA **did not think its job was to research these identities**. It saw itself as an agency to support intelligence consumers, such as CIA. The NSA tried to respond energetically to any request made. But it waited to be asked." (9/11 353)

The Commission tells us how the NSA people explained to the Commission their lack of understanding of what they were meant to do – to produce a warning of an attack on the US. In many words, the NSA people said openly that they were **passive** ("support intelligence consumers, such as CIA") and not **active** ("to keep Americans safe and free"). Please note that Michael Hayden was the NSA Chief at the time of the 9/11 attack.

If this is not enough, the Commission says that the NSA didn't need any additional information from other agencies to solve the puzzle of who were these two whom they estimated to be "part of 'an operational cadre'"

"If NSA had been asked to try to identify these people, the agency would have started by checking **its own database of earlier information from these same sources**. Some of this information had been reported; some had not. But **it was all readily accessible in the database**. NSA's analysts would promptly have discovered who Nawaf was, that his full name might be Nawaf al Hazmi…" (9/11 353)

Nawaf al Hazmi was one of the 9/11 hijackers.

Summary

The Commission's finding is not that the US lacked coordination between the various intelligence services. The Commission's finding is that one particular agency – and in this case, the NSA – did not do its job correctly. If it were to do its job correctly, translating reports of an imminent attack on the US in a timely manner, and using its own data base to support its monitoring efforts, the intelligence they would have produced would have been "operational" – arriving before the attack – and not produced in a manner similar to a "history department" – arriving after the attack.

What the Commission found is something very basic to "Intelligence" – that there is no way to separate "collecting information" from "assessing" it. Both go in tandem with each other. The one who collects information needs to know what he/she is collecting, and in order to do so, the same one needs to "assess" the information. Separating the two creates the same systemic failure that the Commission found at the NSA.

Israel and US response to an attack

Before the Yom Kippur War in 1973, the Israeli equivalent of the NSA did report about the imminent attack. However, the Chief of Military Intelligence "assessed" the information wrongly. The Chief of Military Intelligence was fired by the Commission of Inquiry, and the Chief of the Israeli NSA unit later published a book describing the events that led to his unit's findings that were ignored by the higher-ups.

In the US, the NSA functioned in a very wrong way, not doing their job correctly. The Commission of Inquiry in the US recommended creating a new layer of bureaucracy over the entire Intelligence Community (called "Homeland Security") to coordinate between the various services. But what was really needed was - to send the negligent managers (or Directors) home, and to recommend improving each agency on its own, within itself. More bureaucracy is not going to solve the problem. More bureaucracy was only meant to cover up the mismanagement by these negligent directors, who didn't know how to run their operation correctly. The new layer of bureaucracy was also meant to show the public that the government is doing something, while in fact it did nothing.

Former Director of CIA Richard Helms correctly stated in his book that there is an "…American inclination to find a dollar solution to difficult problems." (96) And if there is any doubt what he meant, he goes on to say, "In secret intelligence the addition of more staff does not necessarily guarantee increased production. In many instances, a lean outfit will outperform its plump neighbor." (96)

In summary

In Israel the "collecting of information" was satisfactory, but everything went wrong due to a wrong "assessment". In the US, even the "collecting of information" was wrong, so there could have been no **good and beneficial** "assessment".

The 9/11 Commission's findings

The Commission stated: "The September 11 attacks **fell into the void** between the foreign and domestic threats." (9/11 263)

Actually, if we include the FBI, there was no "void" at all. The agency that was responsible for domestic threats did get signals on its radar of a domestic threat from various points in the continental US. The only reason they didn't connect the signals is due to the "decentralized organization" and having 56 independent FBI offices.

And the Commission continued:

"The foreign intelligence agencies were watching overseas, alert to foreign threats to U.S. interests there. The domestic agencies were waiting for evidence of a domestic threat from sleeper cells within the United States. No one was looking for a foreign threat to domestic targets. The threat that was coming was not from sleeper cells. It was foreign—but from foreigners who had infiltrated into the United States." (9/11 263)

One needs to read this "finding" several times before understanding the full meaning of it. The Commission says - "The domestic agencies were waiting for evidence of a domestic threat from sleeper cells within the United States." And the Commission rightly added that "The threat that was coming was not from sleeper cells." They were not "**sleeper** cells". They were very **active** cells.

The word that bothers me the most is the word "waiting": "The domestic agencies were **waiting** for evidence of a domestic threat…" The fact is that they were not "waiting". They were already collecting this evidence. However, due to lack of management and coordination, they didn't see the "big picture".

Actually, it seems to me that the Commission only echoed what the failed directors of these services "sold" them in order to somehow explain their mismanagement. After all, it is much easier to blame the criminal than to take responsibility for not succeeding in apprehending him.

Clapper on 9/11

Clapper in his book sums up the 9/11 "mistake" by saying that the US intelligence did not "connect the dots" to prevent 9/11 (JC 154-155). Realizing the wrong set of priorities of NSA in not focusing on the information to provide a warning in real time, he should have said that the US intelligence could not connect the dots, because they were not processed in real time.

In both cases – Iraq and 9/11 – according to Clapper, "Errors were made that led to massive tragedies." (JC - 154) Without these "errors" ("criminal negligence" in police language) massive tragedies could have been avoided.

In SCAN terminology, "errors were made" is use of passive language, which is the strongest signal ever in language, of an attempt to conceal identity.

Question: whose identify is Clapper concealing?

And the list continues.

Benghazi

A lot has been written about Benghazi, however, only the "contribution" of intelligence will be discussed here.

James Clapper says in his book that he met Chris Stevens before Stevens went to Libya. Clapper says that when he ended that conversation: "My last words as he was heading out the door still haunt me. As he glanced back I told him, 'Stay safe.'" (JC 167). Till this point everything sounds ok. But Clapper ends this issue by saying, "We in the IC knew that Chris **was facing** an uncertain and **dangerous situation**." (JC 167)

The question is: what did Clapper, as Director of National Intelligence (DNI), do with this "knowledge"? Did he report it to the State Department? Did he report it to the Military? Or, maybe he kept this "knowledge" within the Intelligence Community (IC).

After Chris Stevens was killed, the IC needed to reconstruct the events that led to the killing, so they would be able to report it to the president.

This reveals another "mistake" by the IC. Clapper reports the events in Benghazi in the following way:

"On Tuesday, September 11, the eleventh anniversary of the attacks on the World Trade Center and Pentagon, a local militia attacked a low-security diplomatic facility in Benghazi, Libya." (JC 168)

Since the first sentence of a statement is the most important one, it is clear that the Intelligence figured that 9/11 is an important date, quite liked by terrorists for attacks on the US, or on American facilities wherever they are. If so, several questions arise: What did the Intelligence do with this "assessment"? Did they instruct the State Department to fortify the place where Stevens was? Or, did they keep this "assessment" to themselves? And this brings up another question: if they assessed it as such, that the attack was due to the date of 9/11, why didn't they use this knowledge in reporting to the president? And if they did, why did they remain silent when the first story was that the attack was due to an innocent demonstration against an amateur video published in the US making fun of the Moslem prophet Muhammad?

In reconstructing the events during the attack in Benghazi, the IC used "…the security-camera video of the looters and vandals…" (JC 179). One only has to wonder: if they could reconstruct what happened, why couldn't they reach the capability of transmitting these "security-camera videos" in real time, to be able to make sure that the attack would not succeed?

To use police language, it would appear that the Intelligence Community puts more emphasis on "serving" (after the fact) and not "protecting" (before the fact). According to James Clapper, the IC has no responsibility for the event or for the loss of life. Clapper found the real culprit.

Clapper says, "At no point in any of these congressional briefings were decisions made by Chris Stevens questioned." (JC 180), and "While I admired Chris, I still have some serious questions about the decisions he made at that time: Why did he remain in Benghazi hours after the US embassy in Cairo had been overrun? Why did he go there on 9/11 in the first place, and why didn't he realize his security was completely inadequate? Confidence in oneself and one's team is admirable, but had he become too complacent?" (JC – 180-181)

It is always a great solution to blame the victim!!!

The Boston Marathon

Let's see how Clapper introduces us to this "nightmare scenario" (JC – 211) – a terrorist attack in which three people were killed and hundreds were wounded, many severely.

"…Two brothers who had immigrated to the United States as minors in 2002…" – what he "forgot" to mention was that these two brothers came from the Chechnya area in the Russian Federation, that they were Moslems, and that they received "refugee" status in the US. Innocent omissions?

These "two brothers" "…had found instructions for making homemade bombs out of common kitchen pressure cookers in the online magazine Inspire, published by al-Qaida in the Arabian Peninsula." (JC 211)

Clapper defends the lack of any "warning" by the US Intelligence Community as due to the fact that "They had made no phone or email communication that we could have intercepted, and there was no human source whom we could have exploited to learn of and thwart their plan." (JC 212)

And Clapper continued, "We learned that the FBI had interviewed Tamerlan in 2011 - two years before the bombing - but had concluded he wasn't a threat at the time." (JC 212)

How did the FBI know to interview these two brothers if there was no "intercept" of any phone call or any email? Maybe Clapper should have read the news media in the US. There it was reported that the Russian Intelligence had contacted the FBI and reported to them that this family is a Jihadist family. Knowing how any American Intelligence agency trusts the Russians, one can figure that the FBI did not receive this information in any alarming way.

I can share with the reader that after the Boston Marathon attack I listened to a radio interview with the mother of these two brothers while they were still on the run, and it was clear to me from her speech that she was the leader of the two brothers - that she was the one who had sent them to commit this "nightmare scenario".

The reason that I mentioned that they were from Chechnya and that they were Moslems, is for the simple reason that the FBI should have been familiar with the Moslem culture to know that in a Moslem society, an individual has no personal responsibility. Regardless of a person's age, as long as the father is alive, the father is responsible for the actions of his children. If the FBI had to start interviewing anybody in this case, it should have been the father and the mother, and only then to move to the brothers.

Now we know why the brothers made their "… homemade bombs **out of common kitchen pressure cookers**…" – did they find the instructions on the internet, or did their mother show them how to use her own kitchen to make the "homemade bomb"?

Talking about the FBI – in the terrorist attack that took place in Florida, it was reported in the news that the father of the terrorist had reported to the FBI, two years before the attack, that his son is a jihadist. And the FBI interviewed the son and released him, just as they had interviewed and released the two Chechnyan brothers. Two years later he went to kill dozens of people.

We have in front of us two incidents in which information was received, but the assessment of this information was wrong.

Nuclear Reactor in Syria

While this event is not well-known in the US, it is relatively well-known in Israel. And Michael Hayden devotes a full chapter in his book for this event, concluding it was a major success for American Intelligence.

Let's start from the beginning.

Hayden in his book refers to "…intelligence services of the Middle East…" and says that "in April 2007, the tough, tireless head of one of them came into my office at Langley." (MH1 – 255)

It is interesting to note that nowhere in this chapter does Hayden mention that the "tough tireless head" of this intelligence service is the head of the Israeli Mossad, although at the time of the publication of his book (2016) this was common knowledge in the Israeli news media. And in fact, in many words, several Israeli ministers hinted that Israel was the one who did the job.

The head of the Mossad brought Hayden, the Director of the CIA "photos of a nearly complete nuclear reactor in the eastern Syrian desert near a town called al-Kibar." (MH1 – 255)

Hayden says that the US Intelligence had already "picked up on the facility as it was being completed through satellite imagery, but its false walls and roofs **made it difficult to identify**." The imagery agency (NGA) labeled it as "enigmatic" but Hayden himself says that this "…meant that it looked important, **but we couldn't exactly tell what it was**." (255)

The photos brought by the head of the Mossad were "…nearly a hundred handheld photos of the site while it was still under construction. You could see the false walls… over a shape eerily similar to North Korea's Yongbyon nuclear reactor… you could see reactor components… a floor into which uranium rods could be inserted…" (256). Hayden concludes that "This was high-quality *tactical* warning." [Italics in the original.]

At this point, Hayden goes on to describe the meeting with the president. There were four points to discuss.

No. 1: "It's a nuclear reactor. High confidence."

No. 2: "The Syrians and the Koreans have been cooperating on nuclear development... High confidence.

No. 3: Did the North Koreans build the facility? "We haven't seen Koreans there [i.e. in satellite imagery] except one group in one of the handheld photos... So we're giving this to you with **medium confidence**."

Let's take a break here. The facility is "similar" to the North Korean Yongbyon nuclear reactor. No other country had built a nuclear facility with such a structure. Koreans were seen in the hand-held picture taken from ground level. However, Hayden took into consideration that satellite imagery must be better than photos from ground level, and as such he reduced the confidence from "high" to "medium". Wrong assessment?

No. 4: Is it a part of a Syrian weapons system? Hayden says, "Of course it is. There are no other obvious uses for it..." (256). However, Hayden continued, "I can't find the other parts of a weapon program. No processing facility. No weaponization effort that we can see. So I can only give this to you as **low confidence**." (256)

Hayden reported the data accurately. It was a huge building built in the middle of nowhere, near the Euphrates River. The Syrians built "a cooling-water intake... for pipes to bring cold water to the facility and discharge hot water back to the river." (255)

But Hayden gave "low confidence" to the possibility that it was part of a weapon system since he hadn't found other parts of a weapon program. Did Hayden consider the option that the Syrians were waiting till the reactor would be "hot" (operational), and then they would build the other components? Once the reactor would be operational, there would be no way to bomb it and risk contaminating the Euphrates River forever with radioactive fallout, making the environment uninhabitable in practically all the nearby countries, including Turkey, Syria, Iraq, and maybe even Israel.

Wrong assessment again?

Incidentally, this "low confidence" assessment brought President Bush to conclude that the US would not bomb the facility as it was not an "imminent danger" to the US.

It is interesting, but the one who had been Chief of the Mossad at the time of the 1967 war, was in the US for discussions with the CIA about the situation.

In his book, Meir Amit relates to the CIA assessment of the situation: "…and it was not basically different from our assessment. To my disappointment, their assessment was technical **and inconclusive**." (240) In other words, there was no plan for action based on the information.

This was not the only mistake in assessment in this "project". There was a discussion in the CIA about whether Assad, the Syrian ruler, would retaliate against US interests all over the Middle East. CIA analysts figured that he would have to retaliate. On the other hand, "…that tireless liaison chief… and his staff were inclined to think that a successful strike could be pulled off without a Syrian response if everyone would just keep quiet about it and not attempt to humiliate." (265).

The results: the facility was bombed, but not by the US. Everyone kept quiet, and Syria did not respond.

The Israeli Prime Minister Ehud Olmert, who ordered the destruction of the nuclear site in Syria, says in his book: "We reached the beginning of September and we destroyed the nuclear reactor in Syria. As we expected, the Syrians did not respond. I wondered if they would withdraw from the secret negotiations. Amazingly, the opposite happened." (759)

Not only did the Syrians not react – but at the time the nuclear site was destroyed, Syria and Israel were holding secret talks in Turkey to see if they could settle the issue of the Golan Heights, an area that Israel took over in the 1967 war, when the Syrians attacked the Israeli towns in the north. The Prime Minister tells us that not only did the Syrians not retaliate, but they also did not withdraw from the secret negotiations, and even, "Amazingly, the opposite happened."

Hayden moves on to summarize the event: "So we chalked this one up as an intelligence success… Our analysis that it was a reactor proved correct, but our analysis of likely Syrian actions was not. And this certainly wasn't a HUMINT success. In fact, human intelligence had been sorely lacking." (268)

Was it a US intelligence success? Without the hand-held photos taken from ground level, the US would have stayed with "…difficult[y] to identify" the facility, and the US still "…couldn't exactly tell what it was." (255). And what are hand-held photos if not a HUMINT success? It might not have been a US HUMINT success, but still a fine HUMINT success.

Moreover, to say that "Our analysis that it was a reactor proved correct…" is only talking about part of the assessment. Let's not forget that Hayden gave "low confidence" that the nuclear site was for a "weapon system". (But once the nuclear site was destroyed, Hayden's assessment was now accurate – that site was no longer a "weapon system". It was literally "not meant to be".)

Yet Hayden considered this to be a huge success of the US intelligence, in spite of the fact that the US intelligence did not recognize the significance of the building, and did not assess correctly the meaning of that building being there. One should wonder if this is the reason that this friendly intelligence service from the Middle East was not identified even once as Israel.

Incidentally, Hayden mentions Israel in other places in his book, but only in a negative way.

High Tech vs. Low Tech Intelligence

The fact that Hayden says that the US satellite picked up the facility "…long after its appearance had been altered and its use obscured" because "the needs of the war there" [i.e. Iraq] "consumed a lot of that resource" (MH1 255-256) points to the weakness of the US Intelligence in relying solely on high tech – satellites, internet, etc.

It is well-known that Israel has its own satellites over the Middle East, built and produced in Israel, and delivered to space using Israel's own rockets. Quite likely the Israeli satellite picked up the same building as the US satellite did. But the Chief of the Mossad didn't bring Hayden, as Director of CIA, the images from the Israeli satellite. He brought Hayden "a hundred handheld photos of the site" (256).

Hayden speculates in the book as to the source of the pictures saying, "Our best guess was that the photos had been downloaded from the computer of a sloppy Syrian scientist." (256) That is their best "guess"? And should it be a "guess", or should we go with what Hayden tells us? Since Hayden was not confident "that the pictures hadn't been altered" he gave the pictures to his "experts" to examine them.

Hayden puts in italics the word "if" when saying, "…*if* we could be confident that the pictures hadn't been altered." In this sentence Hayden tells his readers that he, Hayden, does not trust the Mossad to produce reliable "handheld photos". What does he think? That the Mossad is in the business of fabricating information? One might wonder why Hayden would think that an Intelligence officer is capable of fabricating evidence!!!

And Hayden continues: The conclusion of the CIA experts was "…that the photos were genuine and undoctored **except for one where some writing on the side of a pickup truck had been pixelated out**."

If the photos were downloaded from "the computer of a sloppy Syrian scientist", why would the scientist "pixelate out" the writing on a pickup truck? Very unlikely. Quite likely, the Mossad itself "pixelated out" the writing on the pickup truck.   Hayden himself said that sharing the pictures with them was "remarkable". There was only one point that the Mossad took out – the writing on the pickup truck. The reason must be that the Mossad didn't want the CIA to know how they got the "handheld photos". The writing would have exposed the source of the pictures.

A former Chief of the Mossad, Zvi Zamir, tells us in his book that they received "a certain report" which the Prime Minister Golda Meir, his immediate supervisor, wanted the Mossad to "distribute it to the US". Zamir thought that "such a step might expose the source of the information" (page 81).   At this point, Zamir gives a long description of the argument between him and Golda Meir. Zamir said that Golda did not want to impose on him to give the information to the US by ordering him. She wanted him to consent to her request/demand. After a long back and forth, they reached an agreement: "…that the information would be transferred to the Americans, and I would take care that the security of the source would not be harmed…" (82)

In summary

Unlike the US intelligence that relies solely on high tech, the Israeli intelligence felt that they needed to check the "site" from close by. Just the satellite images were not enough for them. They wanted "low tech" verification – "handheld photos". After all, according to Clapper, the US used satellites to locate 950 sites in Iraq that they "assessed" were WMD sites. The satellites were enough for them. If they were to use "low tech" intelligence, as Israel did with the nuclear site in Syria, **and send people to get "handheld photos" of these sites**, they might have had a different "assessment". The issue of the WMD could have been settled **before** the war, without entering a war based upon only "high tech" and assessment that resulted from wrong information and brought about wrong conclusions.

Snowden

James Clapper defined Snowden's revelations as "...one of the worst thefts of US secrets in the history of intelligence..." (JC 229). He also says that it "...wasn't exactly the IC's – or my – finest hour" (JC 229). Michael Hayden in his book refers to the Snowden Affair as "...the failure of the intelligence agencies to keep their secrets..." (MH1 - 411), and "...as the greatest hemorrhaging of legitimate American secrets in the history of the republic." (MH1 - 421)

But Michael Hayden adds something to his definition to the Snowden Affair. He defines it as "the Snowden **kerfuffle**" (MH1 - 425). One should note that here Hayden does not call it "failure" or any other negative word. Instead, he preferred to use a mild and uncommon word. Compare this label to "debacle" and "case" (278) with which he describes the Russian spy Aldrich Ames penetrating the CIA.

James Comey, former Director of the FBI, fired by President Trump, says about Michael Hayden in his book: "...his briefings were **a river of really great-sounding stuff** that didn't make much sense once the briefing was over and you tried to piece together what you had just heard." (Page 83).

Hayden's use of the word "kerfuffle" forced me to check the dictionary, where I found this word defined as "informal" and "British". Why would Hayden, an American general, well-versed in American English, avoid using everyday language, and instead prefer to "cross the ocean" to use informal British language? One way or another, we need to conclude that the Snowden Affair is sensitive for Hayden, if not more than that.

The full definition describes a "kerfuffle" as "a commotion or fuss, especially one caused by **conflicting views**." If indeed Hayden is aware of this definition, his language gives legitimacy to Snowden. And in fact, we will see later on that he does so openly.

The Intelligence Failure

James Clapper says that once the newspaper started to print the revelations of Snowden it "…riveted the attention of the entire national security enterprise, and galvanized our counterintelligence and security apparatus to identify and locate the traitor." (JC 225)

Sounds good? Not really! Why would this affair "galvanize" the "counterintelligence and security apparatus" after the horse ran away from the barn? Why not to "galvanize" the "counterintelligence and security apparatus" a long time in advance to prevent such an occurrence?

Former Director of CIA Richard Helms says in his book: "In the years that followed I became convinced that no intelligence service can be more effective than its counterintelligence component for very long." (34-35)

James Clapper says that "…our counterintelligence and security professionals put new procedures and online programs in place intended to thwart potential leakers..." (JC 242-243). Simple question: couldn't they have put these "procedures and online programs in place" before such an occurrence? And if they didn't, who is the one responsible for not doing it?

Israel and Personal Responsibility

After the Lebanon War in 1982, a commission of inquiry headed by a justice of the Israeli Supreme Court looked into the events that led to the Christian militia retaliating against the Palestinians in Beirut, a retaliation that brought about a massacre of hundreds of people. This commission determined a long, detailed list of criteria for personal responsibility, and they are: lack of efficiency, lack of proper attention to the job, impulsiveness, negligence, and also "**lack of insight** in not predicting the outcome, when according to the skills of the person filling a certain position, and the personal characteristics required of him to fulfill his duty,

he should have seen the outcome." (Quoted in the book by Eli Zeira –
"The 1973 War" page 192)

For comparison, when the Prime Minister of Israel was murdered, the chief
of the security detail resigned. Other officials were removed from their
position, and new procedures were put into place. How is it possible to
trust the ones who failed to guard the Prime Minister from assassination, to
be in charge of guarding the next Prime Minister?

The same applied to the one who was in charge of security after the eleven
Israeli athletes were murdered by PLO terrorists in the Munich Olympic
Games. He was removed from his position. When terrorists took over the
Israeli embassy in Bangkok, Thailand, and took the ambassador and the
embassy personnel as hostages, the one in charge of security decided to quit
his job before the commission of inquiry would recommend removing him.

We can ask the same question about the leaders of the "counterintelligence
and security apparatus" who failed to guard the secrets of their
organization. How can one trust them to be in charge of guarding the same
secrets in the future? If they already showed "lack of insight" and they did
not "see the outcome" – then removing them from their position is not a
punishment. It is only a necessary step of "self defense" to make sure this
same mistake will not happen again.

Can the NSA prevent another "Snowden"?

So, Clapper is telling us that "new procedures and online programs" were
put into effect after the Snowden Affair. But Snowden was not an NSA
employee. Snowden was an employee of a contract company that worked
for the NSA.

Question: Would these ""new procedures and online programs" prevent the
appearance of another "Snowden"?

Quite unlikely. The NSA is an agency with an estimated 90 thousand
people, if not even more. Michael Hayden himself says in his book: "We
hired several thousand people in the four years after 9/11; their average age
was thirty-one, well below the agency average at that time. It wasn't lost
on any of the new recruits **that we were offering them the opportunity to
legally do stuff that would be felonies in any other venue**." (MH1 - 135)

Like James Clapper, who didn't read American society correctly before the elections, so does Hayden. In his admission, he openly says that he recruited people to commit "felonies" for the US government. What would be the chances that one or more of these new recruits would realize what is requested of him, and complain to the news media?

Taking into consideration that the US Constitution is an integral part of US culture, almost like a "sacred text", the likelihood that the NSA would keep its secrets intact is slim. At any given point, there is one, or even more, who are contemplating in their mind to follow in Snowden's footsteps.

Back to Snowden

Question: how can a top-secret organization such as NSA use "contractors" to run their computers? A top-secret organization contracts out their most sensitive position – their computers (which are the nerve center of the organization that includes ALL secrets) – to an outsider. If this is not a "mistake", what should we call it? In legal terms it can be defined as "negligence", if not even "criminal negligence" bordering on total recklessness.

In fact, after the Snowden revelations, President Obama appointed a commission of inquiry to look into everything relating to the NSA. This commission had five members, two of whom were security/intelligence people (one of them a high-ranking CIA official) and three professors of law.

This commission published "The NSA Report". In the report, we find:

"We recommend that the US Government should move toward a system in which background investigations relating to the vetting of personnel for security clearance are performed **solely by US Government employees or by a non-profit, private sector corporation**." (TNR 177)

The Security Clearance Process

The Commission that produced "The NSA Report" found major deficiencies in the security clearance process, also known as "vetting".

They stated, "We believe that the current security clearance personnel vetting practices of most federal departments and agencies **are expensive**

and time-consuming, and that they **may not reliably detect** the potential for abuse in a timely manner." (TNR 178)

The commission moved to outline the process : "The applicant is asked to provide the names of a score or more of contacts. An investigator attempts to meet with those people whose names have been provided by the applicant." (TNR 179) And they added, "Not surprisingly, very few contacts suggested by the applicant provide derogatory information, especially because they know that their remarks may be disclosed to their friend or acquaintance." (TNR 179)

They also said that "In many agencies, the current personnel vetting system **does not do well** in detecting changes in a vetted individual's status after a security clearance has been granted." (TNR 180)

If so, what is the reason to continue to do something that does not produce results?

Moreover, former Director of CIA Richard Helms says in his book: "Ironically, the most serious known breaches in OSS security were made by **native-born citizens**." (156) And Edward Snowden is a "native-born citizen".

The NSA Report

The commission quoted some findings from the Church Committee from 1976:

"…the system of checks and balances – created in our Constitution to limit abuse of Governmental power – **was seldom applied to the Intelligence Community**… because government officials failed to exercise appropriate oversight and because intelligence agencies systematically concealed 'improper activities from their superiors in the Executive branch and from the Congress.'" (TNR 16), and, "'…even those who are supposed to supervise [our intelligence agencies] are likely to fear [them].'" (TNR 17)

The commission that produced "The NSA Report" said that all the findings of the Church Committee "…shaped much of our nation's thinking about foreign intelligence surveillance for the past 40 years." (TNR 14)

In other words, nothing much has changed.

The commission related to the revelation that the NSA was monitoring the phones of European leaders, and stated that doing so, "…might seriously compromise our relationships with those very nations. It is important to consider the potential effects of surveillance on these relationships…" (TNR 5) And if the intelligence officials still "didn't get it", the commission added that "…if officials can acquire information, it does not follow that they *should* do so. Indeed, the fact that officials can *legally* acquire information (under domestic law) does not mean that they should do so." (TNR 6). The commission continued: "…it is tempting to think that such capacities should be used rather than ignored. The temptation should be resisted." (TNR 6)

The commission produced a common sense comment:

"Any expert with access to **open sources** can provide insight on questions such as the Eurozone crisis and Japanese politics, but insights on the plans, intentions, and capabilities of al-Qa'ida, on the status of the Iranian nuclear weapons program, and on the development of cyber warfare tools by other nations are simply not possible without **reliable intelligence**." (TNR 30)

In many words, the commission stated that the NSA should have their priorities set right.

The commission also found mismanagement again. Note that this is not after 9/11 in 2001, but in 2013 after the Snowden revelations:

"…NSA's data accessing technologies and practices **were never adequately designed to comply** with the governing minimization procedures…". (TNR 59)

The Director of the NSA, General Keith Alexander, explained this lack of compliance by saying: "…there was no single person who had a complete understanding of the [section 215] FISA system architecture." (TNR 59)

And what does a director of an agency need to do when his employees do not have "complete understanding" of the law? Does he need to establish a training program? Not according to this director. He can always blame the employees for non-compliance with the law.

Let's see how the commission dealt with this military general. They issued the following recommendations: "That the Director of the National Security Agency should be a Senate-confirmed position" and "the President should give serious consideration to making the next Director of the National Security Agency a civilian." (TNR 135) They added that "A senior (two- or three-star) military officer should be among the Deputy Directors." (TNR 136)

Since this is the US, and in the US no government official would be relieved of his position due to mismanagement and/or failure, the closest the commission could come up with, is to send a very strong message. The director of the NSA should be a civilian. In other words, a military general is not suited for the job.

The commission also recommended that "…the National Security Agency should be clearly designated as a foreign intelligence organization; missions other than foreign intelligence collection should generally be reassigned elsewhere." (TNR 136) They also recommended to break up the agency: "NSA now has multiple missions and mandates, some of which are blurred, inherently conflicting, or both." (TNR 136) and "…if the nation were writing on a blank slate, we believe it unlikely that we would create the current organization." (TNR 136) They therefore recommended that "…the head of the military unit, US Cyber Command, and the Director of the National Security Agency should not be a single official." (TNR 137), and "Information Assurance Directorate (IAD) of NSA should be organizationally separate and have a different reporting structure." (TNR 138)

In other words, the NSA became "too big to fail". It needed to be split into three different entities.

Back to Snowden

James Clapper says, "NSA officials had no idea that they were hiring someone the CIA considered problematic and untrustworthy." (JC 230)

"NSA Officials had no idea"? In this matter-of-fact sentence, James Clapper condemns the vetting system that the NSA had in place before the Snowden Affair. It is mind-boggling. An organization that is proud of penetrating computers and phones of people all over the globe is so negligent to even consider the fact that their vetting system is faulty, and that there could be such a "kerfuffle".

And Clapper says that "My job was supposed to be getting the agencies to talk to one another." (JC 230) If the CIA did not provide its information to NSA, it only means that Clapper didn't do his job. And if so, what is Clapper's conclusion from the fact that he actually didn't do his job right?

Systemic Failure

Hayden says, "...and I do know that intelligence officers talk about them among themselves at the water cooler, and at the Starbucks and Dunkin' Donuts in the Agency cafeteria, and at diners and steakhouses near the Agency" (MH2 - 146-147).

Two points come to mind: the fact that CIA personnel "talk ... among themselves at the water cooler, and at the Starbucks and Dunkin' Donuts in the Agency cafeteria..." testifies to the fact that the CIA does not observe compartmentalization of information. Hayden says openly that there is a free flow of information between people. In other words, everyone knows everything!

One wonders if this is wise. An organization that holds so many secrets must take steps to prevent secrets from coming out. When Hayden says, "No one expected Stellarwind to stay secret forever. Nothing does." (MH1 - 76), and "...the US government's less than stellar record in keeping secrets..." (MH1 - 256) it sounds as if he looks upon the leaking of secrets as a "weather pattern" that one can only talk about it, but one cannot do anything to change it. If one wants to contain secrets, one must make sure that secrets within one unit of the same organization will stay put in that unit, and not move to the "water cooler"

The NSA Report confirmed this point. "Once granted a certain level of clearance because of a need to do part of their jobs, employees are often in a position to read other material at that classification, regardless of its relevance to their job." (TNR 180) In other words, there is no compartmentalization in the system.

Maybe the NSA should have read the book written by Richard Helms who said, "In the secret operations canon it is **axiomatic** that the probability of leaks escalates exponentially each time a classified document is exposed to another person – be it an Agency employee, a member of Congress, a senior official, a typist, or a file clerk. **Effective compartmentation is fundamental to all secret activity**." (184-185)

Interestingly, Helms himself talks of a process of "osmosis": "Even though I was not directly involved in or consulted on any aspect of the activity, I had by osmosis gained a reasonable idea of what was going on." (178)

Back to Hayden

It is mind-boggling to read the continuation of the Hayden's sentence, "...and at diners and steakhouses near the Agency" (MH2 - 147). Not only do the employees talk among themselves inside the organization, but they feel free to talk about their job (i.e. secrets) outside, at diners!

The Israeli military intelligence has a unit called "Field Security". This unit is in charge of ensuring that soldiers will not talk about their job anywhere outside their post. This unit might even send undercover agents on buses, trains, etc. to listen to soldiers, and if they reveal secrets, or even close to a secret, they court-martial them.

When I taught a class in Singapore for their military, I saw that the mouse pads had slogans calling for soldiers to keep silent and not talk about their job. Common sense. How can it be that a secret organization would be so negligent in keeping secrets? What do the news media need to do? To post an employee in each diner and to sit and eat all day long and write whatever they hear. And if not the news media, maybe the Russians or the Chinese, or any other hostile force.

The Ames "Debacle"

Hayden says that due to "the Ames debacle" the counterintelligence efforts were "reenergized". (MH1 – 278). Why to "reenergize" after a "debacle"? Why not to work on preventing such a "debacle"?

Hayden says that Ames was caught "...during a routine polygraph" (MH1 - 278).

And former Director of CIA Richard Helms says in his book: "...Aldrich Ames's record as **an undisciplined, drunken, and indifferent CIA officer** did not interfere with his continued access to highly classified data until shortly before his arrest. While on duty in Washington, Ames **lived handsomely beyond the constraints of his civil service salary**." (155)

In other words, Ames was only caught "during a routine polygraph" because of lack of observations by people around him, including his supervisors and colleagues.

Again, we see how the US intelligence relies upon "high tech". Why isn't management responsible to watch out for any change in behavior of the people under them? And just as people who are appointed to high-level positions in the government are asked to produce their tax returns, why not ask each CIA employee to produce his/her tax return once a year, and to describe in detail their standard of living. Where they live, how much they paid for their house, their mortgage, the cars they own. Standard procedure that can be requested once a year. This will raise a red flag once one report deviates seriously from the previous year, or if a person's standard of living deviates from his/her reported income. True. It is not "high tech" like polygraph, but it can bring the same results, and not allow a person to operate several years under the radar.

It is not what is done that counts, it is how it is seen

Hayden says that "Jim Woolsey's tenure (1993-1995) was forever darkened by the Aldrich Ames case, even though that Russian spy was actually uncovered on his watch." (MH1 278)

Although Ames operated for several years previously, still the individual who was CIA Director when Ames was caught suffered a loss of respect, and in Hayden's words, his tenure "…was forever darkened…" If one thinks this is a one time operation, let's see how Hayden related to his own tenure: "Fortunately, during my time as director, there were no hostile penetrations of CIA (that have yet been detected)." (MH1 - 279) He does not talk of an actual hostile penetration of the CIA. He emphasizes in parenthesis: "(that have yet been detected)".

But the catchword in his sentence is the first one: "Fortunately". He was just "fortunate". He doesn't even attribute it to his efforts of preventing such occurrence. It is quite likely because there was no such effort. It is just a matter of "luck".

It is no wonder that secrets are not kept. "Nothing does." It is so because nobody is responsible for ensuring that they will be kept secret. And if there is a "debacle" or "kerfuffle" nobody is removed from their position.

Failure in Perception and Attitude

Michael Hayden says: "For me, the center of gravity of this conflict is not a war between civilizations (Christians versus Muslims), but rather a war within a civilization, within Islam itself." (MH2 - 50)

The problem in this statement is the first two words: "For me". As if Hayden is the center of the universe, and his view is the dominant view. The fact is that as an intelligence officer, Hayden should "listen" to the enemy. I don't mean to just "intercept" messages, but to actually listen to what the enemy says.

When Khomeini in Iran called the US "The Great Satan" (and Israel "The Small Satan"), it is not what Hayden was thinking. It is what they were saying. When Bin Laden declared war on the US, it was not what Hayden was thinking but it was what Bin Laden was saying.

When Hitler in Nazi Germany started to talk about getting rid of the Jews, many of the Jews went "the Hayden way" and dismissed what he said as only rhetoric, only to find later that he had meant what he said.

After the Oslo agreement in 1993, Arafat gave a speech in South Africa, and said that when he signed the agreement with Israel he was only following in the footsteps of the prophet Mohammad, who had signed a treaty with his opponents only because he was weak. And two years later, when Mohammad had become stronger, he ignored the treaty and attacked his opponents. When this speech surfaced right away, the advocates of the Oslo agreement dismissed it as just rhetoric. It was not rhetoric. In September 2000, Arafat started a full-scale war with Israel.

Both Hitler and Arafat[2] said what they were planning to do, and what they were doing, and people tried to find the deep meaning behind the words, only to dismiss the words themselves. This is the reason that no Israeli leadership will dismiss the words of the Ayatollahs in Iran, who declare their wish to eliminate Israel from the face of the earth. Israeli leadership cannot say it is rhetoric. They have to take it very seriously. Israel cannot do what Hayden does, when he starts his dismissal of the enemy's words by asserting "For me".

In talking about India testing its nuclear bomb, former Director of CIA George Tenet says in his book: "…both the U.S. Intelligence and policy communities had an underlying mind-set that Indian government officials **would behave as ours behaved**. We did not sufficiently accept that Indian politicians **might do what they had openly promised** – conduct a nuclear test, as the incoming ruling party had said it would. The lesson learned is that **sometimes intentions do not reside in secret** – they are out there for all to see and hear." (GT 45)

Hayden continues by saying, "Brussels, Berlin, Manchester, Barcelona, San Bernardino, and other attacks invite the former conclusion...", meaning, that it is a war between civilizations. But Hayden will not let the facts derail him. He is into "assessment". Just like the "assessment" of the NSA in the Gulf of Tonkin fiasco, or the "assessment" regarding the WMD in Iraq, two "assessments" that led the US into unnecessary major wars. Does the US Intelligence keep the country "safe and free", or maybe with its "assessments" it keeps the US "unsafe and unfree"?

Hayden continues with bringing us the "reality": "...but the reality is that the victims of Jihadist terrorism have overwhelmingly been Muslim..."

What Hayden does not understand, or maybe he doesn't want to understand, is that the "reality" is that the Jihadists do not care if they kill Moslems. It is not even a consideration for them. One only needs to read the book "The Infidel" by the Somali author Ayaan Hirsi Ali, who accurately portrayed the violence that takes place in the Moslem society against its own members. If violence within the Moslem society is no big deal, why would it be a big deal if Moslems get killed in terrorist activities? It is simply "collateral damage" for them, or maybe even less – to the point that it is "meaningless".

Hayden criticizes the Trump campaign by saying, "When we describe this struggle – as the Trump campaign did – as a struggle between civilizations, we adopt the narrative of ISIS and al-Qaeda that there is undying enmity between Islam and the West" (MH2 - 53).

One should note the 9/11 Commission said in their report:

"…both President Clinton and President Bush chose not to seek a declaration of war on Bin Ladin **after he had declared and begun to wage war on us**…" (9/11 102)

In 2013, John Brennan, in his appearance before the Senate Committee on Intelligence in his confirmation hearing to the post of CIA Director said, "We remain at war with Al-Qaida and its associated forces…" (JB 26)

In other words, Michael Hayden's saying that candidate Trump was "adopt[ing] the narrative of ISIS and al-Qaeda that there is undying enmity between Islam and the West" is a misleading statement. The fact (not "assessment") is that both of these terrorist organizations declared war on the US.

In other words, to listen to your self-declared enemy is not to "adopt the narrative". It is called being "careful" and "vigilant". It is the only way to win a war.

"Safe and free" as an objective

When the US Intelligence Community defines its objective as keeping the United States "safe and free", the Intelligence Community is taking the role of the US military. The US has military to keep it "safe and free".

The duty of the Intelligence Community is to provide a warning against an attack. If this is in fact the real and actual objective, then the whole US Intelligence Community is messing up.

In future chapters we will see what happens when a person and/or an organization does not do its job.

Should there be accountability for mistakes?

Hayden tells us that "the core issue in the inspector general's report … was the IG's recommendation that I form an accountability board (a kind of professional jury) to judge the behavior of the analyst who had launched the chain of events. **I declined**…" (MH1 – 279-280)

And he then moved to explain to his readers why there should be no "accountability": "…it had to do with the nature of intelligence and the near-absolute inappropriateness of applying law enforcement models to its conduct." (MH1 - 280) Really? Why in Israel were six Chiefs of Military Intelligence relieved of their jobs? And it was not a result of "punishment". Their performance showed that they were not the right people to hold the position.

And Hayden compares intelligence to law enforcement, where "…the appropriate standard of proof being beyond reasonable doubt…   None of that applies to intelligence…" (MH1 - 280). He concludes: "What might be admirable for a court system is unconscionable for an intelligence agency." (MH1 - 280)

Why would it be "unconscionable for an intelligence agency" to measure the performance of their people? After all, if they are consistently wrong, there must be a reason for it. Maybe they are not trained well. Maybe they are not well-versed in the area they cover – in the culture and/or the people. See for example how the CIA analysts predicted that Assad would retaliate for bombing his budding nuclear reactor, when in fact he didn't retaliate, as the bombers didn't boast about it. This is a simple feature of Arab culture that the CIA analysts were not aware of, and they judged the outcome from their own American eyes.

In his second book, Hayden quotes National Security Adviser McMaster as telling "an audience at the highly regarded Institute for the Study of War… 'He's [President Trump] a business person and what he demands is **results**. And what that has done is, it's changed the way that we do things.'" (MH2 – 163)

And what was Hayden's reaction to this assertion about demanding results? "There is something **inherently discomfiting** in that. There are some problems that cannot be simplified. They are inherently complex." (MH2 – 163)

Why would it be "inherently discomfiting" to demand "results"? After all, this is basic in every profession on earth, no matter which one. Why would intelligence (and in this case, only the US intelligence) be exempt from this basic requirement?

It is no wonder Hayden resists accountability. We see it in the way he ran NSA at the time of 9/11, where the agency intercepted two warning signs on 9/10, a day before the tragedy, and they delivered them only a day after 9/11. If this does not call for "accountability", then what more-significant failure will call for it? For NSA, 9/11 was not a "mistake". It was gross negligence in the way they define their job, and in the way they do it. It is bordering on criminal negligence.

TSA

Hayden is not the only one that resists results within the US intelligence/security system. The Transportation Security Agency (TSA) is the same.

Several years ago it was reported in the news that the TSA did its own survey to check the success rate of their screeners at the airports. They sent their own agents into the scanners, equipped with bomb components in their bags.

The results were that the screeners failed to detect 70% of these agents!!! In other words, they only detected 30% of them. But there was one exception in this survey: the San Francisco airport, where the success rate was 100%. The reason is that this is the only airport in the US that received permission to use a private company to run the security at the airport. The screeners were not TSA employees.

When the Chief of the TSA was asked in a congressional hearing to explain these dismal results, he said that it is no big deal. The security at the airport is not based on the scanners that all the passengers go through. The security is elsewhere. This "sophisticated" explanation was accepted.

A simple question: if the security is not at the scanners, then why put all the passengers through this trouble? No one at the congressional hearing even asked this simple, common-sense question.

The survey only reflected one major weakness in the TSA, a weakness that everyone passing through the airport can see. There are too many TSA employees who are just standing around, and are allegedly in charge. However, the real security is done by the person who sits looking at the monitor to see a 2-dimensional picture of 3-dimensional objects. I am not familiar with this profession, but looking at the monitor would not be any different from looking at pictures taken from above, as in the example we had before regarding the satellite picture of the nuclear reactor building in Syria. Looking at such a picture calls for expertise. I wonder how much training the screeners get before they are asked to decide if an object is a bomb, a component of a bomb, or anything else. Did anyone compare the training that an aerial photo analyst receives before going over satellite pictures, and the TSA employee looking at the monitor? In my unprofessional eye the two are basically the same, while very likely the training is very different.

The TSA might want to check what went right with the 30% who managed to find the bombs, and to apply this knowledge all over the system. In the meantime, the TSA should check again the ones who failed, and if they would fail again, to remove them from their position. Not as a punishment. They can find another position within the TSA system, maybe replenishing trays, but not as an analyst of the X-ray images.

Summary

We see the same situation in both Intelligence and the TSA. There are no expectations of "results". The words "results" and "accountability" are unheard of.

Israeli Security/Intelligence Community and Civilian Authority

Introduction

Many years ago, one of the reading assignments in the SCAN course was a few chapters from the book "I Have Captured Eichmann" by Peter Mann. The challenge in that book was to find a mistake in the pronouns, a mistake that exposes the identity of the author of the book.

In the book, the author brings us the following: the team had already captured Eichmann, and they were holding him in a safe house and waiting for the plane that would transfer all of them back to Israel. The Chief of the Mossad arrived and ordered them that in case the police or anyone else would raid the place, to handcuff themselves to the "prisoner" and to declare themselves as Israeli agents, and to send whoever it was to his hotel, and that he would deal with them. Once the Chief was on his way, the agents discussed whether to obey the Chief's order, and they decided not to obey, and to deal with the situation on their own, without involving their Chief in the situation.

In one of my classes, one of the students asked me, how could the agents disobey an order? How can any organization function when an employee can decide on his own, to disobey the order of their superiors?

I had to explain to him that this is a cultural difference between the US – where hierarchy is set and rigid, and Israel – where "authority" is not carved in stone.

The Israeli Armed Forces

One should notice that in the title of this section, I intentionally avoided using the word "military", as it is quite doubtful if what Israel has is actually "military".

Prime Minister Golda Meir was once quoted that we can forgive the Arabs for killing us, but we cannot forgive the Arabs for forcing **our sons** to kill them. Golda Meir didn't call them "soldiers". For her, they were "our sons". And in fact, most parents in Israel would not consider the three years of their sons' required military service as their becoming soldiers. The parents will say that they are "giving their sons" to the army. And in fact, there are many situations in which the parents will call their son's commander and complain of the treatment their son gets in the unit. This means that any military commander in Israel has to not only to lead his "soldiers", and to satisfy his own commanders, but he also has to be a "public relations" guy, dealing with the parents of the "sons" who were drafted for a mandatory service of three years.

There were several incidents in which an entire unit decided to protest against a cruel commander, and they convened together and decided to leave their post and go home. Of course the military court-martialed them, and sent them to a military prison for two weeks for going AWOL, but the commander was "burnt" for good, and there would be no way that he would ever serve as a commander in the military. The unit achieved their goal of removing their commander at the expense of two weeks in prison. It should be noted that the parents supported their sons' decision to go AWOL.

An American young man who joins the US military on his own initiative, to "see the world", might not see his family at home for several months. In comparison, an Israeli 16-year-old in high school will get his draft notice to come and go through all the tests, so that two years later, when he graduates high school, he will be drafted into the military, and the military will already know the capabilities and skills of this 18-year-old. And if this 18-year-old would not see his family once in two or three weeks, the military would have a time bomb in their hands.

To sum it up, Israel does not have a "military". Not in the sense that the US has, or even other countries have. It will be more accurate to say that Israel has a "militia". And in fact, many times the Israeli military is called "the people's army". After all, all the components of society are represented in this "militia" – from the poorest to the richest. From the extreme left to the extreme right. From the religious to the anti-religious. Moreover since the military brings together people from all parts of the country, it is considered in Israel to be the biggest "matchmaker" in society.

In addition, since a combat unit will remain together after the three-year service as a "reserve" unit, it will serve its members as a social network for many years to come.

At the time of the Vietnam War, President Johnson asked the Israeli Defense Minister Moshe Dayan to send a token Israeli unit to serve in Vietnam, maybe even just a hospital, to show support for the American effort. After all, the United States was supporting Israel militarily and diplomatically. Dayan responded that even if he would like to do so, and if he could even give such an order, no Israeli soldier would obey such an order.

In fact, the only time the Israeli military today functions in other countries is at the time of a natural disaster. When the earthquake hit Haiti, within one day an Israeli military hospital with 220 medical personnel was set up to treat the injured. The same happened in Nepal and in Thailand. An Israeli soldier will understand going out of Israel if he/she is requested to save lives. He/she will obey such an order. But no "son" or "daughter" will obey an order to fight a war that is not his/her own.

A View from Inside the Israeli "Militia"

Giora Eiland served in the IDF (Israel Defense Forces) and reached the rank of Aluf (Two-Star General; the highest rank in the IDF is the Chief of Staff, who has three stars). In his book Eiland gives us a very accurate view of the IDF.

"The assumption is that the military is a hierarchical organization, and at the end of every discussion 'the commander decides and everyone has to obey.' This assumption is not correct at all." (169)

And if anyone is surprised by this assertion, Eiland explains it in another place in his book. "The success of a commander also depends on the **willingness** of his subordinates to help him to succeed. When this component exists – the sky is the limit, and when it is less, and the commanders are only carrying out the orders of the unit commander 'by the

book' – there is an erosion in the capability and the morale of the unit."
(90)

Going 'by the book" is sometimes called in Israel "an Italian strike". This
means that the employee (and in this case the soldier) will only do what is
necessary, and he/she will take their time doing it, slowing down the
process significantly.

And if it is not clear enough to anyone who is not familiar with what goes
on inside the IDF, Eiland describes it clearly for the reader: "Anything
relating to personnel issues **is not based only upon orders and formal
authority**, it is important to hold conversations and to know how to
convince the soldier's commanders." (104). Eiland continues: "The **ability
to convince** the commanders who are subordinate to you, is in my eyes the
most important thing in military leadership. True leadership is the ability to
cause people to do (and mainly to want to do) what is important to you, and
without exerting authority. It is true that as a commander the last word is
always yours, **but it is better not to reach that point**." (106)

Eiland fought in several wars, including one of the most serious battles of
the Yom Kippur War, and took part in the Entebbe raid to rescue the Israeli
hostages. He tells what he learned from his combat experience: "…the
most important lesson I learned from the war was sharp and clear: take care
of yourself (and your unit), **since nobody else will take care of you**. (93)

"Nobody else will take care of you"? Is it only a slogan? Eiland goes on
to explain the success of the Israeli "militia": "The great luck of the IDF in
the Yom Kippur War was that the lower ranks of officers understood
quickly that 'this is what we have and with this we will win.' The
commanders who succeeded in the war were those who understood quickly
that the responsibility to solve problems is theirs, **and they should not
expect too much help from above**." (69), and "As we saw in all the wars,
and mainly in the Six-Day War and the Yom Kippur War, the ones who
won the wars were mainly the low-ranking officers in their mandatory
service and in the reserves." (332)

And as a two-star general, Eiland moves to indict the Israeli military
leadership.

"The ignorance of the IDF leadership on the eve of the Yom Kippur War
was in my opinion a more significant factor than the serious intelligence

mistake." (189). And: "The senior IDF commanders certainly were not stupid, but they did not relate seriously to learning the profession. Most of them lacked the knowledge, the intellectual curiosity, and the self-criticism that are so essential in the military profession." (193) And: "The amateur way of giving orders and the behavior of the senior officers **in the ranks of Chief of Staff or the commanders of the fronts**, that resembled more the behavior of a company commander, all of these reflected terrible ignorance." (195)

The strength of the lower ranks of officers in the Israeli "militia" is what drives the success of Israel in its battles and wars.

Eiland is not the only one with such an assessment. Kenneth Bilby was a journalist reporting on the War of Independence in 1948-1949. In his book he gives an accurate assessment of the success of Israel in 1948, fighting against seven Arab countries that invaded Israel after its declaration of independence.

While Bilby talks about the weakness of the Arab soldier as "lack of individuality, his incapacity to act without orders" (110), the opposite is true of the Israeli soldier. "…when officers were killed and the lowliest non-coms jumped into command." (110)

While Eiland condemns the IDF High Command, Bilby chips in with his observation: "Without question, the entire General Staff of the Israeli Army could have been eliminated in one stroke and replacements would have been found. The Jews had no indispensable men, and the broad base of trained talent on which the Army rested gave it one more whip hand over the enemy." (110)

How come "the lowliest non-coms" can take command? Shlomo Gazit, who was Chief of Military Intelligence, explains it by describing his training in the "Haganah" - the para-military force that was organized before Israel's independence: "There is not much similarity between the program of the course we had then and the courses for squad leaders in the IDF of today. The emphasis in the course we took was on the "commander". We were trained above all for positions of command, to take responsibility and to make decisions. At the time, they perceived the squad leader as someone who is meant to be at least "half a general". Every squad leader learned how to make an assessment of the situation (they called it then "tuning in to the enemy's logic"), when his expected position was indeed to lead a squad, but we received training and principles that would **enable each one of us to command a platoon, a company, or even larger**." (27)

According to Eiland's description, Bilby might be right in saying that the IDF High Command "could have been eliminated in one stroke" and still Israel would succeed in the war, based upon the lower ranking officers - the lieutenants and the captains.

And as Eiland condemns the IDF for not examining the weaknesses of its performance in the war, Bilby says correctly: "When an underdog suddenly finds itself on top, both the audience and the underdog are prone to consider him something special. This is what happened in Israel - in the sweep of victory **the mistakes got buried under the carpet's edge**." (77).

If the situation is so problematic, how does Israel succeed?

There are two answers for it. Bilby mentions one of them in his book: "I once asked one of the top Israeli military strategists what policy the government would adopt if the Middle East became a world battle arena. He answered without a moment's delay: 'If either the Russian or American armies crossed our borders, we would probably allow them to overrun the country without resistance. At the present time this seems the best chance of sparing our country from destruction and of ultimately regaining our sovereignty.'" (112-113).

The other answer is a Biblical one: Israel is described as "a land which the Lord your God cares for; the eyes of the Lord your God are always upon it, from the beginning of the year to the end of the year." (Deuteronomy 11:12)

Half-jokingly I say: why does the verse describe the Almighty's eyes in the plural? I say that the reason is that if He would blink one eye, the Israeli leadership might mess up and lose the country.

If one thinks that this is true only regarding 1948, let's how Giora Eiland describes the US and Israel: "The negotiations between the American **elephant** and the Israeli **mouse**..." (349). And this is not 1948, but 2018, 70 years later.

More about disobeying an order

During the Six Day War, the Defense Minister didn't want the Israeli military to reach the Suez Canal. He wanted the forces to stop around 10 km from the Canal. His reasoning was that if the Canal would remain open, it would be a great barrier against a future war.

There was one captain from the Armored Corps who took his unit to swim in the Canal. Moreover, he asked his people to take his picture with him in the water holding his rifle over his head. The picture reached the news, and "Israel took the Canal". Later on, this captain went up the ranks to reach the rank of One-Star General.

Not only a captain can disobey an order. Dan Halutz, the Chief of Staff at the time of the Second Lebanon War in 2006, tells us in his book that the government approved each military plan he presented to them. However, it took him a week to realize that the Commander of the Northern Front, who was in charge of actually running the war, was not doing what he was supposed to do. In other words, a two-star general was disobeying the orders of a three-star general.

At this point in the book, the former Chief of Staff started a long discussion over the next 80 pages, about what he should do with this disobedient general. Should he fire him? But how can he do that when they are friends? Before he managed to reach a decision, the war came to a close.

One might think this is a joke. Unbelievable. I told one of my cousins about the book, and she said, "There is no way that someone would write about such stupidity in a book." I challenged her to read the 80 pages. When she finished reading, she said: not only is he stupid, but this is stupidity squared! He not only behaved stupidly, but he described his stupidity in a book for everyone to see.

When the Arabs in Judea and Samaria (sometimes called "the West Bank") and the Gaza Strip started their riots in 1987, the Prime Minister at the time, Yitzhak Shamir, called the Military Chief of Staff (Dan Shomron) and told him to take all necessary measures to suppress the riots. The response of the Chief of Staff was that there is no military solution to this problem. End of discussion.

Moshe Arens, in his book "In Defense of Israel", tells us about an encounter he had as Defense Minister with the Military Chief of Staff. At the time terror attacks were at their height in Judea and Samaria. And the Defense Minister wanted to reduce the terrorism, if not to eliminate it altogether.

Let's see the description of the meeting the military and the civilian authority.

"I summoned to my office all the senior generals, including Ehud Barak - whom I had appointed as Chief of Staff instead of Dan Shomron - and I read to them the list of the recent terror events. Preventing these terror attacks, I announced, will from now on be the first priority of the military. I told them, there is a need to increase significantly the number of soldiers stationed in Judea and Samaria and even to position there elite units and special forces." (204)

Imagine that the Defense Minister had to tell the Chief of Staff that his responsibility is to ensure the safety and security in the area. And Arens continues: "When Barak started to argue with me..." – of course he wanted to argue. How could the Defense Minister tell the Chief of Staff how to set priorities for the Israeli "militia"? But unlike Prime Minister Shamir, who didn't argue with the Chief of Staff who resisted his order to take out terrorism in the area, Arens moved to impose his will on the generals.

"...I raised my voice and I said that if he does not succeed in suppressing this wave of terror, [Chief of Staff] Barak himself and all his staff will have to position themselves in the field and take an active part in the task that I had assigned to the military. That's how the discussion ended." (204)

And Arens ends his description by saying, "During the next five months we started to bring an end to the Intifada that had been going on wildly for two and a half years." (204)

It should be noted that Arens, a professor of engineering, did not serve in the military. Moreover, he is American-born. Shamir, who was a Mossad agent before entering politics, understood the military Chief of Staff who refused his order, while the American-born Defense Minister acted as any American Defense Secretary would when talking with his generals.

The response of these two Chiefs of Staff exposed a point about which people outside Israel are not aware. Even when the government might be a right-wing government, the high-ranking officers are mostly left-leaning people, if not even extreme left. This is because the High Command is an "old boys' club" (or in Hebrew: "one friend brings another") where the previous members of the High Command appoint the new ones, usually choosing like-minded colleagues. And since Israel was ruled by the Labor party for its first few decades, the High Command became – and remains to this day – a left-wing club.

Eiland in his book tells about the following encounter he had with an officer after a meeting of the High Command with the brigade commanders. The officer told Eiland: "You generals, the members of the General Command Staff, you have the same opinions, you use the same explanations, the same language, and even the same metaphors. It is scary." (226-227).

Since Eiland himself was a member of the "club" he is "suspected" of being "left-leaning" if not an outright "leftist". Supporting this "suspicion", Eiland brings in his book an incident in which he had to debate a representative from the "Palestinian Authority" at a conference in Europe. But the "Palestinian" didn't show up; and in order to prevent the cancellation of the debate, Eiland offered the organizers that he would represent both sides. He did such a good job that one of the attendees told him that he even represented the Arab side better than the Israeli side. Eiland didn't see anything wrong by representing the "Palestinian" side, and in fact he did a great job, better than his representation of the Israeli side. After all he is a member of the "club".

Eiland mentions in his book an incident in which the Deputy Chief of Staff Yair Golan, at the ceremony for Holocaust Memorial Day in Israel, went on the podium and gave a speech in which he expressed "…his concern about dangerous trends in Israeli society…" (182).

Eiland, as a member of the "club" of High Command continued: "…he was criticized harshly, not so much because of the words he said, but because of the place and time." (182)

Really? Eiland neglects to tell us that Golan said that while there are "dangerous trends in Israeli society" there is no leadership to deal with these trends. This "no leadership" comment was said in the presence of Prime Minister Benjamin Netanyahu who was in the audience with several members of his government.

The Defense Minister Yaalon, who was a former Chief of Staff, and therefore a member of the "club", made a public statement commending the officer for expressing his opinion. Within two weeks, this Defense Minister was replaced. The officer was not. After all, the government cannot fire a "soldier". Only the Chief of Staff can. But he is also a member of the "club". Let's not forget the 80 pages of the former Chief of Staff who had to deal with a disobedient general.

Eiland, concludes this incident by saying, "I think that he did a courageous thing." (182) "Courageous"? There are definitions for such behavior. "Courageous" is not one of them,.

Incidentally, the government recently approved the officer who would replace the Chief of Staff at the end of his term. The self-righteous leftist general who was preaching to the Prime Minister was not appointed, although nominally he was a candidate.

Yair Golan is not the only outspoken leftist of the "club". Since most high-ranking officers might find their way to either the Mossad or the General Security Service, we find the "club" present in these organizations as well.

Not long ago, there was a book published in Israel, "The Gatekeepers"[3], in which six former chiefs of the General Security Service were interviewed at length. (A movie was later made from this book.) Out of the six, five are extreme leftists, supporting the "Palestinian" struggle against Israel. Only one is right-wing; today he is a member of the Likud party, which is also the party of Prime Minster Netanyahu.

In view of this situation of actual chaos in the relationship between the civilian authority and personnel of the military and security organizations, we can also examine the relationship between elected officials and those who are appointed.

History

Two traumatic events took place in Israel that impacted the relationship between the Intelligence Community and the civilian authority.

The former chief of the Mossad briefly mentions in his book – "The Lavon Affair [Hebrew: the 'fiasco operation'] took place in 1954, two years after the Officers' Revolution in Egypt. In general it was a huge failure of our

Military Intelligence, a misstep that left behind it deep cracks in Israeli society." (247)

He referred to an operation in which the Israeli intelligence recruited Egyptian Jews for espionage and sabotage of American facilities in Cairo. This was done as a false-flag operation, in order to bring hostility between the new Egyptian regime and the US administration. The operation failed, and the group was arrested and tried. Two members were executed, and the rest were sentenced to long and harsh imprisonment.

Since failure is always an "orphan", and no one wants to take responsibility, there was a major dispute between the Chief of Military Intelligence and the Defense Minister, where each one of them accused the other of having given the order to carry out this failed operation. The "deep cracks in Israeli society" that the Chief of the Mossad referred to, were the events that brought the Prime Minister to demand a commission of inquiry to find out "who gave the order?" The Labor Party, which was the party of the Prime Minister, refused to go along with the Prime Minister's wish, and the Prime Minister resigned.

The second traumatic event was when there was a dispute between Prime Minister Shamir (who was a Mossad agent before entering politics) and the head of the General Security Service regarding what was the exact order that the Prime Minister gave to the Head of the General Security. Investigation showed that the Head of the Security Service tried to frame the Prime Minister, and when this was discovered, the Head of the Security Service had to resign. Since then, no Prime Minister in Israel meets any of the Chiefs of Intelligence without a secretary being present and taking a shorthand version of every single word being said in these meetings.

The recording of these meetings brought a former chief of the Mossad to comment on this situation:

"Since these briefing sessions were recorded both in shorthand and in tape form, he (Prime Minister Shamir), like others, had his eye on history no less than on the current conduct of the affairs of state. The result was that whereas in actual fact the prime minister was fully aware of the fact that he was briefing an emissary, in terms of the written protocol he rarely could be caught making a policy statement of any consequence." (45)

These two traumatic events crystallized the importance in Israel of the civilian authority over the Intelligence Community, realizing that people who deal with intelligence (espionage and deception) might be tempted to lie even when they shouldn't do so.

One cannot conclude this list of Israeli failures without mentioning the recruitment of Jonathan Pollard, a Jewish American citizen employed by the US Navy, who was recruited by Israel as a spy.

The Pollard case exposed the bureaucratic entanglement of the various Israeli intelligence agencies. Although the Mossad and the General Security Service are directly under the Prime Minister, the defense minister established his own "intelligence service" called "the Bureau of Scientific Relations" that was chaired by Rafi Eitan, who was a veteran Mossad agent. This "bureau" recruited Pollard to supply Israel with satellite images of Iraq, images that the US intelligence refused to share with Israel.

When Pollard was caught, Moshe Arens in his book brings the following: "The Foreign Affairs and Defense Committee of the Knesset (Parliament) established a special sub-committee chaired by Abba Eban (former foreign minister) to investigate the case. After continued discussions, the members of the committee reached the conclusion: 'It is clear beyond any doubt that the Bureau of Scientific Relations chaired by Rafi Eitan decided to recruit and employ Pollard **without consulting the political level and did not receive any approval**, direct or indirect, for this activity.' Rabin and I together were criticized for the inefficient supervision of the activities of this unit, which functions under the authority of the Defense Minister." (138)

The Pollard affair had the impact of Israel moving into the production of its own satellites, delivered into space mostly by Israeli self-produced rockets.

Eiland in his book brings us his take on the Israeli satellite project: "Our impressive intelligence capability was achieved, among other things, due to the Israeli satellite project, that had started about 20 years previously. This project was forced upon the IDF by the Defense Minister Moshe Arens, and it is one example among many of **the short-sightedness that the IDF can suffer from** when facing the civilian authority that is in charge of it." (291)

Israeli Prime Minister

Prime Minister Yitzhak Shamir, who succeeded Prime Minister Menachem Begin, was a former Mossad agent before entering politics. The Chief of the Mossad at the time of his tenure as Prime Minister was Ephraim Halevy, who described Shamir in his book as being "…imbued with a keen belief of ultimate personal responsibility for the very destiny of the Jewish people." Halevy continues by saying that this sense of "personal responsibility" was "…a characteristic common to most or all of those who occupied the post of prime minister in Israel's hitherto short history." (47)

One should note that Halevy is attributing this "sense of responsibility" only to "**most** or all of those who occupied the post of prime minister in Israel…" In other words, he cannot hide his criticism of one prime minister, criticism that he brings in another place in his book.

In comparing Prime Minister Shamir (Likud) to Prime Minister Shimon Peres (Labor), Halevy says that Shamir "…had his eye on history in the broader sense of the term… He certainly was sensitive to his role and place in the annals of his people and country, but being a cautious and suspicious person, he was never in a rush or a hurry to produce instant success, nor did he court populism and instant glory." Peres, on the other hand, "…always threw caution and good counsel to the winds." (51)

The Prime Minister of Israel is not only a "prime" minister heading the Israeli government. At the same time, the Prime Minister is also in charge of the Mossad, the General Security Service, The Nuclear Commission, and the Space Agency. This means that the Prime Minister, among his other responsibilities, is also the civilian authority over the Intelligence Community, except for the important Military Intelligence that is under the Chief of Staff and the Defense Minister. As we already saw earlier, the Chief of Military Intelligence is a frequent visitor at the Prime Minister's office for intelligence and security briefings.

The Prime Minister at the time of the Second Lebanon War (2006), Ehud Olmert, in his book says: "They came to present to me a very complex and sensitive military operation, that would involve many risks, and I was the one who would decide whether or not the operation would be carried out… I had heard of such operations in the past, I knew of their existence and at times even of their results, but I had never been asked to approve an operation like this" (645).

Earlier, we saw that the military secretary of the Prime Minister is an observer at the meetings of the Head of Services Committee, giving the civilian authority (the Prime Minister) the knowledge of what is going on in these meetings.

Ehud Olmert in his book tells us about this military secretary: "The position of the Military Secretary is unique. He is privy to the top secrets of the state, and he reads Intelligence material to an extent and variety that nobody sees except the Prime Minster. Not even the Defense Minister" (639-640).

The Prime Minister is not the "Commander-in-Chief"

Although the Prime Minister wields a lot of power by being in charge of important services, he is not equivalent of the US "Commander-in-Chief".

Former Prime Minister Ehud Olmert describes in his book how he wanted to expand the operation in the Gaza Strip, to occupy the area that connects the Gaza Strip to Egypt, to prevent any smuggling of contraband via tunnels, only to be opposed by the military that didn't want to suffer casualties in doing so:

"But it was clear to me that a military operation in these conditions is almost impossible, with the objection of the Defense Minister, the Foreign Minister, the Chief of Staff and several other generals. One cannot send soldiers to the battlefield when the Chief of Staff and the Defense Minister object." (771)

The Prime Minister and the Intelligence Chief

Meir Amit, a former Chief of the Mossad in the years between the 1967 and 1973 wars, describes in his book several incidents in which a turning point in an operation mandated approval of the Prime Minister:

"First thing we had to telegraph Israel **and to request approval from the Prime Minister** for such a daring move …" (145), and "…mainly because I wanted to consider the matter at leisure, to consult our experienced and expert people, and to get the approval of the Prime Minister before I would take any additional step…" (161)

Amit describes his relationship with the Prime Minister as "ambivalent": "On one hand, Eshkol had trust and appreciation towards me, and I assume also a friendly attitude, he appreciated my work and the work of the Mossad. On the other hand, there was a great deal of suspicion by him towards me, mainly because of the pressures of domestic politics, that were imposed on him by a group of advisors headed by Isser Harel, who saw me as "Dayan's man[4]" and did whatever they could to disgrace me in his eyes." (187)

Amit describes the influence and impact of the **domestic** politics on the work of the **foreign** intelligence service, the Mossad:

"Most of the initiative for an activity **comes from the bottom** and not from the top. The Prime Minister is a busy person, totally immersed in solving political entanglements and in political battles within the party and between parties. When he finds the time to meet the head of the intelligence service, he doesn't always listen to him." (265)

Amit also discusses the role of the Mossad in delivering the information to the Prime Minister. Is the role of the Intelligence Community only to supply the information as it is, or are there other aspects that need to be addressed while delivering the information:

"Therefore the question arises, does the head of the intelligence service need to present to his superiors just a report of the situation and to suffice with that, or should he also analyze this picture **and present various options for action**, and maybe to even go one step further and also **to recommend a specific option**. On this matter there are differences of opinion among the people in the field. I am among those who claim that it is necessary to go all the way, not only to present the data and options to the leader, but also to express an opinion and to recommend an action." (259)

In other words, Amit does not see any contradiction between being an objective and unbiased deliverer of the data, and to also make additional suggestions for action and to even recommend one specific action.

Another former chief of the Mossad, Ephraim Halevy, brings us in his book a description of his meetings with then Prime Minister Shamir:

"…and, more often than not, he preferred to invite me to suggest to him what should be said at a forthcoming encounter." (45)

In his book, Aaron Zeevi Farkash, a former chief of the Military Intelligence, brings us a different approach. According to him, the intelligence officer should only deliver the information to the political level without adding any advice:

"An intelligence agency must not take upon itself the role of an advisor. I used to tell the Prime Minister that he can approach and consult with whomever he sees fit, and with me as well. By means of the process of collecting and assessing information, I of course could study the issue in which he was interested and to give answers, but I had no added value in the field of advising." (33)

Still, Prime Minister Sharon, who had been a general in the military before entering politics, did not accept this position. Farkash describes a meeting he had with Prime Minister Sharon:

"At the end of presenting the intelligence picture on these issues, the Prime Minister asked me, 'So what do you recommend doing?' Apparently my facial expression did not manage to conceal my surprise at the question. Sharon emphasized to me that in his opinion there is reason for the intelligence expert to express his opinion as to what should be done, according to his knowledge of the opponent and the enemy, and from his capability to analyze the cases and the reactions to our operation or our activity." (42)

Aharon Zeevi Farkash also describes in his book an example where the Prime Minister and the government might act in a way that is not based upon the intelligence picture, due to other domestic considerations:

"…the question of distributing gas masks during the Gulf War of 2003. In a case like this, the official, organized Intelligence does not influence the decision of whether to distribute the masks. What influences such a decision above all is the decision makers' stress, **that makes them more attuned to the political and social environment**, both internal and external. If the minister in charge and members of the cabinet or government feel that the news media is pressuring them to distribute the gas masks, the intelligence assessment will not be the decisive consideration." (18)

Disagreement between the Prime Minister and the Chief of the Mossad

Zvi Zamir, another former chief of the Mossad, brings us in his book a major conflict he had with then Prime Minister Golda Meir.

Golda Meir wanted the Chief of the Mossad to relay certain information that the Mossad had to the US, and to relay it "as is" – as raw material. Zamir says, "I explained to her my position and I emphasized that relaying the raw information might endanger our source. I told her that if the information is important to the Americans, we will give them the content of the information, but not the raw material, as it exposes to a certain degree the source… But I told her, "If you decide that we should transfer the material, say so and I will do it." (81)

One should note that the chief ended his refusal with accepting the Prime Minister's authority to order him, and if she would do so, he would comply. However, Golda Meir didn't want to order it. She wanted him to agree to her position, and he didn't feel that he can do so. The two were at a stalemate, until another minister brought about a "compromise": "The agreement of the Prime Minister was that the information would be transferred to the Americans, and I would take care that the security of the source would not be harmed, and if it would be necessary, I would travel to the US myself to make sure of it." (82)

The above-mentioned disagreement dealt with an issue that is very important to an intelligence officer: the security and safety of a source of information. But we also have a case in which the disagreement was in regard to a policy.

The present Prime Minister, Benjamin Netanyahu, wanted to attack Iran in 2012, but was opposed by the military Chief of Staff, the Chief of Military Intelligence, and the Chief of the Mossad. The Chief of the Mossad even actively opposed the Prime Minister's plan by warning the US of the imminent attack.

A debate started in the news media in Israel as to whether an appointee (the Chief of the Mossad) can oppose an elected official (the Prime Minister), and if it is not "treason" to recruit foreign support for the appointee's point of view.

Incidentally, the Prime Minister later secured a liver transplant for the same chief of the Mossad (then retired) in an eastern European country, due to the age restrictions on such a surgery in Israel.

The relationship between the political level and the professional intelligence practitioner
is summarized nicely by Farkash, a former chief of Military intelligence:

"…He (Prime Minister Sharon) was more impatient, and many times he said, 'Chief of Intelligence, it is time for you to think also about the Jews, you always think about the Arabs in this scholarly description'… One time at the beginning of my term as Chief of Intelligence, he also said, not to my face, 'Farkash as Chief of Intelligence annoys me, but I need him.'" (38)

Intelligence and the Government

Eiland, a member of the High Command who does not come from the Intelligence, gives us in his book a view of how the intelligence chiefs present themselves in government sessions.

"The Intelligence people always have a lot to say, **whether their words serve the decision or not**. Nevertheless, till **the draining presentations** of the chiefs of Military Intelligence, the Mossad, and the General Security Service ended… (page 268)

And if this is not enough - "Even if the opening sentence of the chief of the Mossad is 'I agree one hundred percent with everything that the Chief of Military Intelligence has just said', even so he will not give up his right to deliver a speech of half an hour or more. The chief of the General Security Service continues after that along the same lines…. In this way the intelligence presentations, **that even so are frightfully draining**, turn into a sort of trivia game." (269). Eiland summarizes it by saying: "The discussion in the government started in the morning and it opened with long Intelligence presentations, **draining and irrelevant**…" (page 270)

Eiland complains about this state of affairs, but his complaint only demonstrates the fact that the Intelligence chiefs are an integral part of government sessions. All three chiefs are present to offer their "draining" presentations. And in fact, the government does not seem to object to these presentations, even when they are "draining" or even "irrelevant".

Why?

In a way, Eiland explains it. When he comes to compare the information provided by the Israeli Intelligence on Iraq to the one that the US Intelligence had, Eiland says: "We presented to them a book with hundreds of strategic targets in Iraq. We knew how to give a detailed explanation on the character of every such 'real estate site'. The Americans were in shock. It became apparent to us that at this stage, the level of their intelligence on targets in Iraq was extremely shallow." (page 291)

Eiland demonstrates that the Israeli Intelligence is great in collecting information. As for assessing it, the Yom Kippur War was testimony to the low grade that the Israeli Intelligence gets in this area. As a matter of fact, during the years, it seems that whenever the Chief of Military Intelligence gives his assessment to the public, one has to turn it around by 180 degrees to know what really will happen.

For example, three weeks before the Six-Day War, the Military Intelligence announced its assessment that they do not foresee any war in the next five years. The same was their assessment before the Yom Kippur War. It was before a national election, and the Labor party – that was at the time in power – put up ads all over the country that Israel has peace on its borders. When the war between Iraq and Iran started, the Chief of Military Intelligence appeared on TV and assessed that Iraq will win the war, and it will only last about a month. (In fact, it took nine years.) More recently, when the rebellion of the Sunni population started in Syria against the Assad regime, the Chief of Military Intelligence appeared on TV and assessed that Assad will be out of office quite quickly. (From this, I figured Assad will stay in power forever.)

The Israeli Military Intelligence cannot even assess correctly the prospects of peace. When Sadat announced that he is coming to Jerusalem, the news media published on their front page the assessment of the military that he is "bluffing" - that it is a ruse to start a war. One of the explanations of why Menachem Begin (of the Likud) could sign a peace treaty with Egypt, while Golda Meir (of the Labor party) couldn't, was that Golda Meir was entrenched with the military establishment, while Begin was not. He was an outsider.

[As a lesson from the Israeli experience to the present, one should note that three US administrations – starting with President Clinton, and continuing with President Bush and President Obama – failed to reach any accommodation with North Korea, while an "outsider" like President Trump **might** be able to accomplish what all of his predecessors could not. The first three listened too much to the military and Intelligence Community, while the "outsider" said in public that they are wrong all the time.]

And there are numerous examples of this phenomenon. Collecting information = great. Assessing it = very poor, if not even "non-existent".

And Eiland goes on to explain the impact of low quality intelligence on the performance of militaries: "The gap between high capabilities of firepower and a low level of intelligence capability is characteristic of most militaries in the world today in relation to most of the arenas. **This is also true of the IDF, even in relation to the campaign in the Gaza Strip or Lebanon**. At that time, the gap for the Americans concerning Iraq was huge. (Page 291)

One should note that Eiland is not sparing the Israeli Intelligence at all. Not even in regard to collecting information, when it comes to the Gaza Strip and Lebanon.

US Security/Intelligence Community
and Civilian Authority

Introduction

In going over Senator McCain's book, which he published just before he died, I encountered a few points that he mentioned in regard to the US Intelligence in general, and about the CIA in particular.

When talking about the debate in regard to the CIA Enhanced Interrogation Techniques (EIT), McCain said that "CIA officials had **misled him** [former attorney general Michael Mukasey] **as they had other Justice officials**, and, as it turns out, as they **misled senior White House officials, including President Bush and Vice President Cheney**" (98). He goes on to say that, "…most of the CIA's claims that abusive interrogations of detainees had produced vital leads to help locate bin Laden were **exaggerated, misleading, and in some cases, complete bullshit**" (99)

McCain also says that, "…CIA personnel hacked the [Congressional] investigators' computers, an unlawful act, and a violation of the separation of powers, which should have resulted in the firing of officials who had ordered it" (101)

In other words, Senator McCain says that the CIA used their intelligence prowess to spy on their own Congress. A unit of the executive branch spied on the legislative branch.

Moreover, according to McCain, the CIA felt strong enough to also do the following: "One of Tenet's successors [as CIA Director], General Michael Hayden, a vocal proponent of the interrogation program, **ordered an investigation of the inspector general's office** in response to criticism that Helgerson was on a 'crusade' against the program." (83). In other words, according to McCain, not only did the Director of the CIA feel free to spy on Congress, but he felt free to act against other units in the executive branch. If this is not enough, McCain goes on to say that "The CIA planted false stories in the press." (100).

So not only did the CIA spy on the legislative and executive branches, but it also actively manipulated the press to achieve its goals.

Since this analysis will be based upon three books – one published by James Clapper, who served as Director of National Intelligence, and two books published by Michael Hayden, the same Hayden that Senator McCain referred to above, we need to know what other people said about Hayden, and also what Hayden said about himself.

Michael Hayden

James Comey tells us in his book about his meeting with Michael Hayden, when Hayden was Director of the CIA, and Comey was the Deputy Attorney General.

According to Comey, Hayden's briefings "…were a river of really great-sounding stuff **that didn't make much sense once the briefing was over** and you tried to piece together what you had just heard." (83)

James Clapper in his book describes the following event.

When Clapper served as Director of the Defense Intelligence Agency, who was also in charge of appointing military attaches in US embassies, he got a call from JCS chairman General Colin Powell. When he met Powell, the first question Powell asked him was: ""Do you know this Mike Hayden guy?"

At the time, Clapper had only heard of Hayden as "…a fast-rising colonel assigned to the National Security Council staff who was on the brigadier-general promotion list" (JC 71) but Clapper didn't know Hayden personally. Clapper brings us Powell's request: "…he'd been told that someone on the NSC had slated Mike to become the next US defense attache to Moscow, apparently based on his earlier assignment as the Air Force assistant attache to Bulgaria from 1984 to 1986." (JC 71).

And Clapper tells us what Powell requested: "Powell informed me that wasn't going to happen. As JCS chairman, he was deeply involved in trying to forge a new relationship with a post-Soviet Russia and wanted his own trusted agent to represent him in Moscow." (JC 71)

It seems that Powell perceived Hayden as anti-Russian, and at the time he wanted "…to forge a new relationship with a post-Soviet Russia…" He couldn't trust Hayden to do so.

What was Powell really saying? That Hayden could not be "his own trusted agent"? That Hayden was not known to abide by the policy set up from above? That Hayden was known to be one that sets his own policy, and who does whatever he could to accomplish his own policy?

Michael Hayden on himself

Hayden openly says that he is very aware of the power of using pronouns in one's language. In talking about himself as a Director, "I always used **first person plural**: 'we're going to do this.' 'We're going to try that.' **Never first person singular. And never, never, never second person**. The routine use of 'you' would have deepened the chasm that was always threatening to open between me and a talented workforce." (MH1 - 17). He also says that "…government spokesmen (and even retirees like me) have to bend themselves into **linguistic pretzels of passive voice** and **oblique generalizations…**" (MH1 - 118-119)

Knowing Hayden's recognition of using passive voice as a means to conceal information, let's see how he started his second book.

James Comey, Director of the FBI (later fired by President Trump) and Mike Rogers, Director of the NSA, were asked in a Congressional hearing "if the president they were serving was misleading the nation with his claims that they or their British friends had wiretapped him while he was president-elect." The two answered that he was.

Hayden says that the two "were asked" (passive voice), and after they answered, Hayden said:

"That question doesn't get asked very often… let alone get answered – to say nothing of being answered in that way." (1)

Why did Hayden twice use passive voice for the question ("were asked" and "doesn't get asked"), and why did he use passive voice for the answer ("let alone get answered")? Does Hayden use "linguistic pretzels of passive voice" because President-elect Trump talked about "wiretapping", while the NSA and "their British friends" are more involved in "wireless-tapping"? In other words, the bureaucrats used the unfamiliarity of President-elect to be able to produce a technically true statement, but one that is very misleading.

Hayden is not only versed in using language for himself. He even showed that he would go out of his way to determine the language used by others. He describes in his first book a meeting that he had in which he advised the other person "…that he should never again use the words "torture" and "CIA" in the same paragraph. Torture was a legal term, I said. It has specific meaning. It was a felony. Associating it with the agency was inaccurate and would set in motion things that would be difficult, if not impossible, to control. There were lots of words available if he wanted to condemn any policy or practice of the past, but this shouldn't be one of them." (MH1 - 362)

John Brennan

In his appearance before the Senate Select Committee on Intelligence regarding his nomination for the position of Director of the CIA, John Brennan was asked whether "enhanced interrogation techniques" constitute "torture".

Brennan responded by saying, "I expressed my personal objections and views to some Agency colleagues about certain of those EITs, such as waterboarding, nudity, and others, where I professed my personal objections to it..." (JB35)

Please note the following:

First, the change of language from initially using "expressed" to later using "professed". This is an apparent "unjustified change of language" which might be a signal that deception is present in the sentence.

Second, to the best of my memory, in all of the discussions regarding the EIT, the emphasis was on "waterboarding". Nobody talked about "nudity". Here, John Brennan tells the Senate that "nudity" was part of the list.

When the abusive practices were exposed in the Abu Ghraib prison in Iraq, the pictures of "nudity" created a major shock that US soldiers could act on their own to abuse prisoners in such a way. In his testimony, John Brennan is telling Congress that nudity was part of EIT. Officially.

Back to John Brennan

When Brennan was pressed by the committee for an answer to the question as to whether EIT constitutes "torture", he said, "I have a personal opinion that waterboarding is **reprehensible**, and it's something that should not be done. And again, I am not a lawyer, Senator, and I can't address that question." (JB 51)

If we had any doubt that John Brennan was running away from the word "torture", the following confirms it: "…Senator, the term 'torture' has a lot of legal and political implications." (JB 51)

Later he said, "…The enhanced interrogation techniques were **brutal**…" (JB 58)

He was willing to use the words "reprehensible" and "brutal", but not "torture". The word "torture" was too much for both Hayden and Brennan.

The reality is that waterboarding is "torture", but these two high-ranking intelligence officials are more interested not in reality but in the way reality is being presented. Or in other words, they realize that language is more important than reality.

In a way, they expose the environment in which the CIA operated with these EIT. They realized that it is "reprehensible" and "brutal", and even "torture", but they had to "launder" the language to be able to use EIT.

James Clapper

We need a brief "introduction" to our second source of information for this analysis.

In his book, Clapper talks about Intelligence and policy making:

"There is an unwritten, almost sacred writ of the intelligence profession that we in intelligence should avoid engaging in policy formation or execution. We support policy makers by providing them timely, accurate, relevant, even anticipatory intelligence…" (JC 49). He also said that "As a lifelong intelligence officer, I instinctively live by the first, fundamental, unwritten law of intelligence work: Speak straight, unbiased intelligence truth to power, and leave the business of policy making to the policy makers." (JC 127)

It sounds good. But we should note two major points:

The first is a major change of language. While calling intelligence a "profession", Clapper calls the policy making a "business". It sounds as if "profession" is more reputable that "business.

If this is not enough, let's move to the second point. Clapper says that "…and **leave** the business of policy making to the policy makers."

The word "leave" implies that the "policy making" is given to the "policy makers" only because the ones in the intelligence "profession" leave it to them. The intelligence people are looking down on "policy makers".

If this is not enough, let's see another label Clapper has for policy making: "…but we don't participate in making the policy **sausage**…" (JC – 49). Now it is not only "business", but he looks upon "policy making" as a "sausage" – a dish which includes not only "meat" but a lot of other miscellaneous ingredients.

If "business" and "sausage" is not enough, let's see how Clapper relates to a US Senator who didn't go along with Clapper's wish: "I couldn't believe that a senator could be so disrespectful to a lieutenant general (oh, how naive I was), and I directed my staff to prepare a barn-burner response." (JC 69). Clapper's aide prevented him from sending this "barn-burner response", and thus saved Clapper from making a fool of himself. But apparently he still didn't "get it", as he put it openly in his book.

Summary

Realizing that the source of the above information is two people who were entrenched in the intelligence "profession" for a very long time, we can now move to the topic of the interaction between the intelligence "profession" and the policy making "business".

US Security/Intelligence and Civilian Authority

Clapper defines the Intelligence objective as**: "Our objective typically is to reduce uncertainty for decision makers as much as possible**, whether they're in the Oval Office, at the negotiating table, or on the battlefield." (JC – 49)

In other words, by using such a general term ("reducing uncertainty"), Clapper prevents any way of measuring whether the Intelligence is right or wrong. By comparison, in Israel the objective of intelligence is to produce a "warning" against an imminent attack, a definition that enables measuring if the intelligence is on target. Clapper prefers a very ambiguous definition that means practically nothing.

Was Clapper avoiding policy making?

Clapper says that "As DNI, I was careful not to advocate for specific policies in National Security Council meetings." (JC- 49).

Please note that Clapper does not say, "As a DNI I did not advocate for specific policies…" He only says that he was "careful not to" do so. Let's see how Clapper describes being "careful" in his book.

In regard to Korea, he says (in the same paragraph): "Korea was one issue on which I let President Obama know – **privately** – that I thought his policy rationale of not discussing anything else until North Korea agreed to end its nuclear capability and ambitions was flawed…" (JC 49)

By saying "privately" he means to say that he was "careful" – but not "careful" to avoid advocating a policy, just "careful" that he would not get caught doing so.

As for Korea, Clapper mentions that he was sent to North Korea to arrange the release of American citizens who were imprisoned in Korea. Before he embarked on his mission, he was told that he was not to discuss anything at all with the North Koreans, except for the release of the Americans. When he landed in North Korea, his North Korean counterpart, a general with the same rank, wanted to talk with him about policy. Abiding by the orders he had, he told the North Korean general that he cannot talk with him about anything but the American prisoners. From that point on, Clapper's stay in North Korea went wrong. He was able to free the American citizens, but from that point on, the North Koreans were very cold to him.

Reading Clapper's report, I really wondered how any Israeli military person with Clapper's rank would have acted. There is no doubt in my mind that the Israeli intelligence officer with any rank, whether a private or a general, would have loved to talk with the North Korean counterpart about policy. After all, it is a great way to collect information from the source itself. And there would have been no problem to explain it back home.

In another place in his book, Clapper says that "I told the president that, because this was a policy decision, **I was speaking as Jim Clapper and not as the DNI...**" (JC 152).
Why not use the same explanation with the North Korean general? And anyway, there is no way that Clapper can talk to the President of the US, as only "Jim Clapper". He was there as "DNI", and he couldn't shed his title to be able to talk about "policy making".

Summary

Although Clapper is very "careful" not to advocate a specific policy, a point that Prime Minister Sharon had openly asked his Chief of Military Intelligence to do, Clapper found a way to participate in "policy making" - even though he describes it in a demeaning way as "business" and a "sausage". He simply shed his title and talked to the "policy maker" as Jim Clapper. Good solution!

Michael Hayden

While Clapper looks at policy making as "business" and "sausage", let's see what title Michael Hayden uses for the President. "The intelligence community also needs to know the character of **the first customer** and especially how he learns." (MH2 – 78)

Hayden doesn't refer to the President as his "commander-in-chief". The president is only a "customer" although "the first". A business will look upon "customers" as "outsiders" while the employees are "insiders". Hayden is saying that he looks upon the President as an "outsider" to the Intelligence Community.

Hayden also says, "The goal, of course, is for intelligence **to get into the head of the president**..." (MH2 – 77)

And I thought that the goal of the Intelligence is to bring the information they had acquired to the President, and let the President do with it whatever the President sees fit, based upon the President's approach to life. No person in the executive branch, or any other branch, has the goal of entering the head of anyone, let alone the President. In the courtroom, for example, only the evidence is relevant in reaching a decision. "Knowing the inside of a person's head" is only relevant if we want to manipulate the person or control his behavior.

And Hayden goes on to say: "...Intelligence and the President come at this from different perspectives. Metaphorically, they enter the Oval Office through different doors." (MH2 – 77)

Before moving on to see what are the differences that Hayden sees between the two (Intelligence and the President), let's note that this metaphor sees the two as equal. There will not be a situation in which the two will enter the Oval Office at the same time. The intelligence practitioner (I am avoiding using the word "professional") will always enter the Oval Office to meet the President, who is already sitting there, waiting. In other words, the two might enter two different doors, but not at the same time. One is the host and one is the guest. One is in charge and the other is subordinate. But reading the metaphor, one might conclude that Hayden sees the two as equal. As we go along, we will see that Hayden does not see them as equal. And not in the way that the hierarchy really works.

The Metaphor of Two Doors

And Hayden continues: "The Intelligence door is labeled **'facts'** – the kind of data that intelligence steals, elicits, or otherwise acquires to inform decision making." (MH2 – 77)

Hayden forgets to tell us that in most cases the "facts" that he is talking about, are only "facts" that have already gone through a process of "analysis" or "assessment". In other words, there is no such thing as pure "facts". They are always a product of the beholder of these "facts". Or, in other words, there is no such thing as "reality". It is only the "reality" that the intelligence practitioner sees. It is just like a doctor who reviews an X-ray image. One doctor swears that he sees cancer, while his more experienced colleague will say that it is only an "inflammation" due to other factors that accompany the image.

Hayden himself confirms this in the same paragraph when he says, "Intelligence is inherently inductive, swimming in a sea of data and attempting to draw **generalized conclusions**." It is just like the "generalized conclusion" of Iraq possessing WMD. Hayden himself says in his first book, "We compounded our error by stating our conclusions in the NIE in language **that was far too categorical**. No reader of the final product could conclude other than that we were firm in our judgments, despite some thin sourcing of our human intelligence and signals intelligence that (as noted) **was circumstantial, at best**." (MH1 - 50)

In other words, there are not only "facts". There are physical facts, there are circumstantial facts, and on top of it, there is the language one uses to present these "facts".

And if according to Hayden, the "Intelligence door" is "facts", the President's door is labeled "vision", and he continues: "…specifically the one that people voted for in the first place." (MH2 – 78)

Even here, Hayden is wrong. Although it is true that the President is coming with a "vision", this is not the only factor. Just like the intelligence practitioner, the president "assesses" the situation, but does so differently from the intelligence practitioner, due to the fact that the intelligence practitioner might be fixated on something, due to his past experiences.

The North Korea situation is a great example. Three different administrations (Democrat and Republican) dealt with North Korea with no success. Did Hayden consider that this "no success" was partially due to the input that the Intelligence Community provided to these three presidents, input that was faulty, as the Vietnam and Iraq examples showed?

Hayden, in his first book, explains more about the metaphor of having two doors, and now with more details. Regarding the "decision maker", he says that he/she "…can range from a tactical commander, to a cabinet secretary, to a president," and "the 'room' can range from a canvas-covered tactical operations center, to an ornate office, to an oval one."

And he continues: "The intelligence professional must connect with the decision maker. Ideally, that would be in the center of the room…" (MH1 - 428-429)

But what happens if the decision maker and the intelligence officer do not meet "in the center of the room"? Then "…the job of intelligence is to impose itself on the thinking of the other, **no matter how far one has to walk to capture him.**" (MH1 - 428-429)

Now it is in the open – the intelligence is entitled "…to **impose itself** on the thinking of the other, **no matter how far one has to walk to capture him.**" (MH1 - 428-429)

When Hayden talks about "imposing", does he relate to the following – "…the first time American intelligence really **had to try to force its way** through Mr. Trump's bubble of skepticism, they had to engage him on a matter that was being used by other Americans to challenge his very legitimacy as president of the United States: the Russian interference in the U.S. election." (MH2 – 79-80)

And in another place Hayden says: "One wonders how good (or firm) intelligence was **in pushing back against** some of these policy decisions, or at least making their downsides known." (MH2 – 33)

"Imposing", "forcing its way", and "pushing back against" – while I was trained in Israel in "Intelligence 101" that the intelligence provides the information to the commander, and the commander might choose to use it, or even to disregard it. After all, the commander, in a way, is an intelligence officer as well.

Two Doors Metaphor

Continuing with the metaphor of having two doors, Hayden describes from his own sources how the meetings between President Trump and the Chiefs of the Intelligence Community take place:

"Discussion of a topic usually starts with a presidential statement or belief, firmly held…" (MH2 – 163)

Till this point there is no problem. The "policy maker" is defining his "belief firmly held". But Hayden continues the sentence by saying, "Discussion of a topic usually starts with a presidential statement or belief, firmly held **if not especially well informed**." (MH2 – 163)

In this addition, Hayden is giving himself the authority to rate the "belief" of the policy maker, the "belief" that brings the "policy maker" to demand a certain policy. In other words, the **appointed** person puts himself in the position to rate the **elected**.

And Hayden continues: "Intelligence is fixated on the world **as it is**. The president and his policy team **dream** of the world as they want it to be." (MH2 – 78)

Hayden used the right word for the intelligence – "fixated". The Intelligence Community is a prisoner of their own view of the world. And since they are "fixated", they are not able to come out of their narrow view to bring about a change in the course of events. While the intelligence sees "the world as it is", Hayden labels President Trump's view as a "dream". There is nothing wrong with a "dream". Just ask Martin Luther King when he talked about "I have a dream…"

It reminds me of the book about Steve Jobs. Steve Jobs was not a computer guy but a "visionary". There were times in which he came to his programmers, and told them what he wanted them to achieve. If any of the programmers said "it is impossible", or "it cannot be done", Steve Jobs fired him on the spot. And Steve Jobs defined what he wanted in people – A-rated people. Not B-rated people. As a result, Apple under the directorship of Steve Jobs changed society. He didn't accept "the world as it is".

Hayden continues his comparison: "And intelligence analysts trend pessimistic..." (MH2 – 78)

This is the first time that Hayden is not talking about "Intelligence" in general, but of "intelligence **analysts**". Why would "intelligence analysts" tend to be **pessimistic**? Being an analyst in the Intelligence Community does not mean one has to be pessimistic. If one has the capability to prevent attacks on his/her own country, that person should be very proud of their accomplishments, and actually should be very optimistic.

But if one is in a position that no matter what he/she says, the outcome is negative, one quite likely will be pessimistic. Since we already saw that in most cases in the past, the US Intelligence didn't guard the US, and didn't keep it "safe", then, yes, any analyst would even wonder what he/she is doing there.

Hayden continues the comparison: "Policymakers have to be optimistic; otherwise they never would have pursued the job." (MH2 – 78)

While talking about "intelligence analysts" he says that they "trend pessimistic", stating it as a fact; however, when talking about "policymakers" he only says that they "**have to be** optimistic". He doesn't say that they are indeed "optimistic". Since Hayden served in different capacities under three administrations (Clinton, Bush, and Obama), I wonder if his experience told him that all three were not really "optimistic". Does he consider them to be "pessimistic" like the "intelligence analysts"? If so, it might explain why the intelligence functioned "so well" under the previous three administrations, while this new administration brought two former chiefs of intelligence to publish books in protest.

Hayden describes what happens when the Intelligence Community perceives the "policymaker" (i.e., the President) as "not especially well informed."

"Then follows **a large-scale and long-term effort** to better inform the president, to impress upon him the complexity of the issue, to review the relevant history, to surface more of the factors bearing on the problem, to raise second- and third-order consequences, and to explore the feasibility of subsequent moves down the board."

Since Hayden attaches this "large-scale and long-term effort" to his statement that "Discussion of a topic usually starts with a presidential statement or belief, firmly held…" (MH2 –163), he is not talking about the intelligence practitioners' response during the "discussion". He is talking about a "**long-term** effort", beyond the discussion at hand. Quite likely, it is being done even when the President is not present. One might wonder where and how this "large-scale and long-term effort" is being held.

Summary

Hayden produces two components of what the Intelligence would do when the president, **according to them**, is not "well informed".

The first is that the Intelligence is entitled "…to impose itself on the thinking of the other, **no matter how far one has to walk to capture him**." (MH1 - 428-429)

The second is "Then follows **a large-scale and long-term effort** to better inform the president…" (MH2 163)

Unlike Israel, where Intelligence Chiefs **personally** update government officials - either the Prime Minister, or the Security Cabinet (consisting of 8 ministers) **in person** - in the US the practice in different.

James Clapper in his book gives us details on how the Intelligence Community (IC) updates the President: the "President's Daily Brief" (PDB).

This PDB is done six days a week, and it is the IC's "…**dialogue** with the president to address global challenges and opportunities related to national security." (JC 141)

One should note that Clapper is using the word "dialogue" and not "reporting" or even "briefing". The word "dialogue" sounds as if two equals are getting together.

The US IC created a "unit" to be in charge of this important task of "briefing" the president. The people who are assigned to this unit are **"star analysts"** who **"…**normally take one-year tours as briefers…**"**, working in shifts. (JC 141)

Clapper goes on in his book to describe the job of these "briefers". Although they are only "briefers", they are also "star analysts" who work with the authors of intelligence documents "…to edit their writing and analysis in a grueling process that can take place over several weeks or several days…"

Hayden in his book gives us more details on the PDB: "The DNI and the president's briefer would cross West Executive Avenue and gather outside the Oval Office a few minutes before 8:00 a.m. The meeting with the president would last thirty to forty-five minutes…" (MH1 - 156)

President Bush

Clapper says that President Bush "…wanted to have the articles briefed in detail, absorb the material, and ask briefers questions at the same session." (JC 146)

Hayden describes President Bush as "…a voracious reader, but it seemed to me that he best learned in the **dialogue**, which was always lively and intense." (MH2 – 74-75)

We should note that both Clapper and Hayden referred to the PDB as a "dialogue".

Hayden compares the attitude of two presidents - Bush and Obama - towards the PDB. Regarding President Bush he says: "…Bush was **fanatical** about it – he wanted a daily briefing, in person, six days out of seven." (MH1 - 211)

One should wonder whether Hayden's description of Bush as "fanatical" is a "good" adjective or a "bad" one. One can also ask whether this attitude by President Bush towards the briefings helped him in his decisions about running the war, not to mention even starting it.

Hayden also mentions that "…President Bush still insisted on a weekly update on covert actions and sensitive collection…" (MH1 - 211).

How does the ultimate bureaucrat relate to this request? "…so I got thirty minutes every Thursday morning immediately after the thirty-minute PDB." (MH1 - 211), and - "As director of CIA, I got to talk to *this* president every week without any filters." (MH1 – 335; italics in original)

We should note that it is not that the President got an additional 30 minutes, but Hayden himself ("I got…") got the President's ear for 30 minutes. Sure enough – "I took advantage of that window to brief President Bush on my trip to Iraq." (MH1 – 211)

But this weekly 30-minute meeting brings Hayden to expose something that I am not sure he is aware that he is exposing. Since these 30 minutes were every Thursday morning, Hayden says that "…you can imagine what the headquarters looked like on Wednesday afternoons, as items suggested by the staff began to flow into my office… easily 50 percent of the specific operational details I briefed on Thursday morning I learned about for the first time on Wednesday afternoon." (MH1 – 288-289).

So without these 30 minutes of having to tell the President about CIA activities, the Director of CIA would actually be "clueless" as to what is being done by the CIA in terms of "covert actions and sensitive collection".

Moreover, from Thursday morning till the following Wednesday, the Director of CIA would still be in the dark. After all, the President requested this briefing only once a week.

For comparison, let's see how the Israeli Chief of Military Intelligence sees his job:

"The Chief of Military Intelligence must be accustomed to swallowing large amounts of reading material. Even after sifting and supervision, there is a great deal left to read. This is the kind of thing **under his responsibility that cannot be delegated**. There is no way to ever know from which direction a problem will arise, and which information is really important, what is the wheat and what is the chaff. One must be well-versed in the raw material and to compare it to the final product. For this one must develop senses. One learns techniques, how to read fast, to see the main point at a glance, and even with all of these – one drowns in the sea of words." (110)[5]

Hayden tells us that "The president devoted a lot of time to these sessions, and he was **incredibly interactive** with the briefers, and **very knowledgeable**." (MH1 - 211)

So President Bush got a "report card" from a person that officially is under him. President Bush was "incredibly interactive" and "very knowledgeable". Such a "report card" is not found in any book published by either a former Chief of the Mossad or a former chief of the Military Intelligence.

President Obama

If Bush was "fanatical" about the PDB, "President Obama stopped the practice of getting a personal briefing every day…" (MH1 - 211) According to Hayden, President Obama was "…more reflective, preferring to read, and learning in the private moment." (MH2 – 74-75)

Clapper tells us about President Obama "…clearly he had already read and digested its contents" before the actual PDB. (JC 142) since President Obama "…preferred to read and digest the material ahead of time." (JC 146)

Clapper quotes President Obama who at the ceremony of celebrating the tenth anniversary of ODNI's (Office of Director of National Intelligence) launch, said in his speech: "I don't know how astute **a consumer of information I am**, but I can tell you I sure do rely on it. And those who come and brief me every single morning do an extraordinary job." (JC 147)

President Obama defined his position very accurately – he was "a consumer of information". Sounds good? Not really. Let's not forget that as "President", President Obama was not **only** a "consumer", but actually **in charge** of the process.

President Trump

If at the PDB Bush was "fanatical", and Obama was "reflective", then "Trump was a different matter, of course" (MH2 – 79). Trump "…seemed disinclined to learn more, even at first pushing back on the very concept of a daily intelligence briefing, saying that he was a very smart person and did not need to be told **the same things over**

and over again every day, itself a hideous mischaracterization of the PDB." (MH2 – 79).

Was it "a hideous mischaracterization of the PDB"? If according to Clapper, the unit of "star analysts" were working with the authors of intelligence documents, how many times can one discuss such a document?

For Hayden, besides counting Trump as an outsider, Hayden notes that "…the creator had also given him [Trump] a few extra doses of those deductive, world-as-we-would-like-it-to-be, vision-based attributes…" (MH2 – 79)

The "psychologist" in Hayden brings us his analysis of Trump: "He seemed purely instinctive, spontaneous, even impulsive, and although he had little background on the substance or processes of international affairs, he also had little patience with written or even verbal presentations. He seemed to have an eerie confidence in his own a priori narrative of how the world worked." (MH2 – 79)

Hayden describes the PDB of President-elect Trump:

"Briefing sessions for the president-elect were described to me as simple, visual, and chaotic: a few sentences from the briefer, a question, then a tangent with frequent interventions about intelligence, policy, and current press all competing for attention. One familiar with the sessions told me that a literal transcript would read like a James Joyce novel: a series of thoughts that appear as they come to mind." (MH2 – 100)

I wonder what is the difference between Clapper's description of Bush's PDB - "[Bush] wanted to have the articles briefed in detail, absorb the material, **and ask briefers questions at the same session**." (JC 146) and Hayden's description of President-elect Trump's PDB as "…a few sentences from the briefer, a question, then a tangent with frequent interventions about intelligence, policy, and current press all competing for attention"?

Let's not forget how Prime Minister Sharon told the Chief of Military Intelligence that he doesn't want only information, but he wants also suggestions for actions, and even a preferred action.

Hayden also mentions how President Trump violated the sanctity of the PDB with - "It was not unheard of for the president to tweet during sessions (**probably** *not* about the intelligence content)…" (MH2 – 100; italics in original)

While the IC had to adapt from the way President Bush did the PDB, to the different way President Obama did, now they wanted President-elect Trump to adapt to them, and not vice versa. Why not grant him the same courtesy they gave Obama?

And Hayden ends his discussion of President Trump by saying:

"A fairly common question that intelligence people ask themselves after an important briefing session is: did they adequately explain and clearly distinguish what they knew, what they thought, and what they did not know? To that was now added, 'Do you think he got that?' It's not that we have never asked that question before, it's just now more routine." (MH2 – 100)

More about the PDB

Clapper exposes one major point. The PDB that the president gets is not the same as the PDB of the candidates running for office. In Clapper's words, "…one team from my office produced and delivered the PDB, and a completely different team produced and coordinated the cross-agency effort to brief the candidates with intelligence on broad global topics **that were separate from the intelligence President Obama received on his secure iPad**." (JC 345)

In other words, the candidates did not need a "secure iPad".

The Director of National Intelligence (DNI)

In the chapter "The Second Most Thankless Job in Washington", Clapper defines in his book the job of DNI as having "the responsibility of occupying a Cabinet-level position without congruent legislative authorities." (JC 128)

This means that after 9/11, when the US figured that they needed to do "something", and that "something" was defined as "integration of all intelligence services" the Congress created a position of a "Chief";

however, due to pressure from other components in the bureaucracy, the job was created "without congruent legislative authorities". If this high language is difficult to understand, Clapper later expressed it in more common everyday language. The DNI "…had zero line authority over any agency." (JC 128)

In other words, post-9/11 the US has a "chief" of the Intelligence Community, who is actually not a "chief", as he is not in charge of any specific intelligence service, such as the CIA, the NSA, or others.

This reminds me of a young Israeli guy who came to visit Phoenix. After seeing that one can get cola without caffeine and without sugar, and one can get a beer with no alcohol, the Israeli commented: "It is a very interesting country. Everything just **'looks like.'**"

In summary, the DNI is cola without caffeine and without sugar, or beer without alcohol. He only "looks like" a chief.

So, what was the job envisioned for this DNI?

Clapper says that "The DNI was tasked to be the president's senior adviser and to lead, integrate, and manage the consolidated budgets of seventeen disparate intelligence organizations, transforming them into an actual Intelligence Community…" (JC 128)

Hayden says in his book that "…the law gives the DNI two massive tasks: acting as senior intelligence advisor to the president and ensuring the smooth functioning of the whole intelligence community." (MH1 - 161)

Hayden as the ultimate bureaucrat says that his "to-do list" when he became Deputy DNI was the following: "1) kill a program, somewhere, anywhere; 2) move some money from one account to another – it didn't have to be a lot; 3) question (but not necessarily reject) a Pentagon personnel choice…" (MH1 - 163)

The Deputy "looks like" found a few things to do. Does any of it have anything to do with actual Intelligence? No. Just to show that he is "in charge". "In charge" of what?

In talking about the first DNI, John Negroponte, Hayden comments, "He didn't know much about intelligence except as a consumer, but he was politically savvy and bureaucratically smart." (MH1 - 161). Being "politically savvy and **bureaucratically smart**" was enough for Hayden, the ultimate bureaucrat.

Summary

If there is nobody really in charge of the Intelligence Community (IC), since the Director of National Intelligence (DNI) does not have any real authority; and if the President is only a "consumer", and the IC only "briefs" the president and has a "dialogue" with him;
and if the same applies to Congress, and the DNI can lie to Congress without any consequences - why should we be surprised that the IC has a track record of being ineffective, to say the least, if not bordering on "criminal negligence"? (As an example, see the two intercepts by NSA on 9/10 that were only translated on 9/12.)

US Intelligence and the Legislative Branch

Israel

In his book "In Defense of Israel", former Defense Minister Moshe Arens
shares his experience as chair of the Foreign Affairs and Defense
Committee of the Knesset (Israeli Parliament). One problem was that
everything that was reported to the committee was leaked to the press, a
fact that actually prevented anything meaningful from being discussed in
the committee. Arens decided to solve the problem by creating sub-
committees with very few members in each sub-committee. The small sub-
committees allowed more control over the information discussed, as it was
easy to find out who had leaked from a group of 3 than from a group of 15,
for example.

Arens invited the Chief of the Mossad to report to a sub-committee of the
Foreign Affairs and Defense Committee of the Knesset. Please note the use
of the word "invited", as unlike the power of ordering someone to appear
before the US Congress, the Israeli parliament has no such power. The
chief of the Mossad responded "…that he never exposed information on
Mossad activities to the Knesset members, and that he has no intention to
begin doing it now." (73)

Arens says, "I felt that that it is the committee's duty to supervise the
Mossad as well, but he didn't respond to my request." (73) Again, note the
use of "request".

Arens didn't give up. He moved to use his "connection" with the Prime
Minister, who is the one directly in charge of the Mossad. And Arens says,
"I approached Mr. Begin, who as Prime Minister was the immediate
supervisor of the head of the Mossad, and I asked him to order Chofi to
report to the committee. Mr. Begin, who was very strict about proper

relations between the government and the Knesset, agreed with me and ordered Chofi to appear before the committee. From then on Chofi reported to the committee every time he was called to do so, and so did the heads of the Mossad after him." (73)

It is an example illustrating the way things are done in Israeli. Although on paper there are rules for doing things, just as in the US, Israel is a small country, "where everyone knows everyone", and there is less adherence to formality, there is a way to bypass resistance by using personal connections. One only needs to have the will to accomplish one's plans.

US-Israel Cultural difference

The Chief of the Mossad was very **direct** and **open** in his resistance to give information to the parliament ("…he never exposed information on Mossad activities to the Knesset members, and that he has no intention to begin doing it now").

In fact, this is a characteristic of Israeli society. One would not beat around the bush to conceal one's resistance. It would not be uncommon to hear in an argument that one person tells another, "This is B.S." It is similar to the way people act in the UK. When I had a class in the UK, I heard one student telling another, "This is rubbish." Not so in the US. Instead of telling the other person what one might think, it is common to hear, "This is very interesting," which is a euphemism for "stupid". It comes to a point that if an American would like to express interest in something, he/she has to say, "It is **really** very interesting". Without the word "really" it would be meaningless.

This American tendency to conceal resistance can cause problems in communication between a person from the US and a person who comes from a culture that takes the sentence "It is interesting" at face value.

A well-known example is the incident in which the Israeli Prime Minister Menachem Begin presented to the US President Jimmy Carter his plan of autonomy for the Arab inhabitants of Judea and Samaria (also known as "The West Bank"). Carter responded by saying, "It is very interesting." Everyone in US circles knew that this was a total rejection of the idea. Carter's resistance was due to the fact that Mr. Begin's plan talked about autonomy for the "inhabitants", and not for the "land" - a land which is the cradle of Jewish history, the Biblical Land of Israel. Hearing Carter's

"Very interesting" comment, Mr. Begin went back home and declared erroneously that the American President had accepted his plan, only to find out later that he was wrong. This misunderstanding of the American culture (avoiding open conflict) brought Mr. Begin to feel that the US President had misled him, if not even lied to him outright.

The Israeli Prime Minister was not the only one to face a misunderstanding of the American language. Oliver Stone, who interviewed Vladimir Putin extensively[6], describes one point that Putin told him: "Further escalation is already happening because the United States is deploying it antiballistic missile system in Eastern Europe… I was talking to George W. Bush in his house outside the city, and I elaborated on our proposals. The response was, '**Yes, that's very interesting**,' but afterwards **it didn't lead to anything**." (115)

Maybe Putin should have learned more about the American way of speaking! In other words, knowing English (or any other language) is not enough to understand the natives. One needs to also learn the nuances, the idioms, and even expressions one should avoid using.

US Intelligence and Congress

Since Israel is a society in which people are more direct and open while the US is not, we should expect that the US intelligence would say that it cooperates with Congress even when in actuality it does not. Just like the sentence "It is very interesting."

In the transcript of the hearing conducted by the Senate Select Committee on Intelligence regarding John Brennan's nomination for the position of Director of CIA, we find two Senators complaining about the way the CIA "briefs" them.
Senator Rockefeller: "…We did this [looking into the CIA's use of "Enhanced Interrogation Techniques" also known as "torture"] because we heard nothing from the Intelligence Agency. We had no way of being briefed. They would not tell us what was going on. So we had to do our own investigation, and we're pretty good at it." (JB 38)

Senator Mikulski: "…and with the exception of Mr. Panetta, I feel I've been jerked around by every CIA director. I've either been misled, misrepresented, had to pull information out - often at the most minimal kind of way; from Tenet, with his little aluminum rods, to tell us that we had weapons of mass destruction in Iraq, to Porter Goss - not forthcoming." (JB 50-51)

Back to Hayden

As we saw earlier, in regard to the way the high-ranking people in the Intelligence Community perceive the President as "the first **customer**", rather than as a "commander", the same applies to the way they perceive Congress.

Hayden says, "I wanted Congress to be **part of that consensus**." (MH1 - 225) and "I was committed to making Congress a **partner** in all this." (MH1 - 229)

Hayden feels he has the authority of what he will give Congress. He "wanted" and he was "committed." It is not that by law he was under Congress's supervision. His language, again, exposes his inner thought of that he is above them.

And being "part of the consensus" and a "partner" "…required a serious discussion with them. **That discussion never happened**. The members were too busy yelling at us and at one another." (MH1 - 225) Hayden wants us to accept that it was not his fault that "that discussion never happened" – as if the members of Congress had created this situation.

It is no wonder that that Senator Jay Rockefeller (D-WV) once told Hayden: "You don't believe in oversight, do you?" (MH1 - 227)

Hayden responds to this question by saying, "I still don't know what prompted it, since I was briefing him on a sensitive activity at the meeting." But the fact is that the Senator was not stupid. Hayden, with all his language capabilities, cannot hide the fact that at times his listeners know what he is doing when he uses language to run away from saying something. Just like former Director of FBI James Comey said in his book that Hayden's briefings "…were a river of **really great-sounding stuff** that **didn't make much sense** once the briefing was over…" (Page 83)

Hayden said, "We answered the questions, but the times were tough: we were talking about controversial things on behalf of a weakened president with the opposition in control of both chambers and a lot of people

positioning themselves for a run for president. Not good circumstances."
(MH1 - 229)

If they answered the questions honestly and fully, why to comment that "the times were tough"? And why to expand by bringing us the political environment, and to conclude that they were in "not good circumstances"?

Hayden says that, "During my public confirmation in the Senate, critics – led by Wyden, the Oregon Democrat – repeated the charge that **I had never been fully forthcoming** about the program." (MH1 - 184)

The "charge" (or in police language, the "suspicion") is that Hayden "..had never been **fully** forthcoming…" Let's see how Hayden denies this "charge". He writes: "I had provided more than a dozen classified briefings to lawmakers since the program had begun…" (MH1 - 184) That he did. But was he actually "fully forthcoming"? He doesn't say. Or, in other words, Hayden does not deny the charge.

Another "charge" was brought by members of Congress, "…who accused us of using contractors to deflect **accountability** for our actions." (MH1 - 287). Hayden moved to "deny" this "accusation" by saying that he told Congress "…that I was **liable** for contractor actions as I was for those of agency officers." (MH1 - 288).

And one should note how, again, Hayden used language to run away. While the accusation talked about "accountability", Hayden responded about "liability".

We don't really need to "dig" in order to find the deep-rooted resistance to inform Congress, the undeclared resistance. Hayden talks about it openly. After Senator Feinstein's report came out, Hayden said, "One positive take-away was **the clear need** to brief Congress **fully** and **contemporaneously** on sensitive activity..." (MH1 – 400)

Note the reference to "clear need", testifying to the fact that this "clear need" had not been addressed.

But this "clear need" does not prevent Hayden from saying in the same breath, "…I'm close to drawing a second, darker conclusion too. **Be careful what you tell these people**…." (Note the use of "these people", a very demeaning term for the representatives of the public in a democracy.)

If using the term "these people" is not enough, Hayden then moves to rate the members of Congress: "Some are less interested in honest dialogue than listening to rebut and accuse and discredit." (MH1 - 400)

"Dialogue"? "Dialogue" is a word describing two equal partners to the conversation. It is no wonder that Senator Rockefeller asked Hayden about oversight. (MH1 - 227)

Hayden is not the only one who brought Senators to feel that he is not "fully forthcoming". Clapper, as Director of National Intelligence (DNI), said that "…talking to Congress publicly about classified intelligence matters while trying to protect vital intelligence sources and methods is one of my *favorite* things to do - ranking right up there with **undergoing oral surgery and folding fitted sheets**." (JC 150 – italics in original)

Unlike Hayden, at least Clapper is open about his feelings that talking to Congress is like "…undergoing oral surgery and folding fitted sheets" (JC 150)

Clapper, like the Mossad Chief in Israel, was concerned about protecting "vital intelligence sources and methods." Still, Moshe Arens as Defense Minister in Israel insisted that the Chief of the Mossad would report to the parliament, and the Prime Minister agreed with him.

Clapper in his book brings us a question from Senator Ron Wyden (D – Oregon) that "seemed to come out of left field":

"…does the NSA collect any type of data at all on millions, or hundreds of millions, of Americans?" (207)

And before giving his answer, Clapper gives us an "introduction": "After nearly two hours in the 'hot seat', I was tired, and annoyed that, months after we settled…" (207)

At the end of the long paragraph, he comes to his answer:

"I flipped the microphone on. 'No, sir,' I replied and then flipped it off. 'It does not?' he asked incredulously."

Another paragraph, and a longer one this time, and then – "I flipped the mic back on and, controlling my voice, replied, 'Not wittingly. There are cases where they could inadvertently perhaps collect, but not wittingly.'" (208)

And now Clapper moves into a long explanation as to why he didn't answer the question truthfully. He needed his aide to tell him that he had "answered incorrectly."

Hayden in his book, using his linguistic skills, labels these events as: "Suddenly on the spot, Clapper **clumsily** answered, 'No, sir. Not wittingly.'" (MH1 - 409)

The question the Senator asked was quite simple. Clapper's "explanations" after denying it to Congress would in other places be called "lying". Not being "tired", or "annoyed", or even answering "clumsily". It was simple lying. And even if we say that it was an honest mistake, why did both Clapper and Hayden treat other people's mistakes as "lying"?

Did the NSA spy on Americans?

When talking about the East German secret police, the Stasi, Clapper says, "This was what happened when a state surveillance apparatus ran amok with no limits and no checks. The people of East Germany never asked for such intrusiveness, and there was no oversight - no legislative review or judicial restraint over their pervasive, Orwellian surveillance." (JC 81)

And Clapper's lesson from this? "The experience also **tempered my attitude** about collecting intelligence on innocent citizens - in our country or anywhere else." (JC 81)

It only "tempered his attitude". It didn't bring him to conclude that it should not be done.

Hayden, on his part, started his book by saying, "Since this is a memoir, its center of gravity is the past, which will perforce drag in issues like renditions, detentions, interrogations, and **the badly mislabeled 'domestic surveillance' program**." (MH1 - xiii)

It is only "badly mislabeled". It is still a "domestic surveillance" program. Maybe he would prefer not to use this terminology, but one can imagine that Hayden will find another label to launder this concept.

And Hayden produces an interesting denial: "Domestic intelligence collection has always been countercultural in America. **CIA doesn't do it**; it's beyond the agency's charter." (MH1 - 326)

Note that Hayden does not say, "CIA and NSA do not do it." He only denies "domestic intelligence collection" done by the CIA. But Snowden's revelations did not focus on the CIA. NSA is the issue. And Hayden cannot deny it at all.

"Total Belief in the Subject" means that what the subject says is true. However, what the subject does not say, might turn the story upside down by 180 degrees.

Hayden in his book outlines Congress's limitations in overseeing intelligence: "It's hard for Congress to legislate **better analysis or more aggressive collection** or more foolproof covert operations." (MH1 - 154)

Hayden is right on this point. "Better analysis" and "more aggressive collection" should be the domain of the one who is in charge of the intelligence organization, and in this case, Hayden himself. Hayden specifies what Congress can do: "Congress can **move money** (it has already given us a lot), it can **add people** (we were recruiting at record rates), and it can **restructure organizational charts** and **strengthen authorities**." (MH1 - 154) But Congress should not be the one to mandate more common sense in the way the organization is doing its job. This should be done by the organization itself.

John Brennan

In his appearance before the Senate Select Committee on Intelligence regarding his nomination for the position of Director of CIA, John Brennan promised the committee that if he would be approved as Director, he would be more forthcoming. It is interesting to examine his promises.

"...it **would** be my obligation, I think, as director of CIA, to try to be as accommodating as possible to that interest, while at the same time trying to respect whatever considerations need to be taken into account as we do that." (JB 40)

"...and it **would** be my intention to do everything possible to meet this Committee's legitimate interests and requests." (JB 45)

"But, Senator, I **would** commit that I would be honest with this Committee and do everything possible to meet your legitimate needs and requirements." (JB 51)

Note the use of "would be my obligation", "would be my intention", and "would commit". By using "would" he runs away from any commitment.

The following is a quote where Brennan caught himself slipping, and he needed to correct himself: "...but to tell the policymakers, the Congressional overseers, **what they need to hear** - what the Intelligence Community, with all its great capability and expertise, has been able to uncover..." (JB 85)

"What they need to hear" and not "what they need to know", and everything is according to John Brennan.

John Brennan's approach regarding honesty towards the Congress is summarized in the following: "What we need to do is **optimize transparency** on these issues, but at the same time, **optimize secrecy** and the protection of our national security. I don't think that it's one or the other; **it's <u>trying</u> to optimize both of them**." (JB 44)

Snowden

Snowden, according to Clapper, was not only "...not exactly the IC's - or my - finest hour." (JC 229). Snowden was the evidence that the US Intelligence Community was functioning without anyone in either the executive and/or the legislative branches knowing what they are doing.

Besides listing all the damage Snowden's revelations did to US information collecting, Clapper says, "...and most disturbing, we'd lost the trust of the American public, which questioned what we were doing globally on their behalf **and what we were doing domestically to them.** " (JC 250)

Clapper lists whatever was going around the internet: "...the internet was full of stories about how we were spying on ordinary citizens, trying to ascertain if they were cheating on their spouses, growing weed in their basement, or pirating Hollywood movies. **None was true**." (JC 265)

We should note this strong denial, as we will check elsewhere if such a denial does exist regarding other issues.

Hayden also relates extensively in his book to Snowden. He describes "…efforts by NSA and other intelligence services to deal with these new realities. Some of the efforts did indeed raise important questions about the right balance between security and liberty, **and Snowden's disclosures no doubt accelerated and intensified that discussion**. But the disclosures, and especially how they were rolled out, badly misshaped it as complex stories were misreported or, worse still, purposely pushed to the darkest corner of the room." (MH1 - 405)

By saying "badly misshaped", "misreported", and most of all – "pushed to the darkest corner of the room", Hayden does not deny Snowden's disclosures.

"A boyish-looking twenty-nine-year-old" in Hayden's words (MH1 - 404), and "a kid… who… appointed himself as judge over what he had seen, and then, without conducting an investigation or calling out wrongdoers …" in Clapper's words (JC 227), forced upon the US Intelligence Community to do what they should have done from the beginning – to adhere to the rule of law, and to abide by the line of command in the executive branch, and to get approval for their operations from the legislative branch. And since they knew they could not get such approval, they simply went "under the radar."

And although Hayden labels Snowden as "an incredibly naive, hopelessly narcissistic, and insufferably self-important defector," (MH1 - 421), still Hayden says that "…Snowden has been, in his own peculiar manner, **a gift**."

Hayden explains the Snowden "gift": "…redefining legitimate secrecy, necessary transparency, and what constitutes consent of the governed." (MH1 - 422) And Hayden says, "…If we are going to conduct espionage in the future, **we are going to have to make some changes** in the relationship between the intelligence community and the public it serves." (MH1 - 422)

If Snowden's disclosures mandated changes in the way the IC conducts its business, it means that Snowden accomplished what he professed to accomplish – to force an open debate on the way the IC is spying. If so,

Hayden can go in linguistic loops and mental circles, defining Snowden as a "defector", but in many words showing that Snowden was a bona fide whistleblower.

The Interests of the US Intelligence Community

When President Trump announced his executive order to ban citizens from seven Moslem countries from entering the US until the US government organization would be able to improve their vetting process before granting a visa, Hayden was strongly against this ban.

Hayden says that he "...privately heard from intelligence professionals..."(MH2 - 129). Again, we see that current "intelligence professionals" share their knowledge and opinions with retired ones.

Although these "intelligence professionals" acknowledged that "six of the seven countries in the ban (Iran being somewhat an exception) were troubled, fragmented states..." still they were concerned with "...the **operational consequences** of this action".

Although Hayden is proud to tell us that the duty of the intelligence community is to keep the US "safe and free", at the same time he tells us that "operational consequences" should take priority over the security of the American people.

And Hayden specifies what are these "operational consequences": "...the executive order breached faith with those very sources, many of whom they had persuaded and promised to always protect with the full might of our government and our people, sources who had risked much if not all to keep Americans safe." (MH2 - 129)

Hayden goes on to say that "The case officers believed that they were empowered to offer the full faith and credit of the American nation for that task, and now, they told me, that promise was eroding. The ultimate sanctuary, America, was being denied **to their sources and to anyone those sources cared about**." (MH2- 129)

Interesting dilemma. What should take priority for the intelligence community? To guard the security of the American population, or to guard the security of the sources they employ in these "troubled, fragmented states"? And let's say the security and safety of these sources are important, doesn't the IC have the capability to guard them in spite of the ban?

Hayden's main complaint right away was: "And although he didn't quite say it then, he later added that if he did win the presidency, he would be inheriting a messy world."

The person who was in intelligence for so many years, attempting to keep the US "safe and free", was genuinely insulted. How can Candidate Trump talk like that?

Hayden then moved to describe Candidate Trump's assertion: "Messy, by the way, because of the failings of his predecessors rather than any inherent complexities. So where was the world, America, and American intelligence when Donald Trump descended that escalator and promised to disrupt things?" (MH2 –13)

Hayden denied Trump's assertion, using his language skill to deny; but instead he proves what Trump said.

Hayden says, "To begin, the world was an increasingly **dangerous** place, but not nearly **as dangerous** as the new candidate's near-apocalyptic rhetoric suggested that day." (MH2 – 13)

And Hayden continues: "Intelligence officers of my generation will tell you that they have actually lived in a more **dangerous** world..." (MH2 - 14)

Really? And what evidence does Hayden bring his readers?

"Many from the old 'security services' - the electronic surveillance folks - will remind you, at the drop of a hat or a drink, of reconnaissance ships attacked in the late 1960s..." This refers to two NSA ships - one in the Mediterranean, mistakenly bombed by the Israeli Air Force in 1967, and one close to North Korea, where NSA made a mistake (according to Hayden himself) that triggered the escalation of the Vietnam war. In other words, an attack on NSA ships that are close to, or even in, dangerous zones, make the world more dangerous. In many words, Hayden says that NSA is the world, and if the NSA is going into dangerous zones, that means the world is dangerous. Really?

Hayden himself can see that this is not a claim, so he moves to use his linguistic skills to come out of this loop that he himself entered: "But even the most hardened Cold War veteran would be quick to add that they have never seen the world more **complicated** than now." (MH2 - 14)

Now we got it. The world is not "more **dangerous**" as President Trump says. It is only "more **complicated**".

And Hayden starts to list the issues that make the world "more complicated": "...substate actors – groups, gangs, even individuals – who can visit the kind of destructive effects on our society that we used to associate only with malevolent state power. Cyber attacks, transnational crime, and, of course, terrorism quickly come to mind." (MH2 - 15)

It is interesting to note that Hayden puts "terrorism" last on his list. In fact, more American lives were lost to terrorism under the US Intelligence Community's watch than any other item on Hayden's list.

Hayden concludes his "denial" of Trump's assertion by saying: "In many ways our security is now **more at risk from ungoverned spaces and failed states than it is from actively hostile nations**." (MH2 - 16)

By Candidate Trump stating the obvious (although not using Hayden's language), Candidate Trump put himself on the Intelligence Community watch list – just like McCain and Obama before him.

Hayden openly says, "And for the American intelligence community, seeing that from someone who could be president **would have been very discomfiting**." (MH2 – 72)

Hayden tells us that President Trump's executive order was not "...anchored on the judgments of the American intelligence community." (MH2 - 123)

And although Hayden says that "Within government a thousand foreign service officers used the State Department's formal dissent channel to register their opposition to the ban..." (MH2 -127) still, President Trump decided to act against the advice of both "intelligence professionals" and "a thousand foreign service officers". This was based, in his opinion, on the security interests of the US, and not the interests of the bureaucrats.

What would the bureaucrats do?

The Intelligence Community as a "Lobby"

For quite a long time, the US intelligence community has been very much aware of the political process in the public arena.

Hayden tells us: "I think that the intelligence community consensus was that the election of John McCain would have been more disruptive to the way America produced intelligence than the election of Barack Obama." (MH1 - 354)

According to Hayden, Senator McCain would have had more of a negative impact on the "information production" than Senator Obama. This is an interesting assertion, as both candidates were very strong on civil rights, and both of them were against "enhanced interrogation techniques" (EIT). (One should note that I am avoiding using the word "torture" as Hayden doesn't like the word.) If both of them were against EIT, why would McCain would be more disruptive?

Hayden says that "Senator McCain was a known quantity. Patriotic. Heroic. Forceful…" Till this point, Hayden lists all the points that should have qualified McCain to be president. But Hayden continues: "Emotional." And he comes to explain why he labeled McCain as such. "He once angrily stormed out of a meeting I was having on Capitol Hill for Senate Republicans, accusing me of covering my ass while exposing theirs (my summary, not his). He later returned to the session and apologized." (MH1 - 354)

Hayden characterizes McCain as "emotional", and he is not wrong on that account. But actually, the incident Hayden reports would testify for McCain to be labeled "impulsive" rather than "emotional". However, Hayden is not wrong in labeling McCain as "emotional". McCain himself does so in his book. [See later the analysis of McCain's book.]

While Hayden labels McCain as "emotional", he labels President Obama as "The usually **phlegmatic** president…" (MH1 - 411)

Now the comparison between the two is clear – "emotional" vs. "phlegmatic". Hayden, the ultimate "bureaucrat", prefers a "phlegmatic" president rather than an "emotional" one. But why would either of these characteristics have any bearing on "…the way America produced intelligence…"?

If one puts aside "intelligence", and talks only about police, then one can see very easily that the political level has no bearing on the way the police will "produce" evidence. The laws of producing evidence are set, and in fact, they will not be different from one country to another. The chain of holding evidence needs to be intact, and not impaired. The law enforcement community must make every effort that evidence will not be contaminated, so its integrity will remain intact. And so on.

Why would the identity and personality of the political head of state have any bearing on the way the intelligence community "produce[s] information", if everything is set legally?

The only way that the identity of the political head of state would have any influence on the way the intelligence community "produce[s] information" is if their rules are not set in stone, and maybe even violate the law. In such a case, what one president would allow, another one might not.

The CIA has no charter to spy domestically. Hayden himself – as a former director of the agency – strongly denies any domestic spying by the CIA (and this strong denial is a reliable one). This leaves us with the NSA that might go beyond what the law allows, and it is totally dependent on the will of the president. (And even this is debatable as there is also a constitution to take into consideration.) What President Bush, who was traumatized by the 9/11 attack, allowed the NSA to do under the ambiguous order of "do whatever it takes", the "emotional" McCain would probably not allow, while the "phlegmatic" Obama would.

In fact, Snowden in his media interviews said that he expected that Obama, based upon his promises before the elections, would curtail the activity of the NSA; but instead he found that President Obama expanded the activity of the NSA above and beyond what President Bush had authorized. This expansion, according to Snowden, brought him to despair and caused him to go to the news media.

In other words, for a "bureaucrat", a "phlegmatic" president is a lot better than an "emotional" one. A "phlegmatic" president would go along with the bureaucracy; while an "emotional" one, who put civil rights on his banner and had a record of strongly defending them, like McCain, would not.

But the issue is much more than just a comparison of McCain and Obama. First all, Hayden was an appointed figure, while both McCain and Obama were running for office, and both of them at the time had also already been elected as senators. Why would an appointed employee find the audacity to rate who is fit to be elected?   In other words, we are looking at an appointed employee, who despite his high rank is still an "employee"; but he looks down on elected people.

This statement exposes the fact that the intelligence community is not "apolitical". They have interests, and they canvass the political arena, to see if the candidates fit their interests. McCain was not fitting for the intelligence community.

Other Presidents – Obama and Trump

Even Obama was received by the IC with reservations. According to Hayden, "There were some at CIA who viewed the upcoming election with great concern, fearful that a new president would try to prosecute CIA officers involved in renditions, detentions, and interrogations." (MH1 - 354)

And what about President Trump?

From the time "…he got off the escalator at Trump Tower in June 2015, Donald Trump launched his candidacy…" (MH2 –13), and he was already in the cross-hairs of the IC. In Hayden's words, "Little wonder folks like me were concerned about the disruption that a Trump presidency would cause…" as "…a lot of the Trump stuff looked like it would be off the charts." (MH2 – 41)

In another place, Hayden describes his expectations of the Oval Office: "**For us** the bottom line was clear: the Oval Office was no place for routine exaggeration, much less for 'alternative facts'." (MH2 – 45).

Regardless of whether he is right or wrong, why would an employee ("For us…") decide what the Oval Office should be?

In addition, Hayden in this comment tells the reader that the high-ranking employees in the intelligence community are active in the political arena. And one might ask, if McCain is not labeled by Hayden to be fit, what would Hayden do to bring about an outcome that would fit the intelligence community's needs?

And since the Intelligence Community felt threatened by Trump, they were observing him, and even concluding, "Even after a formal intelligence transition team was stood up in Washington, **it was the view of the intelligence community** that New York was still a powerful, controlling, distant, and not particularly communicative lord." (MH2 – 88)

What's wrong with the President-elect taking charge of his transition team? It might be "discomfiting" for an organization where previously nobody had held them accountable for failures, to suddenly have a chief who wants "results".

Realizing that he might be out of touch with a major segment of American society, Hayden asked his brother to invite "several dozen of his friends, all Trump supporters" to meet with Hayden "in the back room of a Pittsburgh sports bar over some Iron City beer." (MH2 – 22)

It is interesting, but Hayden does not report the conversation of this meeting in one place. He spreads it out over several different places. Many pages after giving us the bulk of the conversation, he mentions that at that meeting "someone asked me, 'Mike, in this Trump-intelligence thing, who drew first blood?' It was a great question. And like most great questions, it was tough to answer." (MH2 – 77)

Hayden repeats his non-answer a few pages later when he says, "So I didn't have a good answer for my Pittsburgh friend's question about who drew first blood. And maybe it just doesn't matter. It all ended up with a lot of blood on the floor." (MH2 – 80)

And if the subject didn't answer, the subject did!

Ofer Shelah, a member of the Defense and Foreign Relations Committee of the Israeli Knesset (Parliament) in his book[7] relates to the intelligence community in the following way: "Even in conditions in which the Intelligence is at its best, it will always be in a supporting role **and not a decisive one, and there must always be the capability to win even without it**… The IDF must therefore instill in its commanders that the Intelligence is an excellent supporting tool, **but only supporting**; the technology is a force multiplier, **but not the force itself**." (133)

And if Intelligence, with all its importance, is only in a "supporting role", and in fact it is, and one needs to be able to win a war even if the intelligence is faulty, or even non-existent, why would an employee in this supporting role take the view that the political level needs to support the intelligence community in its "production of information", and not vice versa? The reality is that the Intelligence needs to support the political level in achieving its goals.

Hayden the politician

Hayden tells the reader that "a retired senior **colleague**" called Hayden to consult him as to whether to join the Trump team. He goes on to say that "…the close **adviser** making the request understood the candidate's obvious limits on security questions…" And Hayden agrees that "My **friend** could surely help." But Hayden concludes it by saying that he advised the person not to help Trump, by labeling Trump as "a badly flawed man" (MH2 - 61).

Please note the change of language from "colleague" to "adviser" to "friend". It is debatable if this change of language is justified by the sequence of events as described in the sentences. If so, we are facing a signal of possible deception in the text in regard to the identity of this person. Was there even such a person?

But regardless of the reliability of this event brought up by Hayden, Hayden exposes that he operated actively within the Intelligence Community against the candidate Trump.

Now we are back to the question of what Hayden did once he labeled McCain as unfit to be president. Did he actively campaign among his colleagues/friends against cooperating with the candidate? Or, maybe he did even more?

The Intelligence Community as a "social club"

"IC veterans" have "their private moments" where they air their "irritation" about what is going on. (MH1 - 413). In his second book Hayden talks about "people with backgrounds like mine: intelligence, security, military, diplomatic, and related fields…" and these people "noted to one another" (MH2 – 43), and "…I *do* know that intelligence officers talk about them [important issues] among themselves at the water cooler, and at the Starbucks and Dunkin' Donuts **in the Agency cafeteria**, and at diners and steakhouses near the Agency." (MH2 – 146-147 – italics in original)

These people not only talk among themselves. Hayden goes on to say, "Of course, I have spent time talking with members of the intelligence and policy communities. Admittedly it was easier to gain access to those no longer in government…" (MH2 – 5) He also says that he "…talked to a lot of folks about decision making and the role of intelligence in the Trump administration." (MH2 – 163) In other words, Hayden has direct knowledge about what is going on in the Trump administration, using his networking capabilities within his "social club."

Since Hayden "spent time talking with members of the intelligence and policy communities", then even though "it was easier to gain access to those no longer in government" it is clear that easy or difficult, he still talked to people currently employed by the government, advocating his positions.

After saying that, he felt the need to tell the reader, "It should also be clear that I am no longer in government…" but this does not mean the information he possesses is outdated. Hayden emphasizes that, "…this [=his book] should be seen as an application of my experience to current events as revealed by public accounts and available documents, enriched by conversations I have had with old and new friends." (MH2 – 6)

Note two points:

First, Hayden is talking about two sources of information he currently possesses: "public accounts and available documents". While the "accounts" are public, he does not say so about the "documents". They are only "available". One should wonder if Hayden has classified documents that were made "available" to him by "old and new friends".

Second, when talking about "old friends" one can assume that he talks about colleagues/friends from the time he was in government. But he also talks about "new friends", and they are likely to be currently employed.

The Intelligence Community as a political lobby

Hayden also exposes that there are discussions going on within Intelligence circles as to how to operate in the political arena.

Hayden gives us details on this group of "retired intelligence community circles": "Former CIA directors are not **an especially close-knit group**. They may get together once or twice a year to hear from the current director, but they served different presidents in different times, under different circumstances. It would be hard to get them all to agree that a certain day was Tuesday." (MH1 - 393).   They cannot agree "that a certain day was Tuesday", but as Hayden continues, we will see that there is a lot they do agree upon, and they even act to achieve their agenda.

The consensus about politics is not the only consensus Hayden talks about. He also says, "If you believe, as we did, that the national security community **had formed a consensus** around certain tools because they were effective, and that part of that effectiveness lay in the rejection of more extreme measures…" (MH2 – 58)

What would the intelligence community do once they established such a consensus? Hayden is not silent about it. He goes on to say that the intelligence community has "a special obligation" to "express" their position even "publicly" as they express their "values".

In other words, Hayden is telling the reader that high-ranking employees in the intelligence community decided to act as any other political lobby to promote their values. Just like the NRA, the agricultural lobby, the insurance companies, or the pharmaceutical companies.

In summary, a group of people from a component of society that is **in charge of secrets** is going **public** to promote their "values".

Clapper says in his book that this group of retired high-ranking intelligence employees served him well when he, Clapper, being in government, could not say something: "…I was grateful for former intelligence officials like Mike Hayden, who could appear on TV and say things **I couldn't say as DNI**." (JC 231) He also says, "…Mike [Hayden] would be **an IC surrogate** for many of the difficult conversations to come…" (JC 232), and "…I knew it would be very difficult for anyone still in government to contradict the president, and I recalled how helpful it had been when Mike Hayden had appeared on television to say the things I could not say as DNI." (JC 386)

In other words, employees in government have "an IC surrogate" that enables them to combat a sitting president who wants to implement a certain policy that they oppose.

But we have evidence that these "IC surrogates" are not acting independently. There are high-ranking officials in the IC who brief these "surrogates" to enable the IC to disseminate information to the public, information that they cannot or do not want to reveal themselves.

In his appearance before the Senate Select Committee on Intelligence regarding his nomination for the position of Director of CIA, John Brennan was asked about an article that appeared in the newspapers as follows:

"… John Brennan, President Barack Obama's top White House advisor on counterterrorism, held a small, private teleconference to brief former counterterrorism advisors who have become frequent commentators on TV news shows." (JB 46)

Brennan confirmed the accuracy of the article, saying, "I think these are individuals who have served in the government and are counterterrorism professionals." (JB 46)

Brennan expanded on this briefing, saying that it is not one-time occurrence: "…frequently, if there is some type of event, or if there's a disrupted terrorist attack, whether it's some 'underwear bomber' or a disrupted IED, or a printer bomb, **or whatever else**, we will engage with the American public. We'll engage with the press. We'll engage with individuals who are experienced professional counterterrorism experts **who will go out and talk to the American public**." (JB 56-57)

Former Director of CIA Leon Panetta brings in his book the complaint from Obama's White House about the CIA "unleashing the former directors" (LP 216) of CIA against the release of the so-called "torture memos" by the White House.

Panetta says, "Back at Langley, Rizzo opened our meeting by profusely apologizing for unleashing the former directors. He had meant only to extend them a courtesy so that they were not surprised by the memos' release, he said, not to provoke them into challenging the decision. I told him to forget it, though I did make clear I'd rather he not do that again." (216)

Summary

These former government employees are not only "IC surrogates" functioning independently.   High-ranking officials within the Intelligence Community (IC) brief these former officials of the IC as a tool to communicate with the public, and to impose their will on the administration, when the administration wants to enact a policy that is against the interests of the Intelligence Community.

These former IC employees serve an important function in the IC's tools to communicate, to influence, to create public opinion, and even to bring the administration to change policies.

Writing letters and articles

Hayden tells us that "In January 2008 twelve senior leaders of the intelligence community (including me) signed a letter to the leadership of the Senate opposing a pending journalist shield law..." (MH1 - 114). Later on, he says that he "wrote an op-ed" going against President Obama's policies. (MH1 - 361) He also combined forces with former attorney general Mike Mukasey, and they "drafted an op-ed laying out our objections to the president's decision." (MH1 - 387) "In mid-September we wrote the president urging him to reverse Holder's decision to reopen the criminal investigations." (MH1 - 393). When Hayden "...dutifully submitted the piece" about drones, the government told him that "...no articles about drones would be cleared *regardless of the content.*" Hayden didn't accept this verdict. "I actually think that's a misuse of the review process, but beyond that, it's just plain stupid. That it took two days to convince the government of that fact says a lot." (MH1 – 426 – italics in original). In his second book he refers to a letter with "122 signatures, a pretty powerful list of security professionals who had served in Republican administrations." (MH2 – 59)

Hayden says that the letter signed by 122 professionals brought him to fear that "…Trump would use this as just another talking point about how Washington insiders reflexively opposed him and needed to be swept out." (MH2 – 59). He also mentions that "…one influential (but unidentified) Republican did point out the obvious: 'The people signing that letter will be the establishment - the very people that Trump is running against. It will make Trump's day.'" (MH2 – 59-60)

In other words, Hayden acknowledges that this "letter writing" was a "declaration of war" between the practitioners of intelligence and the president.

Hayden also mentions that **"Within government** a thousand foreign service officers used the State Department's formal dissent channel to register their opposition to the ban on similar grounds as well." (MH2 – 129)

This time, Hayden talks of currently employed government people who collectively decide to voice their "formal dissent".

Meir Amit, a former head of the Mossad, labeled in this way a group of government employees who had signed a group letter: "What troubled me and fired me up was the collectiveness of the telegram…   this telegram, that was written, or at least signed, collectively, appeared to be **a declaration of rebellion**." (116)

Writing letters is not the only step. Hayden also talks about approaching the Supreme Court to fight President Trump's executive order banning people from seven Moslem countries from entering the US until the security people will fine-tune their vetting process: "I did sign up a few days later to an amicus curiae brief supporting the court challenge to the order. I wasn't alone. Five former directors and acting directors of CIA (myself, John Brennan, Leon Panetta, Michael Morell, and John McLaughlin); former director of national intelligence Jim Clapper; and former head of the National Counterterrorism Center Matt Olsen all eventually joined in." (MH2 – 128)

TV

Besides writing letters and articles, "There are now quite a few former intelligence officials on the 24/7 news networks," (MH2 – 247) and Hayden names them.
It is no wonder that Hayden quotes the then Director of CIA Mike Pompeo saying, "There are an awful lot of former CIA talking heads on TV," and Hayden brings Pompeo's comment that "…their obligation to remain quiet about their work 'far extends beyond the day you turn in your badge.'" (MH2 – 247)

Hayden says that he feels that his "…credentials to comment on air are based on my intelligence experience. I am (or at least try to be) the 'fact witness.'" (MH2 – 246)

"…or at least try to be…"? - "Try to be" means that he doesn't succeed. Why doesn't he?

Hayden forgets to tell his readers that he should label himself the "assessment witness" rather than the "fact witness". After all, as he commented on the "facts" in regard to the WMD in Iraq, the facts were "circumstantial".

"Since the inauguration [of Trump], the two most senior leaders of the community **under Barack Obama**, DNI Jim Clapper and DCIA John Brennan joined in with somewhat more basic challenges to the president's character and competence." (MH2 - 248)

One can ask a simple question: on what do "the two most senior leaders of the community" base their "assessment" of anyone's character and competence to be a president? Is their "assessment" (taking into consideration their track record during the years) better than the "assessment" of millions of voters? Not to forget that Clapper himself starts his book by saying that the intelligence community is geared "outward" and not "inward".

Moreover, why would the "character" of anyone be an issue for being a good president? After all, anyone who studies the history of the US presidents since the time of independence would know that there have been very good presidents who had major psychological issues - including President Lincoln, to name one.

If the IC is geared "outward", according to Clapper's own words, how can he doubt "Trump's fitness for office"? Hayden himself says that this comment by Clapper created a lot of excitement among "more traditional senior intelligence alumni **about staying above politics.**" (MH2 - 248)

Hayden also says, "I often appear to be in opposition" (MH2 - 247), and in fact, he afterwards says, "...there is no doubt that the comments of people like me, Clapper, McLaughlin, Brennan, Morell, and others have created the impression in the minds of some (many?) that we are merely the public voice of a deep state intelligence community opposed to Donald Trump." (MH2 - 247).

After bringing the impression of them being "...the public voice of a deep state intelligence community..." he continues, "If we are..." (MH2 - 248)

"If we are..." means that not only does he not deny this impression, but he actually verbalizes, "If we are..." - and the sentence "...we are..." (although it is prefixed with the "if") entered Hayden's language.

And how does he move to refute this impression? "If we are, we aren't very efficient. We don't coordinate on commentary. What you see on air is what you get. If there is broad consistency, it is the product of a **common worldview and shared life experiences**, not an orchestrated theme of the week." (MH2 – 248)

In other words, they are people who come from the same "social club" with the same "common worldview and shared life experiences".

It is similar to what Giora Eiland brings in his book as a quote by an officer (recently appointed to be IDF Chief of Staff) – "You generals, the members of the General Command Staff, you have the same opinions, you use the same explanations, the same language, and even the same metaphors. It is scary." (Page 226-227)

Hayden laments the fact that in spite of all the criticism against Trump, "…it becomes increasingly clear that he will not change, that the office will not shape the man, and that, in fact, it has been and will be the other way around." (MH2 – 249). Isn't this true for anyone who heads an organization, like CIA and/or NSA? Or, maybe Hayden has the idea that his term as Director of CIA and NSA was not meant to make any changes to improve their performance?

Leaks

Writing letters and articles and appearing on TV to voice the opinions of former heads of the intelligence community, entering the political arena, was not their only way to influence the political process.

Let's not forget that McCain said in his book, "The CIA planted **false stories** in the press." (100)

It was not McCain's imagination. Hayden in his second book refers several times to leaks that he acknowledges had come from the Intelligence Community.

For example, when talking about the "2016 race", Hayden says that "…some of the subsequent articles **appeared to be sourced, at least in part, to current intelligence officials**…" (MH2 – 71)

When talking about the time President Trump has already been in office, Hayden says, "…but there is no doubt that some [of the leaks] have come from career professionals." (MH2 – 86) And he adds, "My journalist friends admit to me in a generalized sort of way that a lot of folks are certainly more willing to talk to them." (MH2 – 86)

When talking of the infamous dossier about Trump in Russia [to be discussed separately later on], which Trump blamed the Intelligence Community for producing it, Hayden says, "…So Trump was wrong to implicate the intelligence community **in this one**…" (MH2 – 112). Hayden knows what he is talking about. He caught Trump being wrong "in this one" (i.e. the dossier), but not in other instances.

Hayden talks about the departure of Mike Flynn from his position at the White House, and says, "There was little mourning in the intelligence community when Flynn was asked to resign after only weeks on the job, **and there was probably intelligence community leaking that poured oil on this fire**." (MH2 - 150)

Knowing how much the Intelligence Community leaks information, it brought Michael Morell, former acting Director of the CIA, to say after criticizing the administration: "But, to be clear, critiquing policy is not leaking." (MH2 – 247)

Deep state?

Hayden quotes Trump, who was elected with the "…promise to drain the Washington swamp…" (MH2 – 83), and for Hayden it "..had the air of a hostile corporate takeover." (MH2 – 84)

Hayden even says, "I have also heard it compared within the intelligence community to explorers landing in **a suspicious and hostile environment**, looking to make alliances with some tribes in order to subdue all the others." (MH2 – 84)

One should note that Hayden does not say "someone told me…" or "An intelligence officer told me…" Instead, he says "I have heard…" This is even worse than using passive voice, a linguistic form that Hayden professes to use when he wants to conceal information. By Hayden not telling us from whom he heard it, Hayden conceals very deeply the source of these words. This brings me to suspect that Hayden is actually talking about himself.

Let's see why Hayden conceals this source of information. Since the intelligence community is the one that is already there in the DC area, and the new administration is the newcomer to the DC area, then the "explorers" must be the new administration, and the intelligence community must be the "suspicious and hostile environment". If this is not a "confession", I don't know what a confession looks like.

And Hayden continues: "Resistance to the ways of the incoming team **was quickly identified** as evidence of the 'deep state'…" (MH2 – 84). Again, using passive voice. Who is the one who identified it as such? Hayden does not tell us. And why not? Why not to blame the new administration? But he cannot, since quite likely this "accusation" did not come from the new administration.

And now Hayden moved to deny the existence of "deep state". And the way he denies it is very educating.

"There is no 'deep state' in the American Republic. There is merely 'the state,' or, as I characterize it, career professionals doing their best within the rule of law." (MH2 – 85)

Please note the following:

First, Hayden is not talking about reality. He starts his description by saying "as I characterize it". It might be that someone else will "characterize" it differently. Again, Hayden is moving to impose his language on others in order to avoid sensitivity and inconvenience.

Second, Hayden agrees that there is a "state" composed of "career professionals **doing their best** within the rule of law." But "doing their best" of what? Hayden does not say that these career professional are **doing their job** within the rule of law.

Third, Hayden produces a great denial of "deep state". It is not deep state because it is not "deep". Therefore, it is only a "state". The reason it is not "deep" is because these "career professionals" have the arrogance to act openly as "...**a suspicious and hostile environment**..." to a new administration coming into town. Therefore, the US is in great shape. It does not have a "deep state". And the citizen can rest assured now that the will of the people is secure!!!

Hayden continues: "...but painting this as a dystopian government universe inhabited by secret malevolent forces is simply **inaccurate**." (MH2 – 86) "Inaccurate" but not false, as Hayden himself "characterized" it as not being "deep state" as it is not "deep". On top of that, Hayden continues by saying, "Now the organs of the government that he was about to inherit were the secret, antidemocratic, all-powerful, conspiratorial 'deep state.' **It is not a particularly useful description**..." (MH2 – 86)

It is a "description" but it is "not particularly useful". "Not particularly useful" to whom? To the new administration (the "explorers") or to the intelligence community (the "suspicious and hostile environment")?

Hayden moves on with his "confession": "There is no doubt that large bureaucracies are set in their ways, and I can aver from personal experience that it is hard to get them to change course." (MH2 – 88)

And Hayden continues, "But the 'deep state' **calumny** is neither accurate nor "Calumny"? This is very high language. Why not to actually say that it is a "lie" or "slander"? Because it is not. Hayden uses very high language so the average reader will get lost in his reading. Just as Comey said in his book that Hayden's briefings "…were a river of really great-sounding stuff that didn't make much sense once the briefing was over and you tried to piece together what you had just heard." (Comey 83)

The Israeli Military Intelligence –
A View from Inside

Introduction

Colonel (Aluf Mishneh in Hebrew) Yoel (Joel) Ben-Porat was the commander of the Israeli Military Intelligence unit in charge of intercepting electronic signals (SIGINT) before and during the Yom Kippur War in 1973.

Although the unit intercepted the information that provided a warning of the imminent attack, the "analysts" (also called the "assessors" in Israel) dismissed the information and "assessed" the prospect of war with "low probability". This "assessment" produced the well-known "surprise" of the war, a surprise that shook the country to its core. After 2,500 fatalities and many more wounded, the government of Golda Meir fell, and the confidence and trust of the people in the government's ability and skills was eroded for generations to come.

As a personal note: I am very interested in autobiographies of high-ranking military officers and politicians, both in Israel and the US, and I have read many of them. I was impressed by the books of only two people. The first is "Do Not Sleep at Night" by Giora Eiland, which I referred to earlier in this book, and the other is "Neilah", a book published after the 1973 war by Ben-Porat.

"Neilah" means, literally, "locking". Ben-Porat refers in his book to the fact that the "assessors" were **locked** into their conception, although the data contradicted it. However, due to the fact that Ben-Porat's language is loaded with Biblical and Talmudic language and references, one should also note that "Neilah" is the name of the segment that ends the Yom Kippur (Day of Atonement) service in the synagogue. Both the service that starts

Yom Kippur – Kol Nidrei – and the service that ends Yom Kippur – Neilah – are considered the highlights of Yom Kippur. Ben-Porat's book deals with the Yom Kippur War.

Ben-Porat's book is a major eye-opener not only regarding the Israeli Military Intelligence (MI) in particular, but also about the Israeli Defense Forces (IDF) in general, and even about the Israeli/Jewish culture at large.

Who is Yoel Ben-Porat?

It is interesting to note that Ben-Porat describes his background only in the second chapter titled – "Why Military and Why Intelligence".

Ben-Porat was born in eastern Poland in 1931. "After the annexation of Austria by Hitler…" (BP 32) in 1938, when Yoel was 7 years old, his family had a discussion about whether to run away or to stay. His father wanted to "make aliyah" (to "ascend") – i.e. to immigrate to Palestine (Israel of today), but his grandparents refused to leave, and his parents didn't want to leave them behind. They remained in Poland, and found themselves under Nazi occupation.

"In 1943, I was 12 years old and I was in a concentration camp." (40) The camp was raided by partisans, and Yoel was released, and joined the partisans fighting the Nazis.

When referring to his ordeal during the war, commenting on it from the perspective of many years later, Ben-Porat says, "I understood why the Soviets were defeated in 1941 under **the shock of surprise in 'Barbarossa', and what happened at Pearl Harbor**. All this knowledge was archived for many years, but remained bubbling in the storage of the back of my mind." (43)

The fact that Yoel was not born in Israel, and went through the ordeal of the Holocaust and the Second World War, had a major impact on him, as is evident in his life, behavior, attitudes, and in his book. He labels himself as "Polish and '*Galuti*'" (BP 134) - in Hebrew: a Jew from the diaspora.

After the war, Yoel came to Palestine (Israel of today) in 1947 and joined the Palmach (the elite unit of the underground movement). After independence in 1948, he joined the IDF and served with distinction, going up the ranks to the rank of Brigadier General, and retired in 1985.

US history as a lesson

The fact that Ben-Porat came from Europe, impacted him throughout his life. He was not isolated from the outside world, as many Israelis are, thinking that only Israel exists, and nothing else. Ben-Porat did learn something from the war and the events of the cold war.

He says, "We had the lessons of Prague from 1968 – meaning, a large military exercise that can be masking intentions to invade…" (15)

He also says, "The loaded personal experience of 'Barbarossa' of 1941, and reading about the surprise of Pearl Harbor, about the Battle of the Bulge in Ardennes in 1945, and Korea of 1950, helped me to crystallize a warning perception, seemingly fearful, and also extraordinary sensitivity. I adopted for myself the slogan, 'Never again Pearl Harbor'…" (44) He even says that he encouraged an officer in his unit to summarize the book about Pearl Harbor and to distribute it as a pamphlet in the unit. It came to a point that people complained about his nagging about Pearl Harbor, and "…they heard it from you ad nauseam." (28)

Personally, I can testify that my immediate commander (mentioned in Ben-Porat's book) welcomed us to the unit by saying: "You will be here for three years, and I trust you will do a good job. However, if you will miss one word, I myself will 'kill' you. And you will not be able to justify yourself that you did a good job for the rest of the three years." The idea of warning was instilled into the unit from the lowest rank. We were on alert 24/7/365 for three years of mandatory service. We lived with the knowledge that we are the first line of defense for the country.

Ben-Porat as a commander

Ben-Porat gives his way of commanding the unit – he disapproves of the title "chamber" ("lishka" in Hebrew) that many high-ranking officers used. For him, "…the place where I put my behind…" was an "office". He had a secretary "so there will be some brains in running the office, and also so that there will be someone who knows where the papers are stuck." (81) And even this secretary he shared with his deputy. He also didn't have a driver to drive him around, although he was entitled to it. He calls this "right" to have a driver as "corrupt", and he was happy that this "corrupt right" was cancelled in the IDF, "Thank God".

Ben-Porat quotes one of the founders of the unit who told him, "don't become a 'papernik' (one who swallows paper). I open mail only after one month. And then it is apparent that half of it was solved, and there is no need to do anything, a quarter is in the midst of a solution, and the remaining quarter has no solution." (83) Ben-Porat comments on this advice: "He exaggerated **a little bit**, but this was his philosophy of management."

With rejecting the high life of high-ranking military officers, Ben-Porat says, "…of this idol-worshipping custom, that developed especially after the 1967 war, that the elite of the military, the elite of the money (or the black-white money), and the elite of entertainment used to hold corrupt meetings. The rich provided the place, the wine and the cheese; the entertainer the music; and the generals – the inspiration and the glamour." (124)

Moreover, Ben-Porat says that he had a "hobby" of "…absorbing the ones who didn't adjust and those who due to wrong judgment by officers were defined as problematic or as no-good." (82) He adds that the benefit of doing so was, "They were a real windfall, as we received them above the regularly allotted positions, for free." He ends by saying that most of them became good commanders.

As a commander, he says he had a custom "…not to get into trouble with complaints from Field Security, the Military Rabbinate, the Women's Corps, and the Ombudsman [equivalent in the US to the "Inspector General"]." (82)

One should note his list of priorities. As a high-ranking officer in the military intelligence, field security was important for him. Second was the military rabbinate, quite likely due to his religious background, although he was not observant at that time. The ombudsman was on the bottom of the list.

The Israeli Defense Forces (IDF)

Being in such a high-ranking position, Ben-Porat had a great opportunity to observe the IDF.

Ben-Porat says, "To the career military [unlike the mandatory draft of 3 years] comes more and more mediocrity. The dozens of excellent engineers whom we drafted in the sixties and seventies are starring today in the Israeli electronics industry which they established." (99) He also says on the same page, "The system has no ability to deal with the challenge of quality issues."

In other words, what Ben-Porat is saying is that after the 3-year mandatory service, many capable people feel that they have done their duty for their country, and feel justified in then starting their civilian life.

It is quite customary in Israel among young men and women, after these military years, to take one year "sabbatical" and to go touring the globe in faraway countries, and then come back and go into college and/or work, start families, and "begin life".

The Israeli Military Intelligence

Ben-Porat says that, "the capability of any intelligence service is determined first of all by its collection capability and the variety of organizations and sources of collection. One who doesn't have satellites and high-altitude spy planes will never be number one. Therefore, in the best case we were number three in the international league." (BP 11)

Ben-Porat refers to the fact that the military intelligence is not the only player in the field. He mentions briefly "the civilian competitor" (likely the Mossad), and "friendly intelligence services", and "etc." (56)

Ben-Porat quotes a conversation he had with the Chief of MI a few days before the war, after Ben-Porat readied his unit for the war, and asked his superior to allow him to call up some of the reserves. His superior, the Chief of MI responded, "Yoel, listen well, the duty of the Intelligence is to preserve the nerves of the country. Not to drive the community crazy, and not to destabilize the economy. I don't permit you to think of drafting even a quarter of one reserve soldier." (55)

This response sounds almost identical to what Michael Hayden said many years later in the US, that the duty of Intelligence is to keep the country "safe and free". And in fact, Ben-Porat comments on his superior's response: "I learned something new about the duty of the Intelligence. I never knew this." (55)

Ben-Porat says that two months before the war (August 1973) the Chief of MI charged him and his unit with a written order in which it was stated that "…the main duty of my unit was **to achieve information of warning** in regard to war with Syria and Egypt." (110)

The Unit

Ben-Porat says, "one of the largest and major collection units in charge of information about warning was the "Watchman" unit ["Mitzpeh" in Hebrew]." (12).

Although the unit is within the MI, Ben-Porat says, "the degree of responsibility and the task of warning that is given to us justifies that we should be under the president of the country, or at least the Prime Minister, **as it is done in the US.**" (133)

In the IDF it is well-known that a soldier who serves in a combat unit is perceived as a real soldier, while a soldier who sits behind a desk is called a "jobnik". Meaning, not worth much. While serving my 3-year mandatory service, when I was asked what I was doing in the military, I said that I am a "clerk". A "jobnik". People smiled with pity in their eyes. As a matter of fact, and Ben-Porat related to it in his book, at that time our uniform did not indicate anything relating to "Intelligence". On our hat there was the "communication" insignia, and on our sleeve there was the Central Command patch. We were practically "undercover".

But the fact is that at times these "jobniks" had to be stationed at the front line. And Ben-Porat says, "Since we had to be positioned on mountain tops at the front line, we suggested that our personnel there would be fighters – with the training of infantry soldiers at the level of squad commanders in 'Golani' [an elite army brigade] and with appropriate weapons – and MI personnel combined. This, of course, was never approved. We asked for fewer female soldiers, and after the war we got double… as there were not enough males." (98)

Ben-Porat relates here to the fact that a few days before the war he ordered to evacuate all female soldiers from the front line bases, an order that saved the various locations from chaos, as many locations were under constant bombardment, and the personnel were not even able to go to outside bathrooms.

And in fact, Syrian commando units raided the unit's post on the top of Mount Hermon, at the border between Syria and the Golan Heights, and took over the post, with all its equipment, and took all personnel as prisoners of war. This was a major devastating blow to the unit, as it exposed its knowledge and capabilities. At least the comfort was that female soldiers were not taken captive. The Israeli soldiers in Syrian captivity were subjected to extreme torture, and some of them did not regain their own self after returning to safety.

At the "Pearl of the Crown" post (Ben-Porat's language) that was not far from the Suez Canal, the female soldiers were evacuated before the war. During the war the male soldiers had to stay in the working bunkers under constant bombardment. The only soldier who was killed there during that time was one who decided to go and shave in his room outside the bunker.

Ben-Porat's insight before the war, in spite of the "assessment" of headquarters ("low probability for war") enabled the unit to function during the war, and to give the IDF accurate information in real time.

8200 is not the MI

There is a saying in the unit (today known by its number 8200) that "The MI is not the IDF, and 8200 is not the MI." Still,

"We didn't know anything about the IDF… It was not important, and a shame to load the brain with it. It was according to the American principle of the 'need to know' basis. And also not essential." (70) He also says that knowing details about the IDF's capabilities would be "…unnecessary and counter-productive". (140) He summarizes it by saying, "My senior officers, and also I, were with 'our faces towards the enemy'." (140)

He is proud to declare himself as "an Intelligence officer, careful and crazy for one thing – warning." (46)

The Trauma

The Yom Kippur War in 1973 was a major trauma for Colonel Ben-Porat, more than the trauma that the rest of the country had. His unit, under his command, did its job, and provided the necessary warning, only to find out that doing its job is not enough. In the military channels from the collection unit to the "consumer" – the political leadership – there is one buffer, and this buffer is the "assessment" or "research branch" of the MI.

The Research Branch – general information

The assessment branch (called "Research" in Hebrew) gets all the information from all sources, including Ben-Porat's unit, and puts them all together by country.   Ben-Porat says that while he was a captain he served "…for several months as acting head of the Egyptian desk in Research" (44). This is the branch that produces the "assessment" after allegedly seeing the full picture. In the US, the "assessor" would be called the "analyst".

Ben-Porat says, "During 1956-1957 I served two years in Research during the 1956 Sinai Campaign. A period of fascinating activity." (44)

"The unprofessional reader might assume that the Intelligence acquires – or produces – information, that serves the leaders of the country in the process of reaching decisions. **There is no mistake more serious than this**. Although this is approximately how it ought to be." (147)   Readers of Michael Hayden and James Clapper should read carefully what Ben-Porat is saying.

Ben-Porat summarizes: "I know that the Information Service of the Haganah [pre-state underground] and the Intelligence of the first years of the IDF was a **service of information** and not **a service of assessments**. In 1948 when it was said, 'the Intelligence said' it was the words of information, and not the words of assessment." (151) But by the time of the 1973 war, or the time of Michael Hayden and James Clapper, this had changed.

According to Ben-Porat, "all the Intelligence is done by the head of Research and his group." (72) The "assessors" are "our soloists who spoke for the whole Intelligence Community…" (13), "they are the tip of the spear" (27).

The Research Branch – the intelligence's weakness

According to Ben-Porat, the "research" or "assessment" is the core problem of the Israeli military intelligence. And he goes on to list their weaknesses.

These assessors are "…the catastrophe of the Intelligence since its infancy." (25) He says that "this system is very problematic from time immemorial." (13) "The catastrophe of the Intelligence from the dawn of its history… comes from the system, by which the information comes out – from the pen and mouth of the assessors." (147)

He goes on to say that "the information, which is the justification for the existence of the intelligence, is being judged according to the assessors' **quirks, wishes, and desires**, and they are the mouth of the complex intelligence system for the leader who makes the decisions." (147)

Ben-Porat adds a very important weakness of these assessors – "their ignorance about the Arabs, Arabic, and Islam." (13). He says, "I never understood their boldness and hutzpah to deal with nations and countries, and to predict the future, without the slightest bit of knowledge in history, culture, language, literature, and the Moslem religion." (114)

Not only they were ignorant. Ben-Porat says that they also went further and looked down on the need to know about the history, people, language, and culture. He gives an example that two days before the 1973 war, in the month of Ramadan, when Moslems fast from sunrise to sunset, the Egyptian Army ordered all the soldiers to eat – "…an order that was unheard of before – but it didn't bother anyone as they didn't know what the fast of Ramadan means, and what it means to break the fast. This is a basic example of Intelligence due to only education." (115)

Ben-Porat lists only one Chief of the Israeli MI who had a graduate degree in Arabic and Philosophy before he entered the MI in 1949. No other Chief thereafter.

Besides their ignorance, Ben-Porat also talk of their personalities. He quotes a colleague who rated the assessors as "inflated balloons filled with self-importance" (72).

Ben-Porat wants the situation to change. First of all, he focuses on the assessors' ignorance. "There is a need to uproot the ignorance. There should not be an assessing officer from the rank of major or above who is not an 'engineer for Arabism and Islam', just as it would be inconceivable to task someone who is not a certified aeronautical engineer with planning the wing of a plane." (165)

Ben-Porat even suggests what should be the training for such an assessor: "an academic-level course over one year… that will deal with (a) issues in philosophy, logic, and epistemology, to improve the systematic thinking; (b) issues in behavioral psychology, for decisions in unclear or doubtful situations and failures in thinking; (c) history of assessment mistakes by statesmen, military commanders, and intelligence assessors; and (d) issues in political science regarding totalitarian regimes and the process of decision-making." (166)

If this is not enough, Ben-Porat suggests a way to assess the assessors – "there should be an annual inventory of his assessments that were found wrong, and if he was not right more than five times out of ten (this is likely the rate of professionals who are not artists), they should suggest to him to move to another profession, otherwise one cannot fail as an assessor." (165)

Ben-Porat even quotes Rabin, a former Chief of Staff, ambassador, and Prime Minister, who was quoted in 1982 saying that "…it is recommended that the Knesset (Parliament) Committee for Defense and Foreign Affairs should discuss 'the assessments of the Military Intelligence, that in the last twenty years were mostly wrong.'" (147)

I can easily say that, knowing the Israeli military, Ben-Porat's ideas, and even the conclusions of a possible discussion in the Parliament, would be rejected by the Military Intelligence right away. To suggest that the assessor should be right?   Where did Ben-Porat get this "crazy" idea?

One should be reminded of the idea that was presented to Michael Hayden of creating a "jury of peers" to evaluate the efficiency of the analysts, an idea that was rejected by Hayden outright. (MH1 – 279-280)

And Ben-Porat even says - "when an assessor is caught misleading or manipulating information, **there should be no second chance. As it is done in flight school or courses about explosives." (165)

Ben-Porat gives us what he considers to be the **present** requirements to become an "assessor" - "…it is enough that he will talk at a proper pace, not hesitate, not stutter, his syntax is reasonable, and his pen is eloquent – and here you have an ideal national assessor." (165)

"There is a need to be very particular in choosing the assessors. To be less impressed by their rhetoric abilities, and to relate more to their integrity." (165)

This system of "amateur, reckless, unprofessional and irresponsible intelligence work" (16) is the reason for "…the multitude of unjustified surprises, that occurred either due to lack of correct use of the information, or disregarding it, or a faulty ability to observe reality." (13)

In fact, Ben-Porat himself lists all the failures of the Israeli Military Intelligence, and he even comments that all the failures were only due to wrong assessment, and not any failure in acquiring the information.

The weakness of an "assessment"

Ben-Porat says that the main weakness of the Intelligence is the fact that it is "…mainly a human system. Its critical component – the intelligence assessment – is a purely human system: brain and some senses." (148)

Ben-Porat starts this subject by saying, "The information, which is usually facts, has the 'right of way", while the assessment is set down on the huge minefield of wishful thinking and human errors." (13) He qualifies it by saying, "…although the information is not always facts, and is not always verified facts." (149)

He says that besides the pure logic that goes into "the melting pot of the assessment", there is also "…what I tend to label as the 'Shakespearean stew' – likes and hatreds, feelings of superiority and contempt, anxieties, self-confidence, worrying, flippancy, and more – the list is long." (152) In summary, Ben-Porat says, "we don't have mathematics of a human being." (152)

Ben-Porat also adds other ingredients that can influence an assessment. For example, "…the Israeli MI was influenced by the atmosphere of contempt towards the Arabs, and even added to it." (17) He says that "we should admit that the cleverness, daring, and resourcefulness that the leaders of Syria and Egypt showed in the Yom Kippur War were in absolute and polar contrast to what our assessors were willing to attribute to them beforehand." (149) In short, he says, "The Arabs simply refused to behave according to stereotype." (149)

Another ingredient is the fact that "the Jewish arithmetic is different in its values from the Arab one or the Russian one. One of the most frequent mistakes in assessment is to evaluate the opponent by your own standards, since these are the ones, and the only ones you know." (152)

Ben-Porat brings an example, his observation of the Jewish society. We should remind ourselves while reading the following quote that Ben-Porat himself is a survivor of the Holocaust.

"One of the examples of our inability to completely understand reality is the gap in the perception of reality that was prevalent among the leadership of the Jewish people, in all its branches, during the years of 1943-1944, in regard to what was happening to European Jewry. In essence we are optimistic creatures (even the pessimists among us). We tend to suppress the negative and the dangerous. People do not use the phrase "it will be bad". On the contrary, in our arsenal we have a rich collection of words indicating optimism and suppression: 'It will be good', 'it's not too bad', 'we will overcome', 'I hope', "I believe'. There are among us who are fortunate to be able to add 'with God's help', and if this is not enough they will find refuge in "Israel's Rock and Redeemer', and 'the Eternal One of Israel does not lie' etc." (154)

"Wishful thinking and expectations have a significant statistical representation among the causes of error in assessment." (154)

As for the Arab arithmetic, Ben-Porat brings, "…the likes and hatreds of the Arabs towards each other are of a type that is unknown to us, and not understood by us (see the relationship between Nasser-Hussein, Arafat-Hussein, Arafat-Assad, Sadat-Assad, Hussein-Assad, and more). The dynamics of the conflicts among them sometimes have qualities that are not understood by us." (155)

Ben-Porat says that "…our assessments have a tendency to underestimate, especially in regard to the Arabs, and even towards the Russians. In the global context, the Americans show a tendency of overestimate in their assessments of the Russians. They shoot long, while we shoot short. The result is the same." (155)

[Note: This is a very important observation of the US Intelligence Community when we come to "assess" their conclusion as to whether there was interference or meddling in the elections, and if there was any collusion between the Russians and the Trump campaign.]

According to Ben-Porat, assessment is a profession for "fearful people, meaning careful and level-headed" (161). Assessors who think like "a naval commando or a kamikaze pilot" will not be useful in Intelligence. After all, assessment is not an exact science. "In my eyes assessment is an art, and if it is an art – then artists should be dealing with it. But even among artists there are true artists, half-artists and quarter-artists, and even imposters." (150)

In summary, "pride and arrogance are the height of stupidity." (150) The assessor needs "constant awareness, freshness, and a reasonable degree of self-depreciation and humility." (163)

And even all the above is not enough. "…the assessors did not lack intelligence, and its absence was not the reason for the failure, but the lack of intellectual honesty, which is called in English 'integrity'." (151)

[Note: the Academy of the Hebrew Language recently came up with a word for "integrity". It is derivative of the word "honest". While honest is "yashar", and honesty is "yosher", they coined the word "yoshra" for integrity. This word was not in existence at the time Ben-Porat wrote his book, in 1985.]

"Assessment" vs. an "estimate"

Here, Ben-Porat moves to distinguish between two different terms, for which there is usually a tendency to combine them into one term – assessment and estimate. He defines assessment as talking about "something existing and tangible" (145) while an "estimate" deals with estimating a future occurrence, prediction. At which time, "…there is no assessment, as there is nothing to assess. It is only possible to assume, to guess." (145) According to Ben-Porat, "…there is nothing wrong with guessing – as long as one specifies that it is a guess." (157)

Moreover, according to Ben-Porat, "It is the duty of the assessor to educate the leader, who is not versed in the secrets of the profession, that assessments – have limited accuracy, and they are vulnerable to mistakes." (170)

Please note the absolute contrast to what Hayden says; according to Hayden, the intelligence officer should educate the leader to accept the officer's assessment.

The leader

Unlike Hayden, who saw himself as equal (the metaphor of two doors) if not even above the leader, in experience and knowledge, the picture coming from Ben-Porat's book is the exact opposite.

Let's start with Prime Minister Golda Meir who visited the "Pearl of the Crown" of the unit – its main post in the Sinai Desert. Ben-Porat says that when he presented the situation to the Prime Minister, she stopped him in mid-sentence, and asked him: "Tell me, Yoel, if the Arabs would want to attack us, would we know?" (46) And Ben-Porat says about her question, "A simple question, which testifies to common sense. She didn't use the words 'warning', 'surprise', 'capability', 'readiness', but she asked a question of common sense." (46)

And Ben-Porat goes on to say, "Since the government is in charge of security at the highest national level, its responsibility surpasses that of the MI." (59)

He brings the fact that, "Moshe Dayan and the seventh Chief of Staff [i.e. Rabin] were not satisfied with reading assessments as 'chewed thinking', but whenever a serious issue was on the table, they wanted to review the raw material." (147)

They were not the only ones. Churchill, the British Prime Minister at the time of the Second World War, "was his own intelligence officer" (150). Ben-Porat says that Churchill "…did not decide based upon assessments, but preferred to review hundreds of original pieces of information…" (148) And – "It was known that he listened to advisers and all types of 'brains for hire' but to assess – he assessed by himself." (150).

And Ben-Porat continues – "The National Assessor (i.e. the head of MI) is not acting in the sphere of decision makers. He is only an advisor, sort of a 'brain for hire'. He must present the most exact factual picture regarding the enemy, without any embellishment. After he has done this, he has no advantage over the leader." (166)

Ben-Porat goes beyond this statement. According to him, "the leader has an advantage over the assessor. First, he bears the responsibility for the country and its citizens… And this responsibility, by its own nature, must bring him to act more carefully, out of level-headed judgment, and to minimize as much as possible the taking of uncalculated risks." (167)

This means, according to Ben-Porat, that "…the integrative assessment can be done only by the leader: the Chief of Staff, the Defense Minister, the government and the one who heads it… Only the leader can choose and set up his forces… according to what suits our forces, the degree of risk, pros and cons. These are not the realm of Intelligence… They are out of its jurisdiction, beyond its authority…" (167)

After all, "in regard to assessments, assumptions, and guesswork, the tools of the leader are not inferior to those of the assessor." (167)

In summary, this picture presented to us by Ben-Porat only testifies to his sincerity and humility.

The Leader – Intelligence Officer encounter

Ben-Porat starts by saying that "the information is not the possession of the Intelligence, just as the fire of the artillery or the Air Force is not the possession…" (68) of the ones who fire.

The intelligence officer should present the facts. He quotes the head assessor who told a small group of government ministers three days before the war – "the way the armies of Syria and Egypt are positioned today on the fronts enables them to attack at any moment…" However, "…instead of stopping here, with facts of pure intelligence, reflecting capability, and to leave the guessing, or the assumption, of 'intentions' to the leaders, he glided into assessments, and visions, towards prophecy…" (58)

On the other hand, Ben-Porat says, "when the Intelligence conceals from the Chief of Staff vital information at a time of danger, when the enemy is at the gate, this is insubordination under serious circumstances and outrageous irresponsibility." (68)

Ben-Porat tells how the Chief of MI presented to the Commission of Inquiry a "strange position – that as the Chief of Military Intelligence he does not share his doubts with the Chief of Staff, but functions as a decision maker, as a commander." (120) Ben-Porat labels this behavior as "a completely non-Intelligence worldview" (120).

Intents

Both Hayden and Clapper reject the idea of the Intelligence trying to find out information about the intentions of the enemy's leader, and Ben-Porat agrees with them, but he dwells on this issue in a very profound and enlightening way.

"They said about President Nixon that he was unpredictable." (157) However, Ben-Porat asks the question: "Does it mean that we should conclude from this that other leaders are predictable?" (157), And – "…each one of us is surprised at times by the words and deeds of the people who are closest to us! So how can we descend to the depths of our enemies' intentions…" (157)

Ben-Porat brings the example of the Chief of Military Intelligence, who apologized in 1978 for not predicting that Sadat would make peace with Israel. And Ben-Porat asks, why does he need to apologize if even Sadat's foreign minister resigned immediately once Sadat announced that he is ready to go to Jerusalem? Even a person close to Sadat could not predict what Sadat would do, so why should the Israeli Chief of MI apologize?

He goes on to say that even if we know Arabic fluently, does it mean that we understand the Arabs? After all, the Germans did not understand the Russians, and the Americans did not understand the Southeast Asian countries.

Ben-Porat moves to describe the word "intent" with small details – "the term 'intent' has nine faces – a square of the words 'wants', 'can', and 'decides'. What are 'intents'? is it 'wants'? Is it 'wants and can'? Is it 'wants, can, but did not decide'? or is it 'Can, doesn't want to, and decides'? And so on." (158)

Ben-Porat goes on to say: "In the Middle East a war can start when someone doesn't really want to, and isn't really able to, but he still decides. This was behind Nasser's behavior in 1967 and even behind Sadat's considerations in 1973. In my opinion, a personal drive of political perseverance drove Sadat to believe that he can: if he will not fight, he will be deposed. If he will fight and fail, he will be deposed. But what if he will succeed?" (158)

Absorbing this information and extrapolating from it to the Trump-Intelligence dispute and conflict, can we say that the intelligence community really understands Trump? He is not the "enemy". He is American. But can we say that every single American is predictable?

Moreover, can we say that both Hayden and Clapper really understand what "Intelligence" is?

Examining a failure

We already saw earlier that after 9/11 there was a Commission of Inquiry to investigate the events. The Commission came out with the conclusion that the cause for the failure was lack of coordination between the different agencies. This conclusion was based mainly upon the information that the directors of the agencies fed the commission. The reality was that lack of good management within the agencies caused the failure. Each intelligence organization intercepted information of the upcoming tragedy, however, due to incorrect and irresponsible management, the information was not processed correctly.

Question: Did each agency examine itself to correct the systemic failure? Very unlikely. It is quite likely that each director felt lucky that his irresponsibility was not found to be the cause for the tragedy, and life moved on. But if indeed, the mistakes continue, there is a high probability that the same could occur again.

Let's see what happened in Israel.

The Commission of Inquiry after the 1973 Yom Kippur War recommended firing the Chief of Staff and four high-ranking officers in the Intelligence. At the same time, the Commission found that the political level acted properly and found them to be exempt from any repercussions.

This recommendation of letting the political level go free was not accepted by the public. A reserve officer started a personal demonstration calling for the government to resign. The demonstration picked up momentum, and within three months after publication of the Commission's recommendations, Prime Minister Golda Meir resigned, and the government fell.

But what happened within the Intelligence? Did anyone check what happened? Ben-Porat relates to this issue.

The new Chief of Staff told Ben-Porat: "I was not here during the war, and the failure doesn't interest me. I am building a new military that would be able to cope with the Arabs in the future. I don't look back." (107)

The new Chief of Military Intelligence replied to Ben-Porat, who had suggested to examine the causes for the failure: "I don't want to hear about it. For me it is over. I am starting from this point going forward. I have a defeated branch that I have to take care of, and everyday intelligence issues that must be taken care of as well." (130)

Moreover, the military decided to promote each officer who had served during the war by one rank, even those who hadn't fulfilled the minimal time for promotion. Ben-Porat calls it "a Byzantine act" – "A military that had just ended a war, not in the most successful way, promotes its officers en masse, as they did in the Ottoman Empire when the Sultan changed." (118)

In other words, the top level had decided to "buy" silence.

And Ben-Porat says about this: "The Military Intelligence did not shake itself enough, there was no reorganization and no organizational changes that should have been required from someone who had failed so greatly on Yom Kippur… they didn't examine, and they don't know how exactly they were surprised, and what were the causes for that. If they don't know, they don't understand, and if they don't understand why they were surprised in 1973, they don't have enough data to prevent a surprise in the future." (18)

Ben-Porat wrote these words in 1985. Till today, the Military Intelligence produces assessments that are categorically wrong. The opposite from what reality shows us. And in fact, they don't mind to bring one wrong assessment after another, even announcing it to the public on TV.

In summary: in terms of collecting information Israel is doing a great job. In terms of assessing the information being collected, the "national assessor" (the Military Intelligence) is consistent in being wrong all the time.

Was Ben-Porat commended?

Ben-Porat headed a unit that did a great job. It collected the warning of the imminent attack, and delivered the information on time, with enough margin to enlist the reserves, and change the course of the war. Did Ben-Porat get commended?

Ben-Porat reports a conversation he had with the officer who was slated to be the next Chief of Staff, replacing David ("Dado") Elazar, who had been Chief of Staff during the Yom Kippur War. After telling him about the events that led to the war, the officer asked Ben-Porat: "But did you 'knock over tables' [an Israeli expression to indicate making a fuss and shouting loudly] at 'Dado'?"

And Ben-Porat answered, "No, I don't work with the system of knocking over tables; I work according to the regulations and with the channels of command. As a loyal and obedient officer."

The officer responded: "That's the reason that you are guilty like everyone else." (106)

Ben-Porat also says that "Dado" himself asked several years later: why didn't you come to me? And Ben-Porat answered that there were two levels of command between them. How could he approach him about this, even though they were neighbors?

Here, we are facing a major characteristic of Israeli society that explains why Ben-Porat was considered "guilty" in the eyes of the upcoming Chief of Staff.

As we can see in the various chapters in this book, Israel does not generally adhere to the "channels of command". Bilby, the American reporter during the War of Independence in 1948, remarked that "the lowliest non-coms" could "jump into command". Ben-Porat himself says in his book that just before the war he convened his top officers in the unit and he told them:

"I will not tolerate arguments, and I expect full obedience. I will continue to consult, but when I decide – the decision will be final. Everyone is 'wise and intelligent', but during a war there is no time for arguments. I will not be tolerant and forgiving in any case when an order was not followed completely – not only in its language, but also in its spirit." (73)

And Ben-Porat explains himself – "I said it based upon my lessons from previous wars when my commanders forgave symposiums that resembled a debate club, and in the end lukewarm orders came out, that were nice to everyone." (73-74)

Ben-Porat needed to tell his subordinates that the usual Israeli "party" is over. In fact, that's how the Israeli military runs its operations – via discussions. After all, everyone is "half a general". And when the time comes, and one feels that his commander is not doing his job, the soldier might take the initiative, and via back channels, would bypass his commander, and "knock over tables". Ben-Porat was expected to bypass his immediate superior within the Military Intelligence and go straight to the Chief of Staff.

However, Ben-Porat was not born in Israel. He was born in Poland, and although he lived many years in Israel, he described himself as "a Polish officer". He was very successful. His unit performed spectacularly. But he operated in Israel, not in Poland.

Ben-Porat himself says that "one of his serious mistakes on the eve of Yom Kippur" was that "...I trusted the assessors in MI. Not all of them, but I thought that I can trust the three who were the leaders there. And besides, I thought innocently that they had other sources of information, that I didn't see, and that were more reassuring. And mainly, **I am not in charge of the assessment**..." (57)

"It was not customary in the IDF to push your nose in, to overstep the boundaries of authority and responsibility, but to trust the system that is in charge of it, headed by colonels and generals, that mistakenly I thought – like others – that they are capable and trustworthy, **but wisdom after the fact is not wisdom, but stupidity. And this applies to my words above.**" (139)

The aftermath

Ben-Porat had wanted to advance further in Military Intelligence, but he was pushed out. He served for a while as the IDF spokesman and as

Israel's assistant military attache in Washington, and he was eventually promoted to Brigadier General. But very soon he was pushed out of the military, and forced to retire in 1985.

Who is Trump?

Comey, Clapper and Hayden on Trump

Before we come to address chiefs of intelligence who talk about Trump, we need to realize that in any government bureaucracy there is only one person who heads the government. In the US it is the president, and in other countries, based upon parliamentary democracy, it is the prime minister. For anyone else in the government, even though the person might be heading a large organization, there is still someone above him.

One only needs to go to any US military unit and to enter headquarters, to see the pictures of the people who create the hierarchy of that unit. On top is the president, then the secretary of defense, and under him the secretary of the army, and under him the chief of staff, and so on.

The bottom line: there is only one person in the government who has nobody above him – and that is the president.

Comey about Trump

Comey evaluated Trump as "…such a **deeply flawed person** and leader…" (CO 206). He is a "…politician and hardball deal-maker…" (CO 216). Trump "…was known to be **impulsive**…" (CO 217). Since the time of the campaign, Comey's impression of Trump was that, "…he was a **deeply insecure man**…" (CO 220).

Comey, who served as Director of the FBI – a high-ranking bureaucrat, but still a bureaucrat – describes President Trump as a "fish out of water," and goes on to explain to the reader why a person who heads a "private family-held company" cannot serve as president: "Running a private family-held company is, of course, quite different from running a nation – or even running a large public corporation. You have to deal with various constituencies who don't report to you and to live under a web of laws and regulations that don't apply to a typical CEO." (CO 219).

Clapper about Trump

Clapper, another bureaucrat who did not run a business of his own, or, in other words, was never #1 in any position he filled, talks about Trump the businessman:

"...but his experience was in managing massive sums of money, not large numbers of people, and his businesses had filed for bankruptcy six times." (JC 326)

Out of these three assertions, two of them are true: Trump did manage "massive sums of money", and Trump did file for bankruptcy six times.

Let's start from the last assertion – filing for bankruptcy. The only reason that Trump filed for bankruptcy is the simple reason that any developer of real estate will list each development as an independent legal entity, and if that same business will not be profitable, there will be no reason to keep it going. This does not mean that other entities of the same developer are not profitable.

The "luxury" of declaring bankruptcy, if a certain program is not profitable, does not apply to the government. If any government program has not performed the objective it was designed for (and there are many like that), then even if it has been in existence for many years, it will not be closed down, since it is a government enterprise, and it will continue to drain the taxpayers' money for eternity.

One of the many large government programs that fits this description is the "intelligence community". This government program has a budget of 76 billion (with a "B") per year, and does not produce the results that it is supposed to deliver – keeping the country (by their definition) "safe and free". If this "intelligence community" were a private enterprise, it would have been declared bankrupt a long time ago. If not after the Vietnam war, then after the attack of 9/11, and if not then, then after the Iraq war. But the intelligence community, being part of the government, will continue as it is, regardless of whether it is successful or not.

The audacity of these chiefs of unsuccessful organizations is that they feel the authority to rate a businessman who showed success in his overall business.

Clapper is wrong in his second assertion – "...not large numbers of people..." The fact is that one casino alone employs around 6,000 people. This is about the same number of people who are stationed on one aircraft carrier. I wonder if Clapper, being a general in the military, would consider the commander of such an aircraft carrier to be someone who does not manage "...large numbers of people..."

An aircraft carrier (or a casino) is very much like a small city, with its own police, its own emergency services, etc. The high rank of the commander of an aircraft carrier reflects the importance that the US navy accords to this commander. Trump the businessman has many real estate developments.

The bottom line is that Clapper (or Comey), the bureaucrats, insulated from any repercussions of lack of success by being in the government, only show their readers their lack of understanding of what it means to run a business.

Clapper, who called Hillary Clinton "my former colleague" (JC 359), says that if she were to be elected "...that she might ask me to stick around until she could get a new DNI confirmed." (JC 359) However, he continues, "I didn't expect President-elect Trump to ask, and I don't think I'd have agreed to remain if he had." (JC 359)

This "unbiased" bureaucrat says about Trump: "He has set a new low bar for ethics and morality." (JCC 399) One might understand why a government employee would emphasize "ethics". However, one should ask: since when does any government organization, or any government employee, deal with "morality"?

Clapper continues: "And, close to my heart, he has besmirched the Intelligence Community and the FBI – pillars of our country – and deliberately incited many Americans to lose faith and confidence in them." (JC 399)

"Pillars of our country"? Isn't this taking it a little bit too far? After all, these two – the intelligence community and the FBI – are only organizations within the executive branch.

Like Clapper, Hayden is furious that Trump said that he wouldn't listen to the intelligence community "...because they've made such bad decisions." (MH2 - 68)

Hayden says, "Rejecting a fact-based intelligence assessment – not because of compelling contrarian data, but because it was inconsistent with a preexisting worldview or because it was politically inconvenient – is the stuff of ideological authoritarianism, not pragmatic democracy." (MH2 - 72)

"A fact-based intelligence assessment" is practically an oxymoron. Either it is a "fact" or it is an "assessment". However, "a fact-based intelligence assessment" is a contradiction within itself. Were the 950 sites in Iraq, determined by the intelligence as suspected WMD sites, a "fact-based assessment"?

And rejecting intelligence is the prerogative of the leadership. After all, the intelligence is only one tool that the leader has before reaching a decision. I was trained on the basis that the leader (or the commander) is naturally an "intelligence officer" on his/her own merit. Rejecting intelligence is not diminishing democracy. It is what democracy is all about. That's why once in 4 years the electorate chooses a leader – to lead, i.e. to accept or reject what the bureaucracy is producing.

If Hayden is right, he positions the intelligence community above the elected leader.

Let's go back to Clapper. Till this point, Clapper is reporting to us what he knew about Trump from afar. But Clapper reveals to us that he also met Trump personally. And his description of Trump, when he met him in person, is strikingly different.

"I was struck by how sober, professional, courteous, and civil the conversation was. It was so different – both substantively and tonally – from what the campaigns were saying in public, particularly Mr. Trump." (JC 348)

Should Clapper be "struck" by this difference between Trump the person, and Trump on the stage?

Senator McCain, in his book, describes Hillary Clinton as "contrary to the negative public image promoted by her detractors, very warm, engaging, and considerate in person, and fun." (JM 117)

Maybe this alleged contradiction between the public persona and the private one is applicable to all public figures, including Presidents Bush and Obama. Or, in other words, to everyone who holds public office, including Clapper himself.

Hayden on Trump

Hayden starts by agreeing with Trump's claim that he "heads a powerful grassroots movement" (MH2 - 10). He says that in regard to Trump, "I have tried to be fair, although much of what I write will be judged as unfairly negative." (MH2 - 9)

In many words, Hayden prepares his readers before attacking Trump, that what he says is actually "**unfairly** negative".

Trump and the IC according to Hayden

Hayden starts by saying that "...something even more troubling: the candidate often didn't know what he was talking about, and he may not have known that he didn't know." (MH2 - 45)

As examples of Trump's lack of knowledge, Hayden brings the following examples: "He was stumped by the meaning of the word 'triad'... he admitted to not knowing the names Nasrallah, Zawahiri, or Baghdadi, the leaders of Hezbollah, al-Qaeda, and ISIS, nor knowing the distinctions between their murderous organizations.... Unfamiliar with the Quds Force under Iran's ruthless general Qassem Suleimani, he confused it with America's friends in the region, the Kurds." (MH2 - 96)

It is true that Trump was wrong with these details. The only question is whether this knowledge is expected of him? Or, in other words, is it even meaningful?

In another place, Hayden labels Trump as "Today's populist is a **ruthless** Manhattan billionaire real estate developer..." (MH2 - 26) We should note that Hayden uses the same adjective ("ruthless") for the US President and for an arch-terrorist infamous all over the Middle East. The irony is that the one who advocated waterboarding of detainees, and rejected labeling it as "torture", calls Trump "ruthless".

Hayden continues, "One of the complaints that we cataloged was that Mr. Trump 'has shown no interest in educating himself.'" (MH2 - 65)

Hayden also says, "It really wasn't clear that Mr. Trump actually wanted much advice anyway." Hayden quotes Trump as saying on TV, "My primary consultant is myself and I have a good instinct for this stuff, I'm speaking with myself, number one, because I have a very good brain." (MH2 - 62)

Perhaps Trump needs to "educate himself" in his new job. But who will do this "educating"? Should it be one with a track record of a long list of failures under his belt??

Hayden and Trump's lies

Hayden says he "had a long list of out-and-out lies" by Trump (MH2 – 44). In the list that Hayden produces, there are several that call for attention.

First, the claim "...that there were pan-Islamic legions celebrating wildly on the streets of New Jersey as the Twin Towers were aflame and collapsing." (MH2 -44)

Trump might have been wrong about the location where the celebrations took place. But Hayden should know, being a high-ranking intelligence officer, that all over the Middle East there were Arabs openly celebrating the success of this "military operation". Actually, in the Gaza Strip the Hamas movement distributed sweets on the street – a common way to celebrate in the Arab culture. It might not have been in New Jersey, but the fact is that there were celebrations, and to deny them is to deny reality.

Second, Hayden brings "...one particularly divisive campaign shtick..." in which "...Trump would dramatically read a poem about a kindhearted woman who responds to the plea of a nearly frozen snake and nurses it back to health. Revived, the snake bites and kills her." (MH2 - 47)

When I read Hayden's description, what immediately came into my mind was the Chechnyan family who received refugee status in the US, and then two sons of this family bombed the Boston marathon. It definitely fits Trump's description as the epitome of lack of gratitude.

Hayden ends this description by saying "It was an anti-immigrant crowd pleaser..." (MH2 - 47), but the fact is that Trump was talking about reality, while Hayden conceals from his readers the fact that the Boston Marathon fits the bill.   Hayden should know of these details.

Third, Hayden criticizes Trump for advocating "...the intentional killing of terrorists' families because 'they knew what was happening .... They left two days early, with respect to the World Trade Center, and they went back to where they went, and they watched their husband on television flying into the World Trade Center, flying into the Pentagon.'" (MH2 – 44)

Although what Trump advocated was contrary to western norms and laws, it definitely fits the norms of the Middle East. Any Arab who kills another makes his own family a legitimate target for retribution. It is a fact of life in Arab villages in Israel. When someone is killed, suddenly several people from the suspected killer's family are found dead.

By Arab culture, since 15 of the 19 terrorists who carried out the 9/11 attack were Saudis, Saudi Arabia was immediately responsible for the attack. Not by western norms, but by Saudi norms. One might go against this "barbaric" norm, but it is a fact of life in the Arab Middle East.

Hayden denies Trump's claim by saying that "None of that really happened, of course. Few of the 9/11 hijackers were married. None had family in the United States. We know of no family members, even overseas, who were flown anywhere before or after 9/11." (MH2 - 44)

Is this true? Doesn't Hayden know that many members of Bin Laden's family were in the US at the time of the 9/11 attack, and during the time that US air space was closed to flying, there was only one plane that was allowed to take off from the US – the plane that carried Bin Laden's family out of the US. There is no way that Hayden doesn't know about it. Even if the US intelligence community didn't know about it, due to faulty methods of gathering information, still the news media reported this event. So to say that "We know of no family members, even overseas, who were flown anywhere before or after 9/11" (MH2 - 44) is a misleading statement, if not an "out-and-out lie".

Fourth, Hayden says that "I don't think that Mr. Trump needed any help getting to his 'Islam hates us,' clash-of-civilizations paradigm. Certainly his base seems to welcome it." (MH2 - 49)

The "Islam hates us" "clash-of-civilizations" is not Mr. Trump's "paradigm". It is a fact that there are many quarters in the Islamic world that openly talk against the US as being a "decadent society" that violates what Islam stands for. One might claim that only the fanatics advocate this ideology. To distinguish between the fanatics and the "regular" Moslems, the academics use either the term "radical Islam" or even "Islamists". But the reality is that the so-called "moderates" do not talk against this fanatic ideology. If they do, they are putting themselves in danger of being killed. Hayden should be well aware of this fact.

In summary, Hayden makes a list of Trump's "lies", but actually what Hayden lists is some mistakes that can be easily explained. By listing these mistakes, Hayden is misleading his readers. In some quarters, in which Hayden himself is residing, what Hayden does would be labeled as "a list of out-and-out lies".

Clapper, Trump and Russia

There are many accusations that Clapper brings in regard to the Trump campaign and the alleged Russian interference/meddling (McCain's language). Let's deal with one example.

Clapper describes an event in which, after Trump denied on TV that he had any connection to either Russia or Putin, Trump "...turned from the questioner to face the cameras, and his next words absolutely chilled me: 'Russia, if you're listening, I hope you're able to find the 30,000 emails that are missing. I think you will probably be rewarded mightily by our press.' He turned back to the questioner and said, 'Let's see if that happens. That'll be next.'" (JC 343)

Clapper comments on this event that "...hearing Donald Trump ask Russian intelligence to attack his political opponent – in a very specific, direct way – made me fear for our nation." (JC 343)

Really? I happened to watch this same appearance, and it was clear to me that Trump was making fun of both Clinton and the FBI, who couldn't find these erased emails. It was meant as a joke and not as anything serious.

Hayden says in his book that "One undisclosed CIA location in the United States has T-shirts emblazoned with the words *Deny Everything. Admit Nothing. Make Counter-Accusations.* But it is meant to be a joke." (MH2 – 45 – italics in original) Why does Clapper not use the same ruler to measure what Trump said, and what Hayden describes in his book?

Should we not "fear for our nation" when CIA employees print T-shirts saying "Deny Everything. Admit Nothing. Make Counter-Accusations", and dismiss it as a "joke"? It is a "dark joke", and at times it seems very realistic, in view of CIA behavior in the past. Why does he judge Trump so harshly, and not allow him to make a joke in public? Why is there a double standard for Trump and CIA employees?

Trump's Appearance at the CIA

Hayden discusses President Trump's appearance at the CIA when he "...went to Langley the day after the inauguration." (MH2 - 112)

Knowing of the animosity and hostility existing between the intelligence community and the elected president, it could be considered quite courageous on the part of the President to show up at the "den of lions".

Hayden labels this visit as "...the worst presidential visit to an intelligence agency in the history of the American Republic." (MH2 - 113)

Hayden's description of the reception President Trump received is quite an eye opener about what is going on inside the agency. On one hand, Hayden says, "To be fair, there was some whooping and hollering in the CIA concourse as the president spoke. CIA reflects America, and no doubt there were Trump voters in the Agency." (MH2 - 113-114)

In essence, Hayden says that there were people in the audience who supported Trump. After all, the appearance was on Saturday, a weekend day, and the people who showed up there were "...a self-selected crowd. An Agency-all email had gone out the day before asking people to come in on a Saturday to be part of the event." Meaning, only people who were willing to sacrifice their weekend were in the crowd. Therefore, quite likely the crowd consisted of people who were Republicans or leaning-towards-Republican, or even simply "Trump voters".

But Hayden adds one more sentence: "CIA seniors sat stone-faced in the front row." (MH2 - 114)

And now the "secret" is out. There is a gap between "CIA seniors" and the rest. While the "CIA seniors" sat "stone-faced" – masking their inner feelings about their commander (their "consumer" in their language), the rest were open to express either their approval, or even disapproval. There were people who disapproved of the speech. Hayden says, "At the Farm, the agency's clandestine training site that had the ceremony piped in via direct video link, many officers simply walked out." (MH2 - 114)   They "simply walked out" but they didn't sit "stone-faced".

Please note also the following:

First, "whooping and hollering" is not "cheering".   While "cheering" is associated with a positive response, the description "whooping and hollering" exposes Hayden's view of their "cheering".   In his eyes, what they did was not "cheering".

Second, "stone-faced" is not "poker-faced".   While "poker-faced" means that the person masks his inner feelings, "stone-faced" means that the person is doing his best to transmit his displeasure.

Third, saying that the high-ranking level were cohesive in being "stone-faced" implies that they had discussed their behavior prior to the President's appearance.   Otherwise, how would anyone in that row be aware of how others were behaving?

Hayden concludes this incident by saying, "It's hard to imagine a deeper hole from which to begin an administration." (MH2 - 114) If we just change one word in this "assessment" – "gap" instead of "hole" – we can see the situation clearly inside the CIA.   The high-ranking ones feel the need to show their resistance ("stone-faced"), while the "masses" would not mind to either cheer (aka "whooping and hollering") or to "simply walk out".

Hayden on Trump's tweeting

Hayden comments about Trump's habit of tweeting to his followers about what he (Trump) thinks of current events.   Hayden quotes "...a highly regarded career analyst..." who said that she "never had such a rich source of raw intelligence about a world leader, and we certainly never had the opportunity that our adversaries (and our allies) have now – to get a real-time glimpse of a major world leader's preoccupations, personality quirks and habits of mind."

And Hayden continues by saying, "The president's twitter tsunami must have been a gold mine for foreign services. Pressable buttons, loyalties, exposed nerves, responses to pressure, sleep habits, even his unfiltered id were pretty much on full display." (MH2 – 126)

Hayden expresses here one fundamental truth that he simply doesn't get. Intelligence is not everything. Trump's tweeting is actually his best move to reach the population, bypassing the media that opposes him.

There are instances in which the media didn't quote Trump accurately. One example is the so-called "Moslem ban". What Trump actually said was that he would **temporarily** ban immigrants from seven Moslem-majority countries **until the vetting system will be improved to weed out terrorists entering the country**. The news media did not report this condition at all. They presented it as a "ban on Moslems" without the details or the reason for the ban.

The oath a person takes in court is to tell the truth, the whole truth, and nothing but the truth. The reason is that if it is not "the whole truth" it is misleading. After all, "Total Belief in the Subject" means that most people do not lie. They just don't say everything. And what they don't say can turn the story upside-down by 180 degrees. By not reporting Trump's demand to improve the vetting (which actually was a very serious criticism of the current bureaucracy – including the intelligence community), the news media twisted Trump's move.

Tweeting might be the best move Trump could have made in his campaign for the presidency, and even during the presidency. The fact that tweeting exposes Trump to the population, and to foreign intelligence services, does not bother Trump. He wants the population to know what he thinks, what he says, and what he does. Although Comey labels Trump as "insecure", Trump is actually secure enough that he doesn't care what other foreign leaders think of him. He cares about what the American people think of him. After all, they are the ones to determine if he will remain in office.

Hayden, with his very narrow view using strictly intelligence lenses, does not see the reality as it is.

As for tweeting – at the time Trump was elected he had 46 million followers. And if these 46 million only talk with 2-3 people around them, it means that Trump reaches one third of the population. Recently, it was reported that in the two years after he was elected, several more million people joined his list of followers. In a way, it is an ongoing "poll" or "election" of Trump's strength among the population.

Is the Above an Accurate Description of Trump?

Introduction

Many years ago, when I was teaching in the US while still living in Israel, I met a guy named Asher, in the Jewish community near Washington DC. Asher, who is a nuclear physicist, shared a very important observation of his on the US news media. In talking about one of the weekly magazines, Asher said: when the news media start to talk about what a politician thinks, one needs to know that this is not "news". It is fiction. If one wants to know about who a person is, one needs to listen to what the person **says**. There can be no dispute about what a person **said**. However, there can be a long discussion of what the person **meant**.

In other words, Asher related to the most fundamental rule of SCAN: "The Subject is Dead. The Statement is Alive".

In coming to find out who is Donald Trump, we can only follow what he **said**, and what other people close to him **said**.

In this description of who is Donald Trump, we will look at three books:

First, written by Donald Trump himself – "The Art of the Deal", Ballantine Books, NY 1987. The quotes will be labeled as "AOD".

Second, "Let Trump Be Trump" by Corey Lewandowski and David N. Bossie. These two worked with Trump on his campaign for the presidency. Corey Lewandowski was even the campaign manager at the beginning. The quotes will be labeled as "LTBT".

Third, "Trumponomics" by Stephen Moore and Arthur Laffer. These two economists worked with Trump on his economic plan during the campaign. The quotes will be labeled as "TR".

Family

Trump describes his family as being "a very traditional family" (AOD – 69). In describing his father he says he was "very tough and very relentless" (AOD – 74), and "an unbelievably demanding taskmaster" (AOD – 75). Trump says that his father "never sheltered me" (AOD – 78).

In comparing his parents to each other he says, "They were total opposites… My mother loves splendor and magnificence, while my father, who is very down-to-earth, gets excited only by competence and efficiency." (AOD – 80) (As we go along in this journey into "who is Trump?" we will see how accurately Trump is actually describing himself.)

And he adds, "Looking back, I realize now that I got some of my sense of showmanship from my mother. She always had a flair for the dramatic and the grand." (AOD 79)

Trump says of his childhood family: "We lived in a large house, but we never thought of ourselves as rich kids. We were brought up to know the value of a dollar and to appreciate the importance of hard work. Our family was always very close, and to this day **they are my closest friends**." (AOD 69)

When talking about his siblings, Trump says, "Robert, who is two years younger than I am, is **soft-spoken and easygoing**, <u>but</u> he's very talented and effective. I think it must be hard to have me for a brother…" (AOD 17)

The "but" tells us that Trump does not consider himself as "soft-spoken and easygoing". And in fact, he concludes it by saying, "I think it must be hard to have me for a brother…"

And Trump moves on to explain: "Robert gets along with almost everyone, which is great for me, **since I sometimes have to be the bad guy**." (AOD 17)

When talking about his other brother, Harvey, Trump says, "Harvey is a different type: no-nonsense, not too big on laughs, but he's got an absolutely brilliant analytic mind." (AOD 17)

If Robert is "very **talented** and effective" then Harvey is the "no-nonsense" one, and has "…an absolutely **brilliant analytic mind**" – Trump's set of priorities in a person.

Trump's kids

Being a businessman means in many cases sacrificing family life for success in the business. Not for Trump. When his kids were small, he said, "I always take calls from my kids, **no matter** what **I'm doing**." (AOD 11)

And in fact, Trump's children played quite a role in his campaign for the presidency – "During the campaign, the Trump children did scores and scores of interviews, and on Election Day they did one right after the other." (LTBT 3) His economists say, "We came to view all of Trump's family members as amazing assets with great political instincts (**like their father**)." (TR 51)

In a off-hand remark about his daughter Ivanka, we can see that she plays quite a role in her father's success. "When Ivanka Trump, a key friend and ally, saw the article in the newspaper that morning, **she cut it out and put it at the top of a stack of must-read items for the president** as he sat down behind his desk in the Oval Office." (TR 154) Ivanka makes sure that her father will read what in her eyes is important for him to read.

When talking about Keith Schiller, Trump's bodyguard, who served Trump for many years, his campaign managers say, "The Trump kids think of him as an uncle – an uncle who would take a bullet for their father." (LTBT 28) In essence, long-time employees are like "family".

As a personal observation: what impressed me during the campaign was that Trump's children from his first two marriages supported him fully. This is contrary to what one sees in many divorced families, where the children perceive themselves as "divorced children". Not for Trump's children. Trump divorced their mothers (in the plural) but he definitely did not divorce his children.

Trump's wife

But not only the children support their father. His two campaign managers say about his present wife: "People don't realize that Melania Trump is the rock in the family, and one of the classiest people you'll ever meet. Melania gave us good advice and counsel as the campaign unfolded. She became a huge asset during the campaign and we could not have been successful without her." (LTBT 201)

Trump's childhood

"I was always something of a leader in my neighborhood. Much the way it is today, **people either liked me a lot, or they didn't like me at all**. In my own crowd I was very well liked, **and I tended to be the kid that others followed**." (AOD – 72)

Trump's Education

Unknown to many people, Trump studied in high school in a military academy. There he "…learned a lot about discipline, and about channeling my aggression into achievement. In my senior year I was appointed **a captain of the cadets**." (AOD 73)

He also learned how to deal with strong people. In talking about his coach in school, he says, "Like so many strong guys, Dobias had a tendency to go for the jugular if he smelled weakness. On the other hand, if he sensed strength but you didn't try to undermine him, he treated you like a man." (AOD 73). His campaign managers "testify" that "…Trump was a pretty good ballplayer himself back in high school." (LTBT 22)

Trump also went to college – Wharton School of Finance at the University of Pennsylvania – and graduated. His observation of college: "Perhaps the most important thing I learned at Wharton was not to be overly impressed by academic credentials." (AOD 77) "The other important thing I got from Wharton was a Wharton degree. In my opinion, that degree doesn't prove very much, but a lot of people I do business with take it very seriously, and it's considered very prestigious. So all things considered, I'm glad I went to Wharton." (AOD 77)

His Father's "competence and efficiency"

The influence of Trump's father is expressed in something Trump once said to Steve Forbes: "I have a lot of friends, they take vacations for six weeks and eight weeks and three months and they're never happy. So, I watched my father. So, I like to work" (LTBT 44)

The two economists who worked with Trump call him "…an efficiency expert. He didn't waste a minute." (TR 125-126) Trump in his book "The Art of the Deal" talks about it as well: "I rarely go out, because mostly, **it's a waste of time**." (AOD 7)   He measures others according to this trait: "That's one thing I love about Alan: **he never wastes time**." (AOD 12) "Like Alan Greenberg, Schrager **isn't big on wasting time**." (AOD 18). This emphasis on not wasting time is extended to all his activities: "When I have a meeting, I don't waste time. It's quick, short, and to the point." (A quote from "The Apprentice" in 2005 - LTBT 43) And "Frankly, I'm not too big on parties, because I can't stand small talk." (AOD 15)

His campaign manager Corey Lewandowski "…saw Mr. Trump close his eyes maybe five times. And by 'close his eyes,' he means for three minutes, tops. Donald Trump is an absolute machine. He is the single hardest-working person we have ever seen." (LTBT 92) And – "In all the time we spent together on the campaign trail, we saw no indication of him slowing down… he had the stamina of an ultramarathoner." (LTBT 185). Lawrence Kudlow in his forward to the book "Trumponomics" says that he is "…indefatigable. Donald Trump doesn't stop. He barely sleeps. It's almost impossible to keep up with him." (LK-TR viii) His campaign managers say, "You can't help but feed off the man's energy and his drive to succeed." (LTBT 219)

When Trump is awake, "Donald Trump practically lived on his phone." (LTBT58)

Focus

Being so busy does not mean that Trump cannot focus on the issue in front of him. In talking about himself: "…I plan for the future by **focusing** exclusively on the present." (AOD 2). He goes on to say, "One of the keys to thinking big is **total focus**. I think of it almost as a **controlled neurosis**…" (AOD 47)

The following event illustrates Trump's ability to focus. He quotes David Letterman, who told him: "Tell me the truth. It's Friday afternoon, you get a call from us out of the blue, you tell us we can come up. Now you're standing here talking to us. You must not have much to do." (AOD 43) And Trump's response: "Truthfully, David, you're right. Absolutely nothing to do."

Flexible

Being able to focus does not mean rigidity. In talking about himself, Trump says: "I leave my door open. You can't be imaginative or entrepreneurial if you've got too much structure." (AOD 1) "There is no typical week in my life." (AOD 1) "Sometimes it pays to be a little wild." (AOD 5) "I don't want to rule out anything." (AOD 25) "I also protect myself by being flexible." (AOD 50) and – "I like to keep as many options open as I can." (AOD 16)

His "flexibility" extends to his politics. His economists say of him: "Trump does not require ideological loyalty. There could be disagreement on issues. That was fine with him. There was no "purity test," no dogma." (TR 28)

Listening

Although he is sometimes described as "…a suave New York real estate developer **who loved to hear himself talk**…" (TR 188), Trump does listen to people. "I'm someone who responds to people I have respect for, **and I listen**." (AOD 90) His economists confirm Trump's assertion: "Trump didn't lecture us. He asked for our opinions, straight up. **He listened**." (TR 11) and – "It turns out that Trump **can be a very good listener when he wants to be**." (TR 189)

His Mother's "flair for the dramatic and the grand"

Trump attributed to his mother – "Looking back, I realize now that I got some of my sense of showmanship from my mother. She always had a flair for the dramatic and the grand." (AOD 79)

In fact, the most common adjective that can be attributed to Trump is "Big". He talks about himself as – "I like making deals, preferably big deals." (AOD 1) "I like thinking big. I always have." (AOD 46) His economists say that Trump "…thinks very big…" (TR 8) and – "As it happens, Donald Trump does big very, very well." (TR 158)

Trump summarizes this point by saying – "Most people think small, because most people are afraid of success, afraid of making decisions, afraid of winning. And that gives people like me a great advantage." (AOD 47)

Optimism

Trump labels himself as "an optimist." (AOD 102). He says that people like "my directness and my enthusiasm." (AOD 103) Lawrence Kudlow talks of their love for "his Reaganesque optimism. It was infectious." (LK-TR viii) His economists say, "…we are optimists – just as Trump is." (TR 264)

Trump's Parents "were total opposites"

As his parents were "total opposites" – Trump can sometimes display opposite characteristics.

His campaign managers: "The boss is one of those people who can be hot as an August afternoon at one moment, then turn a switch and be as calm as a spring evening the next." (LTBT 143-144) His economists support this view of him by saying, "He can be brilliant, gracious, and insightful one moment and sophomoric, impulsive, and hurtful the next." (TR 3)

Trump's campaign managers describe him, "…As tough as the boss could be – and he could be tough…" They even talk of "…his 'tough as nails' look, a New York real estate killer look." (LTBT 23) and his "…iron girder stare." (LTBT 23).   They are even very specific: "His wrath is never intended as any personal offense, but sometimes it can be hard not to take it that way. The mode that he switches into when things aren't going his way can feel like an all-out assault; it'd break most hardened men and women into little pieces. Around the campaign, we'd call it getting your face ripped off." (LTBT 163)

At the same time they say that Trump is "…incredibly generous…" (LTBT 22; 43) They go on to say that "People who don't know Donald Trump often see him as a cold, calculating mogul bereft of feelings for people. Yes, the boss can certainly be merciless when business is on the line… But he sees the humanity in people, and he has a soft spot for those who battle demons." (LTBT 70-71) They also talk of "…the side of Mr. Trump few would get to see. The funny, magnanimous, gracious, loyal person…" (LTBT 118)

Opposition

If there is any characteristic which is so apparent in Trump, it is the way he responds to anyone who opposes him.

He says of himself, "I don't hold it against people that they have opposed me." (AOD 6) "I don't mind controversy." (AOD 56) He adds, "…if you're right, you've got to take a stand, or people will walk all over you." (AOD 7) "I'd rather fight than fold, because as soon as you fold once, you get the reputation of being a folder." (AOD 98)

In relating to people who criticize him: "The way I see it, critics get to say what they want to about my work, so why shouldn't I be able to say what I want to about theirs?" (AOD 22)

His campaign managers say of this side of him: "The boss was never one to shy away from a street fight. And Donald Trump is the best counter puncher to ever enter the debate stage." (LTBT 192) "But one thing even Donald Trump's enemies had to admit was that he never backed away from a fight. At times, he seemed to relish them." (LTBT 228) "Donald Trump does not like to lose." (LTBT 218) and – "…he never shows weakness." (LTBT 207)

In talking about "management", Trump says: "In any case, I enjoy seeing the lengths to which bad managements go to preserve what they call their independence – which really just means their jobs." (AOD 3)

And he explains it further: "There are people – I categorize them as life's losers – who get their sense of accomplishment and achievement from trying to stop others. As far as I'm concerned, if they had any real ability they wouldn't be fighting me, they'd be doing something constructive themselves." (AOD 59)

Was Trump talking in this last quote of the US intelligence community? But the book "The Art of the Deal" was published in 1987.

The Boss

If there is any characteristic that produced the clash between Trump and the intelligence community, it is Trump being "The Boss"

His campaign managers say of him: "The boss, as we would come to call him, was someone who liked to call the shots…" (LTBT 37) "The lesson here is that there is only one boss, and when he is ready to go, you go. Period." (LTBT 91) Trump did have a campaign manager, but he was to decide on details that were important to him – "As it would be for the rest of the campaign, Mr. Trump picked the music for the event." (LTBT 78) But "…the boss did what the boss does best: he built excitement." (LTBT 76)

Loyalty

As a "boss" there is one characteristic that Trump singles out in his employees – "loyalty". "When asked what he valued in an employee, Mr. Trump gave the interviewer a one-word answer: loyalty." (LTBT 43)

"He brings out the best in his employees: loyalty, willingness to work, belief in his leadership. We weren't alone in thinking of him this way." (LTBT 219) "In his mind, people are placed into two distinct categories: loyal and disloyal. Once you're in the second category, it's hard to climb your way out." (LTBT 250) "For Donald Trump, loyalty is the currency of the realm, and nothing hurts him deeper than when someone he trusts is disloyal." (LTBT 258)

"Loyalty" is a two-way street for Trump: "…I'm loyal to people who've done good work for me." (AOD 20). His campaign managers confirm it, saying that he always stood by them: "Trump always stood by us when we were under fire from the outside." (LTBT – 44) "And he is not someone who goes back on his word." (LTBT 258). His employees "…knew him to be incredibly loyal and generous…" (LTBT 37-38)

"As tough as the boss could be – and he could be tough – a bond developed between those of us on those flights that was akin to family…" (LTBT 118)

This characteristic – "loyalty" – should remind us of how Comey criticized Trump for even requesting "loyalty", as if Trump had asked him to commit a crime. By Comey labeling his book "Higher Loyalty", he actually expressed his lack of understanding of what Trump had actually asked of him.

Trump's Mind

Comey in his book comments on the way President Trump talks:
"…speaking, in his usual stream-of-consciousness and free association cadence…" (CO 231) "…he spoke in torrents, gushing words…" (CO 238) "…rapid-fire, stream-of consciousness monologues." (CO 248)

Hayden in his book brings the feedback on Trump's speech to the CIA:
"The commentariat was pretty critical after the speech: 'incoherent', 'disconnected', 'confused', and 'muddled' were some of the words used in the reviews." (MH2 – 117)

Both Comey and Hayden are not wrong in their description. I happened to see the speech as it was televised on TV. It is very easy to say that Trump was "rambling", and jumping from one point to another. Did it bother me? Not at all. I preferred to listen to Trump the person, and not to any speech that someone else had written, and that is simply read by the president using a teleprompter.

His campaign managers, although agreeing with the description, see the positive in it –
"Donald Trump's mind works differently than most. His thoughts sometimes come out like pieces of a puzzle. It's only later when you put the pieces together that you realize how much they're worth. Sometimes the puzzle pieces form a masterpiece." (LTBT 47)

As for his memory – "Whatever the topic, Jared would be sure to load the speech up with facts, figures, and a few salient points that would play well as sound bites over many weeks. Mr. Trump would then give the speech, and – we kid you not – the material would stay in his head forever. Not a single detail or group of numbers would slip from his memory. Even when they'd made edits to the text, he could always recall both versions of it in seconds." (LTBT 187)

"In each, he would ascertain what was important for him to know by the questions he was being asked." (LTBT 77)

Trump's most "threatening" characteristic for the intelligence community is the following: "Trump is for common sense… With Trump, it is all about results." (TR – 4)

Trump's Quirks

In talking about himself: "I'm a stickler for cleanliness." (AOD 32). His campaign managers say that he always wanted to be in hotels "…that were less than six months old. He didn't care if it was a Motel 6 or a Four Seasons, just as long as it was brand-new. He didn't like the dust." (LTBT 235)

"…he gets freaked out when people sneeze around him." (LTBT 122) "…if you sneezed around him, he would make you go to the back of the plane." (LTBT 235)

In talking about himself in 1988: "The word 'luck' is a very important word – very important. There's no more important word than 'luck.' But you can help create your own luck." (Quoted in LTBT 17) "Donald Trump is one of the most superstitious men that most people have ever met." (LTBT 17) "And he believes that some people, usually ones with low energy, carry bad luck and need to be avoided at all cost." (LTBT 17)

His campaign managers say: "We were never allowed to celebrate before a win was certain, and we always had to take our losses with grace. Anything else and you'd invite in some bad juju. It's the reason that come election night we didn't have a victory speech – or a concession speech – written ahead of time." (LTBT 17)

Trump in Business

"I happen to be very conservative in business." (AOD 48) and – "People think I'm a gambler. I've never gambled in my life." (AOD 48)

He explains it by saying: "I believe in the power of negative thinking… I always go into the deal anticipating the worst. If you plan for the worst – if you can live with the worst – the good will always take care of itself." (AOD 48)

His way of doing business produces one of the most important points that brought the clash between him and the intelligence community: "That's why I don't hire a lot of number-crunchers, and I don't trust fancy marketing surveys. I do my own surveys and draw my own conclusions." (AOD 51-52)

Another point that would bring a clash between Trump and the IC is his attitude towards bureaucracy:

"In most large public corporations, getting an answer to a question requires going through seven layers of executives, **most of whom are superfluous in the first place**. In our organization, anyone with a question could bring it directly to me and get an answer immediately." (AOD 209)

Trump conducts his own surveys by going down to the street: "When I'm in another city and I take a cab, I'll always make it a point to ask the cabdriver questions. I ask and I ask and I ask, until I begin to get a gut feeling about something. And that's when I make a decision." (AOD 51-52) In 1988 Trump said, "The fact is I go down the streets of New York and the people that really like me are the taxi drivers and the workers, etc. I mean I really get a better response." (quoted in LTBT 73). No wonder his campaign managers labeled him as "the blue-collar billionaire." (LTBT 74)

"Trump, ever the no-nonsense business exec" (TR 14) "…doesn't believe that throwing more money at a problem is the answer. In business, controlling costs has a lot to do with success or failure." (LTBT 55)

According to Lawrence Kudlow, Trump wants to move "…to a new private-sector incentive system that *rewards* **success**." (TR ix)

Trump wants to reward "success"? And how would he "reward" failure? How would he treat the intelligence community with their rate of success/failure?

Trump and Lying

The main complaint that both Clapper and Hayden lodge against Trump is they say that he is lying to the public.

Let's see how Trump himself looks upon this issue. In his book "The Art of the Deal" he says, "The final key to the way I promote is bravado. I play to people's fantasies. People may not always think big themselves, but they can still get very excited by those who do." (AOD – 58)

In order to achieve this goal, he says: "That's why **a little hyperbole** never hurts. People want to believe that something is the biggest and the greatest and the most spectacular. I call it **truthful hyperbole**. It's an **innocent form of exaggeration** – and a very effective form of promotion. (AOD – 58)

On the other hand, he says: "You can't con people, at least not for long. You can create excitement, you can do wonderful promotion and get all kinds of press, and you can throw in a **little hyperbole**. But if you don't deliver the goods, people will eventually catch on." (AOD 60)

And in fact, his economists say: "Yes, Trump was saying and tweeting crazy things sometimes. He would exaggerate. He would put his foot in his mouth. And yet, Trump kept winning and winning… " (TR 56)

One place in which Trump does not use "a little hyperbole" or even "an innocent form of exaggeration" is in his promises to the electorate before the elections. Right after inauguration he moved to implement his promises. After all, he needs to "deliver the goods".

Trump and the press

In talking about himself, Trump says, "I wake up most mornings very early, around six, and spend the first hour or so of each day reading the morning newspapers." (AOD 2)

His campaign managers confirm that on their flights during the campaign, "Mr. Trump sat in his seat reading the New York Times. Though he truly does think the paper's failing and promotes fake news, he reads it cover to cover regularly…" (LTBT 207)

In this description we learn that Trump functions as his own "intelligence officer". Although he considers this specific newspaper as "…failing and promotes fake news…" he still wants to know what the "opposition" to him is saying,

Trump is open about his displeasure of being in the press: "Contrary to what a lot of people think, I don't enjoy doing press. I've been asked the same questions a million times now, and I don't particularly like talking about my personal life." (AOD 33)

However, he continues: " Nonetheless, I understand that getting press can be very helpful in making deals, and I don't mind talking about them." (AOD 33)

So Trump is "getting press". He does it intentionally. In his book "The Art of the Deal" he says, "The point is that if you are a little different, or a little outrageous, or if you do things that are **bold or controversial**, the press is going to write about you." (AOD 56)

His campaign managers introduce us to the concept of "earned media" – "…which is a fancy way of saying free media."

They say that "Donald Trump is the undisputed, undefeated heavyweight champ of earned media. According to mediaQuant, an outfit that figures how much it cost each candidate if he or she had to pay for the coverage he or she was getting, Donald Trump's earned media was near $2 billion." (LTBT 116)

And in fact, it was my personal impression that the news media actually (unintentionally) cooperated with Trump and helped him to be elected. There were times that I asked myself whether there is anyone in the US who gets up in the morning and does not think and/or talk about Trump.

The bottom line is the old saying, attributed to P.T. Barnum: it doesn't matter what they write about you as long as they spell your name correctly.

Elections of 2016 and Russian Interference

Question: Was there any Russian interference during the campaign of 2016, and if so, was there any collusion between the Trump campaign and the Russian effort to influence the results of the elections?

Quote

"We briefly discussed Russia's interference in the election, the hacking of the Democratic National committee's and John Podesta's emails, which U.S. intelligence services concurred had been part of a Kremlin attempt to sabotage Hillary Clinton's chances and improve Trump's." (JM 236) - Senator McCain discusses in his book his conversation with Sir Andrew Wood, a former UK ambassador to Russia.

This one word – "concurred" – in Senator McCain's book "The Restless Wave" brought me to change my activity – from just analyzing Senator McCain's book, to going into other books published around the same time by former chiefs of intelligence, discussing the same issue – accusing President Trump of collusion with the Russians during the campaign to defeat Hillary Clinton.

"Concurred"? One can "concur" only with someone else's ideas. For example, a justice in the Supreme Court will "concur" with a decision of his colleague, instead of writing his own decision. If Senator McCain is right, and "the US intelligence services concurred", then who outside "U.S. intelligence services" originated the idea that this was "…part of a Kremlin attempt to sabotage Hillary Clinton's chances and improve Trump's"?

To answer this question, we will take a long journey into attitudes in the US in regard to Russia. We will start with Senator McCain, and then move to examine the US Intelligence Community, as their attitudes come across in the books published by both James Clapper and Michael Hayden.

McCain and Putin

McCain attacks Putin personally, calling him the "corrupt strongman" (241), and the "crooked ex-KGB colonel, Vladimir Putin" (310) for whom "Crime has most certainly paid…" (236).

McCain also talks of "…the regime's crackdown on the opposition, assaults on the press, endemic corruption…" (252) and "The Duma regularly passed laws altering election rules, laws restricting NGOs, laws suborning the media, laws controlling political parties, trade unions, and the judiciary, laws against 'extremism'…" (253). In short, Russia was not a democracy. In McCain's words, "…the glimmerings of democracy are very faint in Russia…" (256)

McCain talks of "…Putin's antagonism to U.S. interests and values" (237), "…Putin is and will remain our implacable foe…" (236), "He never was, he is not now, and he never will be our partner" (237), due to "…the enmity he has for the United States" (237).

According to McCain, the US is "…in an information war with Russia" (236). In this war, according to McCain, Putin, "…means to defeat the West" (299). McCain even advocates retaliation - "We have cyber capabilities, too. They could be used…" (236).

"I have been an equal-opportunity skeptic of four administrations' policies toward Russia. While I might sometimes have been harsher in my judgments than I should have been, I was not wrong about the big picture. I've gotten plenty of things wrong in a long political career. Putin isn't one of them." (244)

Since McCain says elsewhere in his book that, "A **fight** not joined is a **fight** not enjoyed." (10) and "I like to fight, **and I like people who like to fight, even if they're fighting with me**…" (321) – is it possible that McCain sees a "fight" and/or "war" when it does not really exist?

And knowing that McCain says that "I've gotten plenty of things wrong in a long political career", is it possible that he is wrong also now, even though he says that "Putin isn't one of…" those things that he was wrong about?

What does Putin really want?

A former prime minister of Israel, Ehud Olmert, published his book "In First Person". In his book, Olmert quotes what Putin once told him:

"The Communist regime conducted a stupid policy,' Putin told me. 'I will never allow to harm Israel or endanger it. My best friends live in your country. You have more Russian-speaking people, relatively, than any other country in the world, except for Russia and the former Soviet countries. My teacher from elementary school lives in Tel Aviv. My friends from Saint Petersburg live in Israel. I visited Israel many times. I spent time with my friends in Eilat (on the Red Sea) and we looked at your beautiful girls on the beach. But with that said, I have no intention to cool off my relations with the Arab countries. Russia has great influence in these countries, and also in Iran, and I will not give up this influence.'" (857)

In fact, just this week (December 2018) an Israeli military delegation visited Moscow to coordinate with the Russian military regarding Israel's activity against Hizbullah in South Lebanon and the Iranian presence in Syria. The two militaries even established a telephone hotline to prevent any clashes between the two militaries.

The former head of the Israeli National Security Council, Giora Eiland, recently published his autobiography[8]. Having extensive contacts with both high-ranking US and Russian officials, he has the ability to report to us what Putin really wants.

"And so Russia had (and it still has today) three clear interests. First, that no one, and mainly not the United States, would intervene in its internal affairs, and will not preach to her on the absence of democratization. Second, that all the republics of the former Soviet Union will remain under Russian influence, and that no actions would be taken to push them to join NATO or any other strategic alliance with the West. Third, that the United States will treat Russia as a superpower equal in importance, and that in no case would it try to put Russia in an embarrassing situation in the international arena." (360)

And in fact, McCain in his book confirms the importance of the second interest described by Eiland ("...that all the republics of the former Soviet

Union will remain under Russian influence…"). In talking about Putin's appearance at a security conference in Munich, Germany, McCain describes Putin's address to the conference: "Putin delivered an angry diatribe, **an extraordinary tirade about NATO…**" (257)

If there is any doubt regarding Putin's set of priorities, McCain continues, **"High on his list of complaints were the Baltics' admission into NATO, American support for democratic reform movements**, the color revolutions in Russia's 'near abroad', and the U.S. plans to build a ballistic missile shield in Europe." (257)

The only difference between Eiland's assessment of the Russian interests and McCain's description of Putin's address, is the reverse order of the first two interests. While Eiland positioned American support for democracy first and NATO second, Putin's address as described by McCain positioned NATO first and American support for democracy as second.

Since Eiland is talking about Russia, one might think that Russia and Putin are two different entities. Eiland goes on to explain to the reader:

"One must understand, that the president of Russia Vladimir Putin is like Louis the 14th who said, 'I am the state,' and therefore anyone who wants to know the priorities of Russia must learn the priorities of Putin, and it is not too complicated to do that. In Putin's eyes, the constant policy of the United States is to harm exactly the three Russian interests mentioned above. I thought then that Putin is right, and my conclusion only got stronger over the years." (360)

Summary

While McCain presents the Russian foreign policy as **aggressive and offensive**, and meant to "defeat the west", Eiland, as well as Putin, presents the Russian foreign policy as merely **defensive**.

Why is McCain against Putin?

Is it because Putin is practically a "dictator"? McCain introduces himself as "…a democratic internationalist, a proud one, and have been all my public life." (308) He traveled all over the globe in many countries to advocate human rights. And McCain mentions the fact that there are people in

Russia who are against the regime (i.e. against Putin) who are either jailed, or even killed. Is this the reason for his objection to Putin?

Other non-democratic countries mentioned in McCain's book

China

McCain relates to China relatively briefly, compared to the extensive coverage of Russia/Putin.

China is mentioned briefly when talking about Syria: "...Moscow and Beijing were supplying arms and other assistance to the regime." (181)

McCain refers to China as "our greatest long-term challenge" (301) when talking about trade. McCain himself compares China to Putin (note: not Russia but Putin) saying, "China is the challenge of the century, but Putin is the clear and present danger..." (301).

China is mentioned again in a long list of countries for which "I have done what little I can to stand in solidarity with forces of changes in countries aligned with us and opposed to us..." (332). While Russia is listed first, China is only listed fifth on the list.

McCain devotes four pages to the struggle of Liu Diablo, a Chinese human rights advocate who died "from multiple organ failure caused by liver cancer while under armed guard..." (334).

McCain mentions the "student protests in Tiananmen Square" (335), even attaching the word "massacre" to the event in one brief sentence. According to Wikipedia "the number of civilian deaths has been estimated variously from 180 to 10,454". Is there any mention of this number in McCain's book? No!

In addition, one should note that nowhere in his discussion about China does McCain mention the Chinese leadership. It is always just "China". Unlike Putin.

Egypt

When talking about the Egyptian leader who deposed the elected Islamist president in a coup (and McCain himself referred to it as a coup), McCain says,

"He gave the impression of being a pretty cold-blooded individual, and there was a lot of ego inside the uniform he was wearing… He didn't say, I'm going to arrest every Muslim brotherhood member I can get my hands on, **and kill a lot of people in the process**. But he communicated clearly to us the country needed order, and he was going to accomplish that, **and he didn't really care who he had to destroy to do it** or what we thought about it." (167)

But McCain does not express the same fierce opposition to the Egyptian leader as he does to the Russian one. And if indeed, "we often have important interests involved in relations with dictatorial regimes…" (318), aren't there "important interests" of the US that can be accomplished by cooperation with a "dictatorial regime" such as Putin's?

Saudi Arabia

McCain mentions this country very briefly. For this country he says, "Sometimes we have security interests at stake that loom larger on our list of priorities than the rights denied citizens in the country concerned, in Saudi Arabia, for example, with whom we have enemies in common." (317) And in fact, McCain says, "Our interests will often necessitate dealing with some pretty bad actors" (311), and "Yes, we often have important interests involved in relations with dictatorial regimes that those regimes will try to leverage to get us to turn a blind eye to corruption and human rights abuses." (318)

Is it only "bad actors"?

Ambassador George McGhee[9], US ambassador to the Middle East in the early fifties, brings the following incident:

"In my meeting with Faisal and on several other occasions I was greatly assisted by a personable young Saudi employee of the embassy. He was an excellent interpreter, guide, and friend. On one occasion, to my surprise, he confided in me the difficulties he and his wife were having with their **slave**.

The **slave**, a young girl, did little work, was protected against any infringements upon her rights, and was proving more costly than a servant. **Slavery, I found, was at that time still common, particularly on the part of the royal family**. I was deeply shocked." (191-192)

Slavery was commonly used in Saudi Arabia in the early fifties, and "particularly on the part of the royal family". What about today? Have things changed? But according to McCain, "Sometimes we have security interests at stake that loom larger on our list of priorities than the rights denied citizens in the country concerned..." (317)

And what about September 11, 2001? For this attack McCain says, "I was angry and I wanted retribution." (69) Didn't McCain know that 15 of the 19 hijackers were Saudis? But despite this he didn't write more strongly against Saudi Arabia in his book.

According to Arab custom, the entire family of the attacker is responsible for the act of the individual. This means that according to their own custom, any Arab who kills another Arab from another family or tribe subjects his own family to swift retribution. And in fact, in Arab villages in Israel, if someone gets killed in a fight, very soon afterwards several people from the attacker's family are suddenly found dead.

At the time of the 9/11 attack masterminded by Osama Bin Laden, many members of Bin Laden's family were in the US. The plane evacuating them back to Saudi Arabia was the only one that was allowed to take off from the US, when the skies over the US were closed to all other aviation for three days. Any comment by McCain?

One should ask, is there any Arab leader in the Middle East who doesn't have blood on his hands? Leaders in the Arab Middle East are mostly elected by the bullet rather than the ballot.

Summary

We see a lack of fury by McCain against regimes that killed many of their opponents. Apparently the US has mutual interests with China, Egypt, and Saudi Arabia, interests that "...will often necessitate dealing with some pretty bad actors" (311). Yes, it is quite likely that opponents of the regime in Russia are facing very serious consequences, either jail or even death. But why to single out Russia? The three above-mentioned countries are only an example, and they are mentioned here only because McCain refers to them in his book. While it is quite likely that Putin is also a "bad actor", why to choose one "bad actor" among many others, to tunnel all your fury against him?

And even if the three above-mentioned "bad actors" get a "discount" for behaving badly domestically only because they can serve US interests globally, should one conclude then that there are no such interests between the US and Russia/Putin, and therefore Russia/Putin do not deserve a "discount" as well?

When McCain says, "I hate Putin, though. I make no bones about that. I've been accused more than once of taking Putin's crimes 'personally'. And I have. I have indeed. Vladimir Putin is an evil man. There is no better word for him" (294)

When China kills between 180 to 10,454 in Tiananmen Square, McCain does not call it "evil". When an Egyptian leader kills hundreds and maybe thousands, he is not "evil". But Putin is "an evil man". Why to single out Putin?

US and Russia – No benefit in cooperation between the two?

Eiland in his book brings an interesting encounter with his Russian counterpart, Igor Ivanov. Ivanov told Eiland that the day before he met Eiland, he had received a phone call from the US Secretary of State, Condoleezza Rice. She started the conversation by reminding Ivanov that the next day there would be a discussion in the UN Security Council on the American suggestion regarding how to solve the issue of Cyprus. Rice wanted to know if Russia would support the American position, or at least not veto it.

At this point, Ivanov told Eiland: "Cyprus? We have no interest in Cyprus, and we can support this suggestion or that suggestion, but the Americans have been working on this suggestion for 5 years, they consulted with all the world, but for some reason they didn't find it right to ask us. Now, 24 hours before the vote in the Security Council, Madam Rice remembered that we have veto power and she decided to be nice with me. Why should I help her?"

Ivanov was simply saying that the Russians were offended that the US didn't find it right to talk with them, even about something that doesn't matter to them.

And what about Iran?

Eiland in his book brings an interesting encounter with his Russian counterparts – a Russian offer to limit Iran's capability to enrich uranium. This was even **before** the negotiations started with Iran, that eventually ended with President Obama and several European countries signing an agreement to limit the Iranians in their quest to reach the bomb.

In Eiland's words: "And so the Russians told me the following in my visit: We intend to offer to Iran to establish together a plant for enriching uranium on Russian soil. After all, Iran claims that its only wish is to use nuclear power for peaceful needs (to generate electricity). And so, the shared plant will supply Iran with fuel rods on two conditions: first, all the knowledge will be Russian and will remain in Russia, and the second, after the use of the fuel rods in the nuclear reactors that will be built for this purpose (the first in Bushehr) the used fuel will be returned to Russia (otherwise it would be possible to use them to produce a bomb via plutonium). My hosts, the head of the Security Council of Russia Igor Ivanov and the head of the Russian committee for nuclear energy, added that if Iran would refuse the offer, the Russians would be willing to support the West in pressure and sanctions on her." (361)

Eiland adds that the Russians had two conditions: "first, that the United States would publicly support this offer, and so the 'Russian offer' would become the basis of the agreement with Iran. Second, that neither France nor any other country would compete with Russia in anything connected with supplying nuclear reactors to Iran." (361)

Eiland says that when he brought the idea to Israel, he was criticized very strongly: "How do you think that Israel would convince the United States to support Russia in the suggested agreement with Iran? How would we look if we support Russia in their negotiations with Iran, when the American position is that Iran is part of 'the Axis of Evil' and therefore it is forbidden to talk with her?" (362)

And Eiland concludes: "I understood, and not for the first time, that the government of Israel tends to prefer PR (Hebrew: Hasbara[10]) over diplomatic activity. Hasbara is an activity that is intended to tell how bad our enemies are. A diplomatic activity is usually done in secret, and its aim is to cause another country, neutral, to do something that will serve our interests. The importance that is given in Israel to Hasbara at the expense of diplomatic activity causes the country great damage, but it serves the politicians not badly." (362)

Is this true only of Israel? Eiland brings us the American side:

"A year later, at the end of 2005, at the annual strategic meeting between the United States and Israel, I asked Nicholas Barnes, the deputy Secretary of State who led the dialogue from the American side, why the Americans had not accepted the Russian offer the year before. His general and evasive answer caused me to understand two points: first, and in contrast to the American declarations, preventing an Iranian nuclear bomb is not an uppermost American interest. **Their apparent priority shows that continuing the personal attacks on Putin is more important to them**. Second, as the Russians had claimed in all my meetings with them, the United States does not understand Russia, and does not even try to understand, and it is a shame" (363)

Is the US lack of understanding restricted only to Russia, or maybe it is true regarding other countries as well?

McCain says that when he met the Egyptian leader he suggested to him, "Be magnanimous in victory…" (167). Being "magnanimous in victory" might be true in American culture, but it is definitely not true in the Arab Middle East, where "being magnanimous" is perceived as "weakness". It is no wonder that Egypt and Saudi Arabia, mentioned by McCain, are not "magnanimous in victory" towards their defeated opponents.

We saw two examples – Cyprus and Iran – where approaching the Russians with respect could have produced great results. Now, one might wonder what would have happened if showing respect to the Russians could have helped with the North Korean case?

If the United States can benefit from showing respect to the Russians (even as just a show), why to say, "…the West, led by the United States, must accept that Putin is and will remain our implacable foe…" (236), and "He never was, he is not now, and he never will be our partner" (237). As if anti-Putinism is engraved in stone.

Back to McCain and Putin?

Was McCain simply "anti-Russian" within the US political establishment? If so, he was not the only one.

James R. Clapper, former US Director of National Intelligence, in his book says that as Director of the Defense Intelligence Agency he was called to JCS chairman General Colin Powell who told him not to appoint Mike Hayden as US Defense attaché in Moscow. Clapper quotes Powell as being "deeply involved in trying to forge a new relationship with a post-Soviet Russia and wanted his own trusted agent to represent him in Moscow." (71) In other words, Powell considered Mike Hayden (the same Hayden mentioned several times in McCain's book) as "anti-Russian".

It seems that the US defense and intelligence community has its own "anti-Russians" within.

What is the reason for the strong negative emotional reaction towards Putin? Why "I hate Putin"? Why "...my animosity toward Putin, which I unapologetically acknowledged..." (241)?

Comparing Putin to China, Egypt, and Saudi Arabia, one must conclude that McCain's animosity must be deep-rooted, **not only** because Putin is brutal against his opponents. It must be something else.

McCain says, "I've been accused more than once of taking Putin's crimes 'personally.' And I have. I have indeed." (294)

He acknowledges taking Putin "personally". Why?

Is it the point that McCain mentions, "The Putin cult of personality, that bare-chested, give-the-finger-to-the-west machismo..." (249)? The "bare-chested" (=gender-related) description should bring us to wonder if it is connected to the fact that Putin is the only one in the book who received three times the (gender-related) label "man". Nobody else got it three times. Putin is the only one. Something to think about!!!

McCain and Trump

Another person that Senator McCain "has an issue with" is Donald Trump.

There are ten chapters in the book "The Restless Wave" by John McCain, and throughout these chapters, McCain is writing against Trump, although not necessarily by name.

In the beginning section, "Accumulated Memories", McCain says, "We don't build walls to freedom and opportunity. We tear them down." and "…to refuse the obligations of international leadership for the sake of some half-baked, spurious nationalism **cooked up by people who would rather find scapegoats** than solve problems is unpatriotic." (9)

In the first chapter, "No Surrender", McCain says, "I wish every American who out of ignorance or worse curses immigrants as criminals or a drain on the country's resources or a threat to our 'culture'…" (20)

In the second chapter, "Country First", McCain deals with his campaign against Obama in 2008. He mentions that he forbade any attack against Obama that had to deal with "Questioning his patriotism, his **parentage**…" relating indirectly to Trump's challenging Obama to show his birth certificate.

The third chapter, "About Us", deals with McCain's fierce attack against EIT (Enhanced Interrogation Techniques), a euphemism for torture. In this chapter McCain says, "In the following presidential campaign season that was soon to begin, the eventual Republican nominee and next President of the United States insisted torture 'absolutely works' and swore he would bring back waterboarding 'and worse.' His statement was made out of **ignorance**, attributable to his **lack of experience** in a role related to the defense of this country. It also exposed his apparent **lack of appreciation for the importance of our values** to our security." (Page 103)

In the fourth chapter, "In the Company of Heroes", McCain talks about his travels to Iraq and Afghanistan and meeting the soldiers fighting for the US. In this chapter McCain briefly commends the "administration" of Trump (not Trump personally as he does for Obama), saying that "…the Trump administration wisely announced that henceforth, conditions on the ground would determine troop levels…" (146).

One might think that this chapter will end with no criticism against Trump, but McCain couldn't avoid it, and in the last paragraph he says, "I think we have all had over the last year or so reason to wonder about the direction of our country **and some of the people leading it**. I would like to be again in the company of Americans who embody our nation's greatness, and who know it is something more profound and dearer than **a politician's campaign slogan**." (149)

In the fifth chapter, "Arab Spring", McCain describes the events in the Arab Middle East and his criticism against Obama for not reacting after the Syrian regime used chemical weapons against the opposition. Towards the end of the chapter he commends Obama for "his candor… and I respected the sincerity of his convictions" (192). However, he then goes on to refer to **"the thoughtless America First ideology of his successor"** (192).

In chapter six, "Fighting the Good Fight", McCain describes his fights with Senator Teddy Kennedy. Even in this chapter he finds a way to criticize Trump – he is against "…the spread of nationalism that barely distinguishes enemy from friend, seeing every relationship as purely transactional with a winner and a loser" (201).

When talking about his and Senator Kennedy's attempt "…to pass comprehensive immigration reform" (205), he says, "…in this political moment, as old fears and animosities that have blighted our history appear to be on the rise again, **exploited by opportunists who won't trouble their careers or their consciences with scruples about honesty or compassion for their fellowman.**" (205) He goes on to say that the prejudiced people "…believe the President shares their prejudice…" (206). When he talks against Steve King and Steve Bannon, he adds, "…and **those parts of the America First crowd** that misunderstand American culture and exceptionalism" (210).

Countering Trump's assertion that Mexico is sending criminals to the US, McCain says, "…the great majority of unauthorized immigrants… …are not the rapists, killers, and drug dealers…" (212). In his defense of "illegal immigration" he says, "There are politicians today who would have Americans believe that illegal immigration is one of the worst scourges afflicting the country" (214), relating to Trump's "…insulting references to unauthorized immigrants…" (216).

In chapter seven, "NYET (Know Thine Enemy)", McCain describes the well-known dossier that floated around with allegations against Trump. [See more in the section dealing with the dossier.]

In chapter eight, "Know Thyself (Defending the West)", McCain talks about the Russian interference in the last elections. Here we find McCain talks of "…the President's campaign demagoguery" (301) against the Trans-Pacific Partnership trade deal.

In regard to the way Trump perceives Putin, McCain says, "Last year he implied that our government was morally equivalent to Putin's regime: 'We have a lot of killers, too. You think our country is so innocent,'" (301). One can summarizes McCain's criticism of Trump by, "President Trump **compares us neutrally** to the regime of a murderer and thug…" (301)

[It is interesting to find that the same words that McCain uses to criticize Trump – that he compares the US to "the regime of a murder and thug…" – also describe something that McCain does himself. When he talks about the EIT (Enhanced Interrogation techniques) which the US used against terrorists, and especially of the abuse that US soldiers inflicted on prisoners in the Abu Ghraib prison in Iraq, and which McCain went very strongly against, McCain says, "The North Vietnamese could be cruel, and would inflict pain to get what they wanted from us. **But they never did anything like this**" (84).]

In chapter nine, "Part of the Main (American exceptionalism)", McCain talks about advocating human rights around the globe. He says, "I have never once gone to Hanoi and not raised human rights issues with my hosts… The world expects us to be concerned with the condition of humanity. We should be proud of that reputation. **I'm not sure the President understands that.**" (326)

Although he commends President Trump for "…quickly identifying with the protesters [in Iran]…" (328) he goes on to say, "It is hard to know what to expect from President Trump, what's a pose, what's genuine. As in other areas, the character of the President will likely be reflected in the content and conduct of foreign policy." (328-329)

In chapter ten, "Regular Order", McCain talks about his being diagnosed with a brain tumor and his struggle with the disease. In this chapter McCain describes his vote not to repeal Obamacare, one of Trump's promises during his campaign. In spite of his doctors telling him not to fly in his condition, he boarded a flight to reach the Senate to vote against Trump.

The only section in the book that has no mention of Trump, either directly or indirectly, is the section called "Hidden Valley", McCain's place north of Phoenix.

Summary

Except for talking against Putin, the book easily can be classified as a manifesto against Trump and his policies. Even the criticism against Putin is intertwined with McCain's criticism against Trump.

Changes in language in McCain's book

There are several places in Senator McCain's book in which there are changes in language that can easily be classified as "unjustified changes in language", indicating quite likely deception in the statement.

Two of these sets of changes in language refer to illegal immigration and Senator McCain's extensive travel.

In regard to illegal immigration, there are places where McCain is calls it "illegal", "unlawful", "unauthorized", and "without permission".

In regard to his extensive travel, there are places where he calls it a "trip", "visit", "travel", or even without any noun – "I arrived…"

There are more places in which there are changes in language.

The Dossier

In regard to this well-known file that contained information about candidate Trump, we find two sets of changes.

The first, in regard to the type of information included in the dossier:

"They were shocking **allegations**." (238)
"The **allegations** were disturbing, but I had no idea which if any were true." (238)
"I had an obligation to bring to the attention of appropriate officials unproven **accusations**…" (241)

There is another place in the book that gives us an insight into McCain's meaning for the word "accusations".

"The Voting Rights Act of 1965 and the Detainee Treatment Act forty years later were to an extent a response to **accusations** that our proselytizing on behalf of the God-given dignity of all people was cynical." (314)

In this place it is quite clear that the "accusations" were justified, as the Congress felt the need to address these "accusations".

Since in all these three places McCain refers to the information included in the dossier without any division between two types of information, there is no apparent reason to change the language between "allegations" and "unproven accusations". As such, we are facing a situation in which the sentence does not justify the change of language between "allegations" and "unproven accusations". The conclusion is that quite likely deception is present at this point of time.

One should note we find a similar change in language between "allegations" and "accusations" in another place in McCain's book, in regard to a Russian defector, Alexander Litvinenko. This defector "alleged" that the FSB (Russian internal security agency) "…had planted the bombs to improve Putin's prospects for succeeding to the presidency" (246).

In regard to this allegation, McCain says, "Some Western journalists reiterated the **allegation**, while others disputed it. I've no idea if it's true. But I wouldn't be shocked if it were. Litvinenko would pay a terrible price for this and other **accusations**." (246)

In this quote, there is a distinct difference between the allegation (about planting the bombs) and the accusations, since the accusations relate to "**other** accusations". Therefore, we cannot conclude that we are facing an "unjustified change of language", and therefore no suspicion of possible deception.

Although we are not facing an "unjustified change of language", we are facing another troubling signal – the sentence "I've no idea if it's true."

There are 20 places in the book where McCain says, "I don't remember/know".

"I don't remember" as an answer to a specific question might be legitimate. However, in an "open statement", as in the text in front of us, i.e. in McCain's book, the phrase "I've no idea…" is illegitimate. There is a lot that a person would not know of the events that took place even recently, not to mention events from many years ago. Therefore, the phrase "I've no idea…" should be considered as an attempt to **conceal information**.

The rarity of the use of this phrase ("I've no idea") should lead us to suspect that there might be **deception** at this point in the book.

SCAN information: one should note that "concealing information" is not "deception". One can "conceal information" only if one bases the statement upon memory. In other words, one cannot "conceal" if there is nothing to conceal. In a way, "concealing information" gives credibility to the text, as it is a signal that memory is playing. On the other hand, deception is a different signal altogether. One should take into consideration that both signals – concealing information and deception – might be present at the same place in the statement.

The second change in language is in regard to the reason McCain felt the need to bring the information to the attention of "appropriate officials":

"I did what **duty** demanded I do." (239)
"I did my **duty**, as I've sworn an oath to do. I had an **obligation** to bring to the attention of appropriate officials unproven accusations…" (241)

Again, there is no apparent reason by the sentences to change the language between "duty" and "obligation". The conclusion is that quite likely deception is present at this point of time. In other words, quite likely McCain did not bring the information in the dossier only due to "duty"/"obligation".

One should note the merging of these two "unjustified changes in language" in the same sentence. When the language changes from "allegations" to "accusations", it also changes from "duty" to "obligation". We are facing two signals of deception coming together at the same place.

Russia and the elections

McCain uses two different words to relate to the Russian activity in the US at the time of the campaign before the elections – "meddling" and "interference".

"He **meddled** in our election…" (295)
"He **interfered** in the last French presidential election…" (295)
"He did it with the same means he used to **interfere** in our election." (295)
"…and get briefed by our embassy and by Montenegrin officials on the extent of the Russian **interference**. They reported back that the Montenegrins were alarmed about more than Russian **meddling** in their country's politics." (296)
"…he was **meddling** in our election at the same time." (296)
"He will try to **interfere**, he already is, in our next election, and the election after that, and the election after that." (299)
"And some House Republicans investigating Russian **interference**…" (300)
"…Putin's **interference** in our last election achieved all his objectives." (300)
"…**interfering** in an American presidential election with the intention of helping elect the candidate they believed would pose the least resistance to their ambitions." (310)

Again, there is no apparent reason to change the language between "meddling" and "interference". As such, we are facing a situation in which the sentences do not justify the change of language between "meddling" and "interference". The conclusion is that quite likely deception is present at this point of time, i.e. regarding this issue.

One should note that in another place McCain used another word - "intervention" - to refer to the US acting on behalf of one group in another country. It is clear that the use of the word "intervention" is justified by the sentence.

"I've been accused of being too quick to propose that the U.S. **intervene** militarily in other countries' civil strife in support of embattled democratic movements." (322)

McCain's vote in the Senate

Although McCain was diagnosed with very aggressive brain cancer, and he had already started treatment, he insisted - against his doctors' advice - to fly to DC to take part in the vote to repeal Obamacare. McCain voted against the repeal; his vote was the deciding vote that caused the Republican party to fail in its attempt to repeal.

For the reason of why he voted not to repeal we face a change of language.

"I was thanked for my vote by Democratic friends more profusely than I should have been for helping save Obamacare. That had not been my **goal**." (369)

"Among the people who called to thank me was President Obama. I appreciated his call, but, as I said, my **purpose** hadn't been to preserve his signature accomplishment..." (369)

Again, there is no apparent reason to change the language between "goal" and "purpose". As such, we are facing a situation in which the sentences do not justify the change of language between "goal" and "purpose". The conclusion is that quite likely deception is present at this point of time.

Summary

It is interesting to note that all these changes in language have one common denominator: they deal with President Trump, and McCain's fierce opposition to him.

The dossier: the dossier contains allegations/unproven accusations against Trump.
Russia and the elections: in McCain's words, "...interfering in an American presidential election with the intention of helping elect the candidate they believed would pose the least resistance to their ambitions" (310). In other words, saying in many words that President Trump is in a way a Russian sympathizer.
The vote not to repeal Obamacare: to defy President Trump, who listed it as one of his main promises before the election.
"Illegal immigration": the changes in language in regard to "illegal immigration", indicating deception, are in regard to President Trump's

promise to build a wall on the southern border that will stop illegal immigration.

The only changes in language that do not show apparent connection to President Trump are the changes in language in regard to McCain's extensive travel.

All in all, the decisive majority of the signals of deception in McCain's book relate to President Trump.

The Dossier

Introduction

We already saw that there are two sets of unjustified changes in language in regard to the dossier – the first, "allegations" vs. "accusations"; and the second, "duty" vs. "obligation". These changes in language are in conjunction with the rarity of the use of "I had no idea", which shows up only twice in the entire book, indicating deception as well. These signals should bring us to check McCain's account of the appearance of the dossier very carefully.

Background to the introduction of the Dossier

Chapter seven, "NYET (Know Thine Enemy)", starts with McCain saying, "I regularly attend an annual security conference in Halifax, Nova Scotia." (235) He mentions that the time was November 2016 and "that it occurred just after the U.S. presidential election…" McCain goes on to say that he "…spent most of my time in Halifax reassuring friends…" as to the results of the election, i.e. Donald Trump becoming US President.

The Statement

"…a retired British diplomat, who had served as the United Kingdom's ambassador to Russia during Vladimir Putin's rapid ascent to the Russian presidency, Sir Andrew Wood…"

Note the long "social introduction" of a title (a very long one) and name.

"…asked to have a word."

Throughout the book, McCain mentions many conversations. Language-wise, he calls them "talking", "speaking", "discuss", and "conversation". There are only two places in which McCain uses the phrase "to have a word". One is this place here, and the other is before voting in the Senate against repealing Obamacare: "I had a brief word with Chuck Schumer right after I entered the chamber to confirm that I was likely to vote no." (366)

Chuck Schumer, as the leader of the minority Democratic party in the Senate, was in charge of the efforts to keep Obamacare intact. McCain, being officially part of the Republican party, was having a "brief word" with him, informing him before the vote of his intention.

The conversation with Senator Schumer was likely to be kept secret until the vote; or in other words, the two of them were conspiring against the Republicans. And in the same way, using the same terminology, the conversation with Sir Andrew Wood was likely to be a conspiracy. But the question is: by McCain's account, McCain didn't know **at this point of time** that Sir Andrew Wood was asking for something secret and conspiratorial.

Question: at the time of writing his book, McCain already knew that this conversation was going to be conspiratorial. So, what's wrong with him using the phrase "to have a word" at this point?

Answer: One should take into consideration that the statement is given at the present time, in regard to the past. So, **at the time of the statement** McCain is familiar with the incident. However, if McCain is reliving the incident, as is usually the case when someone writes a statement, then at the time that McCain met Sir Andrew Wood, McCain didn't know that the conversation was going conspiratorial. Therefore, saying "to have a word" at this point of time before the conversation was even held is improper, as it demonstrates McCain's knowledge at the time of the statement, and not at the time before the conversation.

To sum up this point: even though a subject, at the time of writing the statement, knows everything, still, from the beginning of the statement a truthful subject "suffers" a major "loss of memory" or "amnesia" concerning what happened later. The subject relives the events while writing the statement.

To use terminology which reflects McCain's knowledge **at the time of the statement** would actually indicate that McCain is not reliving the event – a strong indicator of deception.

Did McCain ask Sir Wood as to what he wants to talk about? McCain doesn't say.

Note: If the subject didn't say it, it didn't happen.

Question: Why wouldn't McCain ask Sir Wood as to what he wants to talk with him about? Did McCain already know what was the objective of that meeting? Let's not forget that McCain said that Sir Wood "asked to have a word", indicating that he knew it was conspiratorial.

McCain goes on: "I might have been introduced to him before at a previous conference, but **I don't recall** ever having a conversation with him."

As an answer to a specific question, "I don't remember" might be legitimate. But McCain's book is an "open statement", and in an "open statement" a person cannot legitimately say "I don't remember/recall". "I don't remember/recall" in an "open statement" is a signal of concealing information.

McCain is defined by himself as a Putin-hater, and throughout the book he writes against Putin as evil incarnate. One might wonder if McCain would not like to get the knowledge from one who was in Moscow "…during Vladimir Putin's rapid ascent to the Russian presidency…" If McCain did meet Sir Wood before, he quite likely talked with him about Putin.

Therefore: since it is quite likely that McCain did meet Sir Wood before, and talked with him about Putin; and since McCain, as a self-declared hater of Putin, would not forget anything relating to Putin; and all this combined with the phrase "I don't recall", which is a signal of concealing information – why would McCain present this encounter as just a chance encounter with someone he really doesn't know?

McCain continues: "Nevertheless, I agreed to sit down with him for a few minutes."

Why "nevertheless"? Earlier, McCain said, "I spent most of my time in Halifax reassuring friends that the United States government consists of more than the White House…" – and Sir Wood, being a former UK ambassador to Russia, would easily be classified as a "friend". Why not to welcome such a "friend" warmly?

McCain goes on to say, "We found a room off the main conference hall, with a few chairs scattered around a coffee table." (236)

Why the "unnecessary details"?

And then he goes on to mention two people, along with their titles, who joined them. In other words, McCain wants us to know that he was not alone with Sir Wood.

McCain then says, "We briefly discussed Russia's interference in the election, the hacking of the Democratic National committee's and John Podesta's emails…"

We should note that McCain tells us that there were two different issues that were "discussed" here: first, "Russia's interference in the election", and second, "…the hacking of the Democratic National committee's and John Podesta's emails…"

If we have any doubt about it, McCain continues, "…which U.S. intelligence services **concurred** had been part of a Kremlin attempt to sabotage Hillary Clinton's chances and improve Trump's."

"Concurred"? One can "concur" only with someone else's ideas. So, who outside "U.S. intelligence services" originated the idea that this was "…part of a Kremlin attempt to sabotage Hillary Clinton's chances and improve Trump's"?

And why was it only "**part** of a Kremlin attempt…"? What else there was there, besides "interference in the election" and "hacking"?

At this point, McCain goes into a long dissertation against Putin, which goes over one full page – from the middle of page 236 to the middle of page 237.

Is this "dissertation" against Putin necessary at this point? Or, is it meant to slow down before the real issue? One should remember that in many statements, slowing down is a signal of deception coming later on. This is due to the fact that people do not really want to lie, so they will postpone the lie as much as they can.

McCain continues, "After a few minutes Sir Andrew came to the subject that was his reason for approaching us." (237)

"After a few minutes…" is an "unnecessary connection" indicating that some significant information might have been omitted at this point of time.

"…Sir **Andrew**…" – if before he was "Sir Andrew Wood", now he is "Sir Andrew" – first name basis. Quite likely the discussion over one page in the book asserting an "information war with Russia" brought the two to a "meeting of minds".

"…Sir Andrew came to the subject that was his reason for approaching us."

One should note two points:

McCain had already written a page and a half without actually reaching the reason that "Sir Andrew" wanted "to have a word".

"…the subject that was his reason for approaching **us**" – it is true that McCain didn't say earlier that "Sir Andrew asked to have a word **with me**…" It was just "asked to have a word". But McCain's reaction to Sir Andrew Wood's request was clearly telling us that the British diplomat wanted to talk with McCain. The fact that McCain later said that two people joined the conversation did not diminish the fact that "Sir Andrew Wood" wanted "to have a word" with McCain. So, now we have two questions: first, why didn't McCain say initially, "…wanted to have a word **with me**"? And second question: why now does McCain not say "…approached me" and instead he says "…approached **us**", when clearly McCain says that the two other people only "**joined** us"?

Using "Total Belief in the subject", can we conclude that when Sir Andrew wanted "to have a word", since McCain doesn't say that Sir Andrew "approached me", that in fact Sir Andrew did not approach McCain? And that maybe, therefore, McCain had approached him earlier?

This would explain the "I don't recall ever having had a conversation with him". It would also explain the phrase "to have a word" which quite likely indicates conspiracy.

McCain continues: "He told me he knew a former MI6 officer by the name of Christopher Steele, who had been commissioned to investigate connections between the Trump campaign and Russian agents as well as potentially compromising information about the President-elect that Putin allegedly possessed."

"He told me…" – and not "…told us…" although three people are present besides Sir Andrew.

"…Christopher Steele, **who had been commissioned**…" – using passive voice. Passive voice is the strongest signal of an attempt to conceal identity. Was this concealing of identity (regarding who had commissioned Steele) on the part of Sir Andrew, or on the part of McCain?

[In the book "The Snowden Files"[11], Snowden says that the NSA in the US reached an agreement with GCHQ, UK's counterpart organization to the NSA, that the NSA will spy on British citizens while the GCHQ will spy on American citizens. This is to enable each organization to claim that they are not spying on their own citizens. This is in spite of the fact that the entire budget of the UK's GCHQ is funded by NSA. Since in front of us there is a "former MI6 officer", is it possible that he "was commissioned" by his US counterparts?]

"…Christopher Steele, who had been commissioned to investigate…"

One might ask how can a former MI6 officer even "investigate" allegations relating to espionage **after the fact**? Even with all the connections such a former MI6 officer might have, still there is no way to "investigate" such allegations unless the investigator catches one or both sides in the actual act of sharing information, or if one or the other confesses.

"…who had been commissioned to investigate connections between the Trump campaign and Russian agents as well as potentially compromising information about the President-elect that Putin allegedly possessed."

Two different issues are discussed here:

Connections between the Trump campaign and Russian agents,
Potentially compromising information about the President-elect that Putin allegedly possessed

Note that while #1 talks in definite terms, #2 talks about "potentially" and "allegedly". Why not to say, "**Possible** connections between the Trump campaign and Russian agents…"? It seems that the first issue had been decided even before this former MI6 officer "had been commissioned…" And if so, why to "investigate"?

McCain continues: "Steele had prepared a report that Wood had not read and conceded was mostly raw, unverified intelligence, but that the author strongly believed merited a thorough examination by counterintelligence experts. Steele was a respected professional, Wood assured us, who had good Russian contacts and long experience collecting and analyzing intelligence on the Kremlin. Both Steele and Wood were alarmed by what he had learned and worried that it would not be further investigated."

"Steele had prepared a report…"

Note that while Steele "…had been commissioned **to investigate**…", McCain does not quote Sir Andrew as saying that Steele "investigated". McCain only quoted Sir Andrew as saying that Steele "had prepared a report".

"If the subject didn't say it, it didn't happen" - and if Sir Andrew, or McCain, did not say that Steele "investigated", then he didn't do so. If so, the information included in the "report" was given to Steele before "he had been commissioned…"

"Steele had prepared a report that **Wood**…"

If earlier he was "Sir Andrew", now he is not "Sir" and not "Andrew". Just the last name - "Wood". Why the "downgrading" from "Sir", and why the formality showing up in the language?

"Steele had prepared a report that Wood **had not read**…"

An "open statement" only answers the question of "what happened?" "What didn't happen" is not within the scope of the statement. There is a lot that didn't happen, and the person would not mention it. To produce a sentence in the negative ("what didn't happen") means that the person giving the statement is branching out from the question of "what happened?" Such a sentence should be considered a very important one.

Question: if Sir Andrew "had not read" the report, why would he come to McCain to present such a report? If Steele "had been commissioned" by an "unknown entity", why wouldn't Steele use his sources in the MI6, or even among his US counterparts, and present this report to them? Why to go in such a roundabout way, to approach McCain, asking him to give this report to the appropriate investigative organization?

"Steele had prepared a report that Wood had not read and **conceded was mostly raw, unverified intelligence**…"

The "conceded" cannot relate to Wood as he "had not read" the report. The "conceded" must relate to Steele. So "conceded" continues the sentence from before: "Steele had prepared a report and conceded was mostly raw …"

"Conceded" means that someone other than Steele and Wood had already read the report and objected to bringing "raw, unverified intelligence". So Steele had to "concede" that in fact it is "raw and unverified".

Question: who had read the "report" that Steele had prepared, and criticized it, bringing Steele to "concede"? And if so, why to continue with using such "raw, unverified intelligence"?

"…but **that the author** strongly believed merited a thorough examination by counterintelligence experts."

McCain quotes "Sir Andrew" as saying that "a former MI6 officer by the name of Christopher Steele… had been commissioned…" Then McCain moves on to say that "**Steele** had prepared a report" – not "Christopher Steele" but only "Steele". And now McCain changes in language to say "the author".

Is it possible that "the author" is **not** actually "Steele"? That quite likely we are facing here two different people - the one who "authored", and the one who "prepared a report" (i.e. Steele). While Steele "conceded" that it is "raw" and "unverified", and quite likely did not see this report going anywhere, "the author" who "had commissioned" Steele to "investigate" (which he didn't…) still "…strongly believed merited a thorough examination by counterintelligence experts."

Again, the question should be asked: why the roundabout route going through McCain, and not going straight to US "counterintelligence experts"? Unless "the author" needed McCain to proceed with this "raw, unverified intelligence", knowing that McCain was very strongly anti-Trump.

And if one wants to be a conspiracy buff, one might even wonder if McCain himself was the origin of this "raw, unverified intelligence".

"Steele was a respectable professional, Wood assured us, who had good Russian contacts and long experience **collecting and analyzing intelligence** on the Kremlin."

Wood, through McCain, is talking of two different issues in intelligence. The first is "**collecting** information", and the second is "**analyzing**" it. Knowing these two different issues, we can go back to the "report" Steele had prepared. McCain (or Wood) does not say how Steele "collected" the information, except for saying that he has "good Russian contacts". However, Steele himself "conceded" that the information he produced in the "report" is "raw, unverified intelligence". Meaning that in "analyzing" the information, Steele "conceded" that the report does not contain anything significant.

The irony of it all is that one who has "good Russian contacts" "had been commissioned to investigate connections between the Trump campaign and Russian agents".   Why shouldn't Steele be "investigated" the same way?

"Both Steele and Wood were alarmed by what he had learned and worried that it would not be further investigated."

Till this point, we had only Wood reporting on Steele. This is the first time that the two of them are of one mind.

"…and worried that it would not be further investigated." This confirms the meaning of "conceded" – that there was someone, or even more than one person, who had already read the report and labeled it as "raw, unverified intelligence". (This is quite likely intelligence jargon, i.e. inside language.) That person or persons did not see any reason to "further investigate".

Another question: If Wood "had not read" the report, how could he be alarmed by what Steele had found?

At this point, McCain talks of "candidate Trump's admiration for Vladimir Putin…" although he says that he was "skeptical that Trump or his aides had actively cooperated with Russia's interference". He goes on to say, "But even a remote risk that the President of the United States might be vulnerable to Russian extortion had to be investigated." (238)

At this point of time, McCain brings the following description:

"Our impromptu meeting felt charged with a strange intensity. No one wise-cracked to lighten the mood. We spoke in lowered voices. The room was dimly lit, and the atmosphere was eerie."

"The room was dimly lit" – "light" in an "open statement" strongly relates to a sexual innuendo in the background. And in fact, later on it was found that some of the allegations against Trump were that during his visit in Moscow, he was involved with some very kinky sex in his hotel room.

The only question is: at this point of time, Wood "had not read" the report, and McCain was only "approached" by Wood bringing the existence of the report to McCain's knowledge. How would McCain know at this point of time that there are allegations against Trump relating to sex?

McCain continues, "Wood described Steele's research in general terms."

Question: if Wood "had not read" the report, how could he "describe" the information even "in general terms"?

Moreover, earlier McCain said that Steele "had been commissioned to **investigate**", and he only "prepared a **report**", and now McCain changes the language to call it "**research**". There is no apparent reason for such a change in language, and if so, we are facing an "unjustified change in language" in regard to Steele's product, indicating that deception is present in the statement at this point of time.

One should not forget that we started this analysis of the "dossier" with two "unjustified changes in language" - the first, "allegations" vs. "accusations", and the second, "duty" vs. "obligation". Now, we have a third signal of "unjustified change of language" = deception.

McCain continues, "He had not read it himself, but vouched for Steele's credibility."

Again, repeating the negative sentence of "what didn't happen" (=important).

Please note that, according to McCain, Wood didn't vouch for the credibility of the research. Wood only vouched for Steele's credibility.

McCain continues, "I was taken aback. They were shocking allegations."

Note that till this point, according to McCain, Wood didn't read the report, and he didn't know what was inside it, and could only talk about it "in general terms". McCain says that he was only approached by Wood at this meeting with this report, and at this point of time could not have known the "allegations", or even "shocking allegations". If so, how can McCain state **at this point** that there were "shocking allegations"?

McCain continues, "When Wood offered to arrange to provide me a copy of his **research**..."

Again, "research" and not "report".

"...I knew that were Steele as **reputable** as Wood claimed..."

While earlier, McCain said that Wood "...vouched for Steele's **credibility**...", here McCain changes in language and uses "reputable" instead of "credible".

Again, there is no apparent reason for such a change in language, and if so, we are facing an "unjustified change in language" in regard to Steele's "credibility"/"reputability", indicating deception is present in the statement at this point of time.

This signal of deception goes along with the use of the word "claimed". "Claimed" (instead of "said") indicates a doubt on the part of McCain regarding what Wood said.

McCain continues, "When David returned [from London], and shared his impression that **the former spy** was, as Sir Andrew had vouched, a respected professional…"

If earlier he was a "former MI6 **officer**" now he is a "former **spy**".

It is quite doubtful if this change in language is justified by the sentence. If so, we are facing another "unjustified change in language", indicating deception in regard to this "officer"/"spy".

McCain continues, "…I **agreed** to receive a copy of what is now referred to as 'the dossier.' I reviewed its contents."

"Agreed"? According to McCain, his aide David Kramer went to London to "…meet Steele, confirm his credibility, and report back to me." If so, after his aide returned from London, how did he agree to receive a copy of the dossier? He continues by saying, "I reviewed its contents." But McCain didn't say previously that his aide had brought the dossier from London. (And if the subject didn't say it, then it didn't happen.)

If he agrees only at this point, then he needs to ask them to send him a copy from London. But he doesn't say anything about his aide either bringing the dossier, or going back to London to receive it. By him saying, "I reviewed its contents", it comes across that the dossier was already in the US, so why to agree only at this point? This whole sentence does not fit the sequence of events.

"I reviewed its contents" – McCain had said earlier that "Wood had not read" the dossier, and McCain also didn't say that he "read" it. He only "reviewed" it. "Review" indicates going over the material quickly. But if these are "shocking allegations" why not to "read" them carefully? Why only to "review" them?

McCain goes on to say that he "…called the office of the director of the FBI, Jim Comey, and asked for a meeting. I went to see him at his earliest convenience, handed him the dossier, **explained** how it had come into my possession."

"Explained" and not "told him". McCain uses language indicating that he knew that the way he received the dossier was questionable, and it needed an "explanation".

"…come into my **possession**" – and not "…had come to my knowledge". Why "possession"? "Possession" indicates ownership. Was McCain the owner of this dossier?

McCain continues, "**I said** I didn't know what to make of it…" – the prefix "I said" only means that at this point of time McCain tells us what he said to Comey, but it is not necessarily true. We might be facing a truthful statement that could contain a lie from the past. In other words, McCain might have lied to Comey, but not to the reader in his book. Since he accurately reports what he said to Comey, the sentence itself is true, but we don't know whether what he told Comey was true.

Later on McCain asks: "Why had I been given the dossier?" (241)

Please note that again McCain uses passive language about receiving the dossier. He cannot say who gave it to him.

Question: did anyone give him the dossier? Or maybe nobody?

At this point, McCain goes into a long dissertation over several pages to describe how he was known as "anti-Putin". There is only one point he does not mention at all – that he was also known as "anti-Trump". McCain expresses animosity towards these two men, almost equally. The only difference is that for Trump he does not use the term "evil", as he does for Putin. But otherwise, the book can easily be seen as a manifesto against Trump's presidency. In almost every chapter of the book.

Summary

There are many signals in McCain's language that there is deception is regard to this dossier. The language he uses, and even the order of events, does not follow the presentation that McCain wants the reader to accept – that Wood approached him with knowledge that he might not have known beforehand.

Conclusion

One cannot rule out that Senator McCain himself might be the "engine" behind the dossier. It would "kill two birds with one stone" – his hatred (McCain's language) towards Putin, and his fierce opposition to Trump.

McCain and the Intelligence Community

There are plenty of places in the book where McCain shows great displeasure towards the behavior of the intelligence community.

McCain devoted a major part of the book to discuss the EIT (enhanced interrogation techniques), which according to McCain were equivalent to torture of detainees.

"CIA officials had **misled** him as they had other Justice officials, and, as it turns out, as they **misled** senior White House officials, including President Bush and Vice President Cheney." (98)

We should note that McCain avoids labeling this activity as "lying". Instead, he used a milder word – "misled".

"…most of the CIA's claims that abusive interrogations of detainees had produced vital leads to help locate bin Laden were exaggerated, misleading, and in some cases, **complete bullshit**." (99)

We should note that here also McCain avoids labeling this activity as "lying". Instead, he uses a much more "colorful" term.

There is one place in which McCain does use the word "lying" for a CIA report – "It **lied** about the value of intelligence extracted from abused detainees." (100)

He does the same when talking about CIA personnel engaging in "a violation of the separation of powers" (101) in "…an attempt by the Agency to **spy** on committee investigators…" (99), and when they "…**hacked** the [Senate committee] investigators' computers…" But he avoids calling it "illegal", and instead labels it "an unlawful act" (101).

This is not the only time the CIA spied on American government organizations. "One of Tenet's successors, General Michael Hayden, a vocal proponent of the interrogation program, ordered an investigation of the inspector general's office in response to criticism that Helgerson was on a 'crusade' against the program." (83)

And this is not the only time that Michael Hayden is mentioned in McCain's book. In another place, McCain says that a major government delegation was sent to change his mind about the EIT (=torture). DCI Mike Hayden was a member of this delegation. McCain says that, "It was clear that Hayden wanted legal cover from Justice that would allow the continued use of the EITs, and, perhaps more important, that protected the CIA from legal jeopardy for their past use." (93)

Please note that Comey in his book described Michael Hayden's briefings as, "…a river of really great-sounding stuff that didn't make much sense once the briefing was over and you tried to piece together what you had just heard." (CO 83).

According to McCain, not only government organizations were targeted by the CIA. The news media (and the public at large) were targeted as well. McCain writes that "The CIA planted false stories in the press." (100)

Let's return to the quote from McCain's book with which we started this chapter:

"We briefly discussed Russia's interference in the election, the hacking of the Democratic National committee's and John Podesta's emails, which U.S. intelligence services concurred had been part of a Kremlin attempt to sabotage Hillary Clinton's chances and improve Trump's." (236)

Hayden says in his book, "Rejecting a fact-based intelligence assessment – not because of compelling contrarian data, but because it was inconsistent with a preexisting worldview or because it was politically inconvenient – is the stuff of ideological authoritarianism, not pragmatic democracy." (MH2 – 72)

We only need to go to George Tenet, Director of the CIA at the time of 9/11, who said in his book: "It would have been helpful to have clarified that the use of the words 'we judge' and 'we assess' meant **we were making analytical judgments, not stating facts**. As the founding father of CIA analysis, Sherman Kent, wrote in the *Foreign Service Journal* in 1969, 'Estimating is what you do when you do not know.'" (GT 332)

Question

According to McCain, the CIA "misled… Justice officials… and… senior White House officials, including President Bush and Vice President Cheney." McCain also says that the CIA produced "complete bullshit" in their reports about EITs (aka torture).

In addition, McCain says that CIA personnel engaged in "spying on [Senate] committee investigators" and "hacking" their computers in a clear "violation of the separation of powers".

Is it possible that this behavior continues even today during the Trump presidency?

McCain himself says, "There are senior officials in government who are trying to mitigate those effects" of the "…thoughtless America First ideology of his successor" (i.e. Trump) (192).

In another place McCain says, "Congress and, I hoped, the people the new President would appoint to senior national security positions would… **restrain the occupant** from impulsively reacting to world events" (235).

Question: Is it possible that the allegation of collusion between the Trump campaign and Russia, is the product of collusion between McCain and "…senior officials in government who are trying to mitigate…" the effect of Donald Trump's election to the presidency?

The Search for Bin Laden – US Case Study

Background

The attack of 9/11, masterminded by Osama bin Laden, took place during the first year of President G.W. Bush. Throughout the Bush presidency, for seven years, bin Laden was not found. It came to a point that President Bush declared in 2006 that "…the capture of bin Laden was no longer a 'top priority.'" (LP 289) bin Laden was only found and killed on May 11, 2011, less than 3 years into the Obama presidency. What made the difference?

The Obama Presidency

Upon inauguration, President Obama appointed Leon Panetta to be Director of the CIA. Panetta was not an "intelligence professional". He was not even an "intelligence consumer". He started in public life as a US representative in Congress from California.

According to Panetta, upon his appointment, President Obama gave him his priority.

"President Obama had ordered that capturing or killing bin Laden **was to be the most important objective** of America's intelligence services. I understood the order, and recognized that it came directly from my commander in chief. With the president's clear direction…" (291-292)

We should note two points:

First, Panetta looked upon President Obama as his "commander in chief". Unlike his predecessor Michael Hayden, who looked upon his president as a "consumer".

Second, Panetta says, "I understood the order". He didn't ask himself too many questions. This was the priority of his "commander in chief", and he moved to implement the order.

Panetta emphasizes that after he was already confirmed by the Senate as Director of CIA, he met the President who told him that he had "…meant what he said. He was emphatic and unambiguous: Killing or capturing Osama bin Laden was to be the single most important mission for the CIA. I understood and agreed." (290)

Panetta replaced Hayden as Director of CIA. Panetta tells his readers of his meeting with Hayden at Langley.

"Hayden had a stack of notes and methodically ticked off his points, emphasizing the quality of the CIA's staff and its need for independence." (205)

Panetta brings us the list of issues that Hayden presented – Iraq, "Israelis on Iran". Nothing on bin Laden. Instead, Hayden presented what was important for him – "…more needed to be done to truly make CIA the 'national human intelligence manager' the coordinator for all human spy operations across the government, as the post-9/11 reforms had dictated." In other words, Hayden was into big words. Hayden was interested in how the CIA is doing within the US. However, as for its missions - no bin Laden.

Hayden was interested also in other points – "…the president-elect shouldn't back off from the aggressive counter-terrorism policies of the Bush administration… to urge the president to protect the CIA's right to detain and interrogate terrorism suspects outside of the judicial 'read them their rights' context… he warned against suggesting that officers had ever engaged in torture…" (205) In other words, Hayden, again, was interested in how the CIA is perceived domestically. However, as for its mission – no bin Laden.

The bottom line: during the last years of the Bush presidency, the CIA was headed by the "professional intelligence officer" whose life was dedicated to Intelligence. At the time of the 9/11 attack he was heading the NSA, and due to mismanagement of how to deal with intercepts "in real time", he was not able to prevent the 9/11 attack, although the NSA possessed the information. With this track record, he moved to the CIA, and quite likely used his style of mismanagement to run the operation. The result was that bin Laden was not found. Obama replaced Hayden, and appointed Panetta to run the CIA – a man who was not entrenched in Intelligence, but who had common sense and knowledge in good management. Within less than 3 years bin Laden was found and killed.

Let's see how Panetta managed to succeed.

Director of CIA Panetta

Panetta says, "I asked a senior group of CIA officials who the person responsible for finding bin Laden was." (292)

Actually, Panetta wanted to find out what had happened at the CIA in the seven years after 9/11 in regard to finding bin Laden. It was a great first question to ask. After all, Panetta was not an "intelligence officer", but he knew something about management and responsibility.

What happened during the seven years that bin Laden was not found?

Panetta says, "The head of the National Clandestine Service **raised his hand. So did** the head of the Counterterrorism Center. **So did** the head of the center's Pakistan-Afghanistan Department. **So did a few others**." (292)

And if the reader does not realize what the situation is, Panetta tells us: "If I've learned **one lesson in management** over the past forty years, it's that **if everyone is in charge, nobody is**."

A revelation. For seven years after 9/11, the CIA suffered from lack of this "one lesson in management" – there is no way that several different departments will all be "in charge", without anyone coordinating what all of them are doing at the same time. The same situation that brought the FBI to not be able to connect the dots, the same situation that brought the NSA to not to realize what they are facing, due to not having the interceptors coordinating with the database, is the same situation that ruled at the CIA during the Bush presidency. For only one reason – there was no good manager at the top. There was only someone who could preach to others with great language and with great mantras, but with no substance to support it.

It is said that a president is successful only if the president knows how to choose good people to serve under him. President Obama knew how to choose the right person to be director of the CIA. Not an "intelligence professional". Not one who is entrenched in the Intelligence "culture", but who knows "one lesson in management".

Comparison: US – Israel

After Arab terrorists killed 11 Israeli athletes in the Olympic games in Munich, Germany, Prime Minister Golda Meir ordered the Mossad to make sure that every one of the terrorists would be killed. It took three years, and even with a few mistakes, but within three years all the terrorists who had been involved in the Munich attack were dead. Not only the terrorists who had been in Germany, but even the ones who had sent them. Three of them were in Beirut, Lebanon, so an Israeli military unit, teaming up with the Mossad, raided Beirut and killed the three of them in their places. Three years. Around the same time that it took the CIA headed by Panetta to find and kill bin Laden.

Protect and Serve

The motto of the police is "Protect and Serve". While "protect" relates to securing the community and preventing crime, "serve" relates to the investigation after a crime was committed.

Many police departments are strong on "serve" (finding the criminal and bringing the criminal to justice) but they are not as strong on "protect". The fact is that Giuliani as mayor of New York City, along with his police commissioner, proved many years ago that the police can successfully "protect" with the right strategy. With "zero tolerance" the police can reduce the rate of murder.

The same applies to Intelligence. With the right strategy (i.e. management), the CIA headed by Panetta was able to find bin Laden and bring him to justice in less than three years. The CIA and the other Intelligence organizations, NSA and FBI, can enhance the "protect" in the equation with the right strategy (i.e. management). After all they do collect the signs. They just don't connect the dots, due to lack of proper management.

In summary

We should admire Leon Panetta as the one who, with good management and common sense, managed to capture bin Laden, and brought him to the justice he deserved.   We should thank President Obama for choosing the right man for the job.

Ideological Gap Between
the Leader and Intelligence –
an Israeli Case Study

Background

For 29 years, from the time Israel became independent in 1948 until May 1977, the ruling party in Israel was the Labor party. Today this party would be classified as a "center-left" party. In 1977, the Likud party headed by Menachem Begin won the elections and established a new government with a different ideology than the one which had reigned supreme for 29 years.

One should note that in Israel, "right" and "left" are not determined by the economic view of society – capitalism vs. socialism. This might have been true many years ago, before the Six-Day War in 1967, when Israel extended its tiny borders to include the Golan Heights, Judea and Samaria (aka "The West Bank"), the Gaza Strip, and the Sinai desert. However, after the war, the definitions of "right" and "left" gradually changed to refer to the way the parties look upon the "territories", and especially the area which historically was the cradle of Jewish history – Judea and Samaria. This is to say that anyone who advocates that the area should be given to the Arabs to establish a new independent Arab country there (in addition to the other 22 already-existing Arab countries) would be defined as "left". On the other hand, anyone who acknowledges the strong historical attachment of the Jewish people to the area, as the cradle of Jewish history and culture, and who does not give up on Jewish presence in the area, would be considered "right".

In the 29 years of Labor government, most of the high-ranking officers of the Israeli military were left-leaning, if not entrenched completely in the leftist ideology. For them, the area is not "Judea and Samaria" but the

"West Bank", and they do not consider the area to have been "liberated" during the war, but "conquered".

In 1977, Menachem Begin, a right-wing prime minister, faced a military headed by leftist high-ranking military officers. Let's see what happened. At this point, we will see the picture as it comes across from a book published by the Chief of Military Intelligence at the time of transition from Labor to Likud, and during the time Israel negotiated peace with Egypt.

Who is Shlomo Gazit?

Shlomo Gazit, Chief of Military Intelligence from 1974 to 1979, published his book (in Hebrew) "At Key Points of Time" in 2016, when Gazit was 90 years old, many years after the events that he is reporting. [It would be more accurate to translate the title as "At Decisive Junctions", but the above-mentioned title is the translation used in the book.]

Gazit defines himself clearly by saying: "I have no ideological attachment to Judea and Samaria. Anyone who has such an attachment, and it determines his world view, has no mutual basis for a discussion with me." (289) So, we know where he stands.

As a matter of fact, while the Six-Day War was still raging, Gazit put out a paper with his recommendation of what to do with the "conquered" ("liberated") area – to allow the Arabs to establish an independent country there.

It is interesting to follow more of Gazit's way of thinking. "**I am pessimistic** about Israel's ability to be the one to determine the wheels/process of history. The smaller the country is, the fewer opportunities and abilities it has for doing so." (253) He also says, "…**time is not in our favor**. Today we can still reach an agreement based upon a strong Israel; tomorrow this might be closed to us. An agreement that is made from a position of weakness, of total coercion – might bring the end of the Third House." (335)

[Note: "The Third House" represents the third period in Jewish history of Jewish self-rule in the land of Israel. The first two "houses" were the First and Second Temples in ancient times.]

In 1978, when talking with the Foreign Minister at the time, Moshe Dayan, he said: "…I want to emphasize that the outside world is 'fed up' with the conflict, and if we wouldn't succeed in solving it ourselves, they might enforce an arrangement and a solution that will quite likely be less comfortable for us." (291)

His worldview also influenced his opinion on how to deal with the Arab-Israeli conflict: "This was not the only time when I was in conflict with my colleagues in the military and security establishment. They did not want to miss the opportunity to eliminate the people who were at the top of the Palestinian diplomatic and operational establishment." (305)

And he explains his approach: "I disagreed with them **on the level of principle** – my approach was that Israel as a country is not free to behave and act as if it was a partisan organization, free of legal and moral considerations." (305-306)

However, realizing that he cannot advocate his true opinions – i.e. complete detachment from the area with its historical and religious significance – he continues, "Nevertheless, I knew that in the practical discussion I should present **only professional counter-considerations**." (306) In other words, he needed to conceal his true opinions.

Gazit's relationship with Prime Minister Begin

Gazit says that, "In the two years that I served as MI Chief under Menachem Begin's government, the relationships and contacts between me as MI Chief and the Prime Minister were **civil**, but **far from being warm**." (272)

One can imagine why. After all, a prime minister who is so emotionally connected to Judea and Samaria, as it is the "Promised Land" for him, has to deal with a high-ranking officer who says, "Anyone who has such an attachment, and it determines his world view, has no mutual basis for a discussion with me." (289)

But Gazit is not going to bring us this apparent reason. As he said, he prefers to bring the reader "professional reasons" – "**I don't know** if it was a result of private history between us or because of the personal style of the Prime Minister's work. Begin didn't understand what is Intelligence and

how the government can and should be helped by the Intelligence work."
(272)

Note his use of "I don't know" in an "open statement". There is no way a person can legitimately say "I don't know" in an "open statement". If you don't know something, you wouldn't report it. But if you know that you don't know, you produce a signal of "concealing information".

Mr. Begin, not trusting the "national assessor", moved to isolate the Military Intelligence from his negotiations with Egypt. Instead, he used the Mossad, the organization that is directly under him. And the Mossad arranged a meeting in Morocco for the Foreign Minister Moshe Dayan and the advisor to President Sadat of Egypt. When Sadat announced that he is prepared to come to Israel and to talk to the Knesset (Parliament) the Military Intelligence was "in the dark" as to the events behind the scene.

As a result, the Military Intelligence produced an "assessment" that "…Egypt was trying to drive a wedge into the relationship between the US and Israel, and Cairo has no way to achieve it but with a demonstration of positive and moderate diplomatic intentions." (267) He explains himself by saying, "…we were not ready to recognize that what seems impossible is possible." (274)

In fact, four days before Sadat arrived in Jerusalem, the Chief of Staff at the time was interviewed and said that "…according to his assessment, Sadat does not intend to come to Israel and to make a true peace with us, and that his declaration is only an Egyptian exercise to defraud us." (275)

Gazit ends this colossal failure of "assessment" by saying: "…it was a classic case of Intelligence that is an expert to collect and research information **about the other side**, while it doesn't know much, and is even prevented from researching and looking for insights, in regard to the policy of its own leaders and country." (272)

In other words, Gazit didn't consider that Begin did not feel any attachment to the Sinai desert, unlike his attachment to Judea and Samaria. Gazit simply didn't understand the Prime Minister.

Gazit says - "Naturally, the Security issue was in the center of the negotiations, and because of that **it is strange** that the Prime Minister didn't approach the Intelligence even once. **We were not asked questions, we**

were not asked to give assessments, and of course we were not included in the internal discussions of the Israeli negotiators." (283)

One point to consider: there is a possibility that in 1971, Sadat might have been willing to conduct negotiations with Israel regarding Sinai. The Prime Minister at the time, consulting her military advisers, concluded that Sadat was "bluffing". The fact that she was too close to the "national assessor" – the Chief of Military Intelligence – prevented her from realizing that "…what seems impossible is possible." (274)

Historians today credit Begin's successful achievement of peace with Egypt to the fact that he isolated the military from any involvement in the negotiations.

The Military Intelligence and the Leader

This is a chapter in the book "Covert Warriors, The Israeli Intelligence – An Insight from Inside" by Ephraim Lapid, a former high-ranking officer in the Military Intelligence.

"…the dream of every Chief of Military Intelligence is that since he is responsible for the national intelligence assessment, his assessments and analyses will be accepted by the leader. But the Chief of Intelligence should not be offended if the leader rejects his assessment due to his own considerations. On the other hand, the leader should understand that once he accepts the assessment of the Chief of Intelligence, it becomes his own assessment as well." (362)

Lapid also says, "…the leaders listened to the Chiefs of Military Intelligence over the years, since they are 'the national assessor', but the significant contribution of the Intelligence to the strategic decisions **was much smaller than the feeling of importance attributed to this status.**" (363)

Ofer Shelah, a member of the Knesset (Parliament) Committee on Defense and Foreign Affairs published his book – "Dare to Win". In his book, he says,

"Even in conditions in which the Intelligence is at its best, it will always be in a **supporting role** and not a decisive one, and there must always be **the capability to win even without it.**" (133) He also says, "The IDF must therefore instill in its commanders that the Intelligence is an excellent supporting tool, but only supporting; the technology is a force multiplier, but not the force itself." (133)

A Lesson for the US

Since Gazit talks in a way that is almost identical to Michael Hayden – being pessimistic, with a perception as if time is not in our favor – one should wonder if the US needs to isolate the entire intelligence infrastructure (also known as "the Intelligence Community") from the process of negotiations with other countries (for example, North Korea) to reach better results. No different from this Israeli case study.

What is "Intelligence"? –
Another Israeli Case Study

Background information

In the mid-seventies, Iraq and France signed an agreement that France would build a nuclear reactor in Iraq.   The construction was due to be completed by the end of 1980, but it was delayed until towards the end of 1981.

Note: Iraq participated in the Arab effort against Israel in 1948 (Israel's War of Independence), and at the end of the war all of the Arab countries signed a ceasefire agreement with Israel, **except** Iraq. In other words, Iraq has remained during all these years in a state of war with Israel. In fact, even during the Six-Day War (1967) and in the Yom Kippur War (1973), Iraqi military moved into Syria to participate in the war. Moreover, Saddam Hussein periodically threatened Israel. And indeed, during the first Gulf War in 1991, Iraq launched 39 Scud missiles at Israel.

During the construction of the nuclear reactor in Iraq, information was revealed that Iraq is planning to use the reactor to produce enough material for military purposes.

During the years 1979-1981 there were several "mysterious" explosions in the ships that were supposed to deliver parts of the reactor to Iraq. But this did not prevent the construction from going on.

Till this point, we are dealing with the effort of collecting the information about the Iraqi nuclear program, and the covert operations to prevent it from being completed.

Since the efforts to prevent the construction were not successful, the Mossad and the Military Intelligence together established "…a work group… that was meant to examine all the available information from various sources, and to assess it, with operational implications." (Lapid 305)

What to do with the Iraqi reactor?

In May 1977 there was a change of government in Israel. During the transition the Iraqi reactor was discussed (304).

The Holocaust Syndrome

Lapid in his book describes Prime Minister Menachem Begin as being influenced by the fact that "…his parents, brothers and sisters were murdered in the Holocaust…" and "he therefore considered the Iraqi reactor to be a threat in the magnitude of a second Holocaust to the Jewish people." (304)

Deputy Chief of the Mossad Nachik Navoth mentions "the Holocaust Syndrome" extensively in his book – "Since the Second World War, Israel could not free itself of the Holocaust Syndrome… the doubt continues even today." (203) He also says that "After more than 60 years (about three generations in historical terms) it is apparent that the Jewish people is not yet free of the most terrible catastrophe that was ever perpetrated on nations by others, since the time that the Almighty created the world, and man created Satan." (223) He goes on to say that "maybe it is correct to say that the source of the creative power that brings about wondrous things, in spite of the Holocaust and the annihilation of whole parts of the nation, is the desire and the expressions of power that come to guarantee that there will not be another Holocaust." (229)

Navoth also brings an example – "in a meeting with the political level in Israel, Kissinger used images from the Holocaust to evoke the primal fear of the leadership for another terrible catastrophe, and to bring Israel to political concessions to the US. In reality, as observers said at the time, this approach brought Israel to harden its positions…" (81-82)

In other words, the attitude of seeing Israel as the "bully" of the Middle East is actually an incorrect reading of the map. Israel is a very tiny country, with a width of 9 miles from the Mediterranean Sea to its eastern pre-1967 border. Even after 1967, with the added area of Judea and Samaria (aka "the West Bank") the width of Israel from the sea to the Jordan River is approximately 40 miles. This geographical fact mandates a very different approach to "risk management". After all, as one Iranian general once said, his country can tolerate a nuclear attack, as they have a large area and 80 million people, so they can lose even 50 million; but Israel is a "one-bomb country," and he was right. The margin of error for Israel is absolute zero.

This is the reason that the first Prime Minister of Israel, David Ben-Gurion, proceeded to develop the nuclear option. All the efforts of the US to prevent it, couldn't stop him. The nuclear option was registered in his mind as "preventing another Holocaust".

Back to the Iraqi reactor

Former Chief of Intelligence Aharon Yariv was appointed to head a committee to consider all options regarding the Iraqi reactor. The committee brought a report in March 1980 saying that, "…it is better to attack the reactor before it is activated, but it is recommended not to do it at the current time 'in order to involve others in the early prevention activities.' The report warned that attacking the reactor after it is activated might cause radioactive pollution in Iraq…" (Lapid 306)

Till this point the report stated facts – radioactive pollution is very likely expected when a nuclear reactor is damaged – as in Chernobyl and Japan.

The report continued that the attack, "…would greatly damage Israel's international position, disrupt the peace process, and unite the Arab and Moslem world to the point of a war on Israel with Soviet backing." (306) These are not "facts", but predictions. In other words, they are an "assessment".

In October 1980, in a meeting of the Ministerial Committee for Defense, the Iraqi reactor was on the table. The Chiefs of Intelligence – both the Mossad and the Military Intelligence – were against a military operation. The Chief of Staff supported it.

Lapid says that even within both organizations there was an internal dispute as to whether or not to destroy the reactor in a military operation. "The opposition of the Chief of Military Intelligence was very strong. He presented a document to the Prime Minister, the Foreign Minister, and the Chief of Staff, in which he listed all his reservations regarding the suggested operation, and pointed out a professional opinion that Iraq would not be able to produce a nuclear bomb before the beginning of the nineties. He also raised his concerns about a sharp American reaction and Arab response." (306-307)

The reservations of the Chief of Military Intelligence brought that Chief of Staff to decide to bypass him. "He ordered the activation of collection measures, not via the Chief of MI but directly with the Chief of the Collection Branch, Col. Lapid [the author of the book]." (308)

Israel bombed the reactor in June 1981 and demolished it. "The Arab world did not react to the attack, and the reactions in the international arena were few and relatively mild." (309)

Years later, the Chiefs of Intelligence admitted they were wrong. The Chief of the Mossad said, "I was not right – Begin was right. The attack on the reactor did not bring the results that we had assumed." (310). The Chief of Military Intelligence said: "I admit that I was proven wrong in everything regarding to the political damage that I expected from the US." Even Yariv, who had initially predicted dire consequences, stated, "Our negative positions were not proved." (310)

The NTSB in the US, the organization that investigates aircraft accidents, treats "close calls" as **an actual accident**. When two aircraft come into dangerous proximity to each other, the NTSB moves in to investigate what caused this "close call", and to recommend how to prevent such "close calls" from happening again.

When Chiefs of Intelligence are wrong in their "assessment" they create a "close call". It calls for and NTSB investigation.

Iran and the Bomb

Realizing the difference between the size of the US and the size of Israel, one can understand now why the present Prime Minister of Israel, Benjamin Netanyahu, functions with one issue constantly on his mind – the Iranian race to achieve the nuclear bomb.

No agreement between President Obama and Iran could pacify Netanyahu. For Netanyahu it has not been an issue of diplomacy. It is an issue of "preventing another Holocaust".

The Syrian Nuclear Reactor

This issue was dealt earlier in the book. The difference between the US, with a wide margin of error, and Israel, with a zero margin of error, comes across clearly in the way the two countries dealt with the issue.

When Director of CIA Michael Hayden talked with President G.W. Bush about it, it was a discussion about "confidence" as expressed in the intelligence assessments – "high", "medium", or "low". For Israel, it was not an issue of "confidence". It was an issue of "preventing another Holocaust". The Prime Minister at the time, Ehud Olmert, wanted the US to bomb the reactor, but once President Bush declined to do so, due to Hayden's "low confidence" that it is "a weapon system", the Prime Minister had no choice but to bomb it.

UK and Israel

The UK Chief of MI6 was once interviewed in the newspaper in Israel. He said openly that there are times in which the British Intelligence service does not share information with the Israeli Intelligence. He said that if they spot a suspect of terrorism, they start a surveillance of that suspect.

As a matter of fact, the Chief of the MI5 reported to the Parliament that at one point of time, they conducted fifteen thousand investigations of people suspected of terrorism.

The Chief of the MI6 said to the Israeli newspaper – The Israelis function with a different set of rules. There will be a time when instead of surveillance they will simply kill him. And he added, we don't feel like sharing the information due to concern that by sharing it, we would actually kill the suspect.

What is "assessment"?

An "assessment" is not mathematics – an exact science. It is based upon the worldview of the one who created the "assessment". It is a very subjective area, unlike reports of events, which are "facts".

The ability of the "intelligence practitioner" to "assess" is not different from the leader's ability to "assess". Moreover, the ability of the Chief of Military Intelligence to "assess" is no different from the ability of any taxi driver or barber to "assess". Everyone in Israel knows that the "practitioners" of these two professions always have an opinion on what is going on in the country. And in many times they are correct.

When the Chief of Military Intelligence brought an "assessment" that the Iraqis would not be able to produce a nuclear bomb before the nineties, he didn't say much. As a bureaucrat, as long as the problem is delayed, it is ok with him. To come later and admit that he was wrong, with a mistake of such a magnitude, does not relieve him from the huge responsibility that he took upon himself. Securing the country is not an ego play.

A former Chief of the Mossad, Meir Amit, said in his book, "It is apparent that even people with analysis capability can be mistaken with **very bitter mistakes**." (105) In order to prevent it, Amit says, "I also emphasized to be careful **not to merge raw material and facts with a concluding assessment**." (124)

Amit also talked about "…uncontrolled desires for power, a lack of boundaries between beliefs and political views, **and between facts and assessments**, and readiness to take all measures to achieve goals." (101)

Former Director of the CIA George Tenet said in his book, "It would have been helpful to have clarified that the use of the words 'we judge' and 'we assess' meant **we were making analytical judgments, not stating facts**." (GT 332)

Tenet continues: "As the founding father of CIA analysis, Sherman Kent, wrote in the *Foreign Service Journal* in 1969, 'Estimating is what you do when you do not know.'" (GT 332)

Another former Chief of the Mossad, Zvi Zamir, said in his book regarding the assessment of the Chief of Military Intelligence: "…It is true that the clearer and sharper the assessment is, if it is a mistake then it is a clear and sharp mistake…" (123) However, if the Chief of Military Intelligence makes a mistake, "…it is not a risk that the Chief of Intelligence takes upon himself, **but a risk to the State of Israel**." (124)

Summary

The Chief of Military Intelligence at the time of the discussions about the Iraqi reactor was wrong. It was not the only time he was wrong. He was wrong in every "assessment" he produced. He didn't even mind to go on TV and announce his "assessment", only to find out later on that he was wrong. But the fact that he was wrong didn't prevent him from going on and on and producing one wrong "assessment" after another.

It comes to a point today, that when the Military Intelligence produces an "assessment", I know that I need to turn it around by 180 degrees to know what will happen. When the rebellion against Assad started in Syria, the Chief of Military Intelligence appeared on TV and "assessed" that Assad will be out of power within a month. So I knew he would remain in power for ever.

There is one thing for which I commend the Israeli Military Intelligence. They are consistent. This enables the average person to really know what will happen.

The Middle East – Facts and Assessment

The book *Prisoners of Geography*[12] by Tim Marshall has some interesting insights.

Facts

"The legacy of European colonialism left the Arabs grouped into nation states." (138)   The borders of Lebanon, Syria, and Iraq were determined in 1916 by an agreement between the British and the French, known as "The Sykes-Picot" agreement. Jordan was created artificially by the British later, after installing a Hashemite "king" over the area east of the Jordan River. In Marshall's words, "In the Middle East, power does indeed flow from the barrel of a gun" (165), and "Sykes-Picot is breaking; putting it back together, even in a different shape, will be a long and bloody affair." (167)

However, the idea of a "nation" is foreign to the Arab world. It is an area where the family and the tribe are dominant. The loyalty of the individual is not to the artificial "nation", but to the blood relationship structure – family, extended family, and even a tribe.

Please note that this phenomenon is true not only of the Arab world. One only needs to read the book "Three Cups of Tea"[13] about Pakistan and Afghanistan to realize that neither of these is actually a country or a nation. Each "country" consists of several tribes, and the "nation" is actually dominated by the largest tribe, while the other tribes are relegated to the dust bin of history.

Similarly, Syria is not one country. The bloodshed that has been going on there for several years now only illustrates this fact. The same applies to Iraq, that is also not one country. Iraq actually consists of three distinct ethnic areas. The same applies to Libya.

Let's discuss the Arab areas that are close to Israel – the Gaza Strip, and Judea and Samaria (aka the "West Bank").

The so-called "West Bank" is an area which is around 75 miles north to south and 30 miles east to west. In total, a little bit over 2,000 square miles. Although Marshall says that "in this century, however, there is a fierce sense of nationhood among the Palestinians" (154), let's see what really goes on in the area. You will see very quickly that this is Marshall's only wrong statement in the section of his book about the Middle East.

The "Palestinian Authority" was established in 1993 by the agreement between the Israeli Labor government headed by Rabin and Peres with the PLO headed by Arafat. This "authority" established its center in Ramallah, a city north of Jerusalem.

In this area there are very few large cities – from north to south are Jenin, Nablus, Ramallah, Jerusalem, Bethlehem and Hebron. To the west of Nablus there are two smaller cities, Tul Karem and Qalqilya.

In fact it is quite doubtful if the "authority" is ruling these cities. Although there is a nominal governor appointed by the "authority" to run each city, in actuality there are "warlords" that control their immediate area. There were times in which the nominal governor wanted to impose his will, only to be rejected by the local militias that even killed the official militia that came to impose the governor's will.

The same applies to the Gaza Strip. People think that the Hamas rules the area. However, this is true only to a certain degree. The fact is that there are areas that no Hamas militia will enter, as the local warlord will use its firepower to eject them.

And the same situation applies within Israel, in the Arab villages. When there are local elections as mandated by law, the village will vote according to families/tribes, and the largest one will take over the city, and disregard the smaller tribe.

This is a fact of life in the Arab world, and in other areas where the Moslem religion is dominant, for example – Somalia. Somalia is defined in the west as a "failed state". The fact is that all over the Middle East there are "failed states" everywhere.

The only exception to this point is Saudi Arabia. This is only country in the world that is named after one person – ibn Saud, who managed to defeat all his opponents and to take over the area in the 1920s. In order to establish his kingdom, ibn Saud, with his infinite wisdom, and Arab tradition, married a daughter of each tribal head in the area, and had children with each wife. This brought all the tribes in the area to have "stocks" in the kingdom. In other words, Saudi Arabia is a blood-relationship society. This is the reason that Saudi Arabia has thousands of "princes". It is also the reason that the so-called "Arab spring" skipped Saudi Arabia. Why would anyone fight against his own family? Why would anyone fight his own relatives, even if they are distant relatives?

Summary

The idea of "nationhood" is not accepted anywhere in the Middle East and even beyond, in some other Moslem countries. The bottom line: the Arabs residing in the areas labeled as "the Gaza Strip" and "the West Bank" will not aspire to establish a country. Their loyalty is to their immediate families and tribes. They have no use for a structure called "state" or "nation".

Assessment

When the outside world talks about a "Palestinian" state, the outside world uses it own lenses to look at the situation. To advocate establishing a "Palestinian" state is an exercise in futility. Albert Einstein said once – to try more than once to do the same thing and to expect different results is "insanity". Or, in other words, "stupidity".

Israel

The irony is that three of the four countries surrounding Israel – Lebanon, Syria, and Jordan – are "leftovers" of the colonial era. (Egypt is an exception.) The only country that is not "colonialist" is Israel. The country is in an area that was inhabited by the Jews thousands of years ago, and they returned to their homeland when the opportunity allowed it. And in fact, there was a Jewish presence throughout the centuries in the land, but as a minority.

One only needs to read the books written by various Americans who visited the Holy Land – e.g., US President Ulysses Grant[14] and William Seward, President Lincoln's Secretary of State[15], who both visited the Holy Land in the late 19th century, on two different occasions. They observed the desolation, and commented that the area is waiting for the Jews to return to cultivate the land. Mark Twain visited the land before them, in 1869, and described his identical impressions in his book "Innocents Abroad".

It is not easy to accept that what has been happening in the last 140 years is in fact "the return of the exiles". It is contradictory to every historical rule. No nation that lost its independence ever returned to its full rights after such a long time. No language that was extinct as a spoken language, as Hebrew was, ever returned to be a living language spoken by children and adults alike.

It is no wonder that 50% of all UN decisions are against Israel. Israelis know it and dismiss it with the saying, "That's life". In Hebrew, the acronym for the UN is pronounced "Oom". Ben-Gurion is famous for referring to it as "Oom-Shmoom".

When Joshua entered the land, it took around 500 years from the time of Joshua till the first united kingdom of David. We are now 140 years since the beginning of the modern immigration (not including the many smaller immigrations before that) of Jews returning to the land. If it took 500 years from Joshua to David, we can wait another 350 years to establish what King David did.

The funny point is that the outside world does not recognize this "assessment". The Israeli leadership of today, regardless of party, does not recognize it either. They do not talk in terms of "rights" to the land. They talk in terms of "security". The Arabs talk in terms of "rights", and the outside world is very impressed by it. They go along and they believe that at some time in the future there will be a "Palestinian" state. After all, both the outside world and the Israeli leadership do not realize that Israel is in a unique historical process.

What do the Arabs want?

One only needs to listen to what they say to know what they really want. They don't talk about "independence". They don't talk about having a "country". They only say that they want "Palestine". In other words, they don't want Israel to exist. That is the reason for their existence. And Marshall in his book is right. If Israel would not exist, the other Arabs countries would move to divide the area between them. After all, that's what they did after 1948.

A "Palestinian" state is not in the cards. In other words – "it is not meant to be". Not because of Israel. It is not meant to be because the Arabs do not really want a country. What a wonderful world!!!

One last point: The above description is not a "fact". It is an "assessment". In Hayden's language it is labeled as a "fact-based assessment".

Scientific Content Analysis (SCAN) – Basic Concepts

The SCAN technique is the result of many years of research into verbal communication, and the linguistic behavior used by people when talking or writing. SCAN analyzes a text or statement strictly according to the words used. SCAN has a long track record of successful results in law enforcement investigations, and is currently being used in many police departments and other government agencies in many countries.

The basic concept of the SCAN technique is that no human being can say everything that is in his/her mind. Before a person can write or talk, the person needs to decide if the information (or opinion) present in mind at that specific moment is important enough to transmit to the listener or reader. Or maybe it is not important enough, and therefore the person will not transmit it. This is "the editing process" which is the engine behind every statement. As the speaker or writer goes through this process, so the listener or reader can step into the person's shoes, and reach conclusions about what was present in the person's mind at the time that the text was delivered.

The editing process does not end in choosing which information is important enough to enter the statement. After this stage the person needs to move into another phase, still before delivery, and this is phrasing the information. Here the person needs to decide how to lay out the story, how to build the sentence (syntax), in what order to write the sentence, and which words to use to describe the event or the information.

All these points are taking place in the person's mind at a very fast speed, a speed that is measured in milliseconds. This fast speed might even prevent the person later on from knowing why he/she chose this particular way to describe the event. There are times in which the **statement** itself gives the answer while the **person** cannot do so.

If one were to ask the person, "why did you choose this way to write the sentence?" or, "why did you choose this word and not another word?" in most cases the person would say, "Just because," or, "I don't know." However, when the analyst brings the person the reason for the language in the story, the person is able to confirm if the explanation is the right one. The reason behind the choice of information, and its wording and phrasing, are present in the person's mind; however, this information is "background information" or "passive information." It is not present in the front of memory, or in other words, "active information."

This above-mentioned description of what is going on in the person's mind brings us to an important and basic rule in SCAN: "The Subject is Dead. The Statement is Alive."

People who are not familiar with the SCAN technique ask me, "Don't you need to know who is the person giving the information – their personality, behavior, and/or facial expressions during the delivery of the text?" The answer is no. The analysis does not deal with **people** but with **the statement**.

Here we can move to another basic concept, and this is the "copyright" the person has on the text. This means that the analyst cannot add to or subtract from anything in the text, either from outside sources, or even from logic. In front of the analyst there should be only the text. In a way, the text of every statement is "sacred." The analyst cannot change it, nor can the person who delivered the text. The words have a life of their own. "The Subject is Dead. The Statement is Alive."

In order to be analyzed with SCAN, a statement must be an "open statement". This refers to information that a person gives, without being guided by any questions of the listener to lead the story in a certain direction. The only question the listener is allowed to ask is, "What happened?"

The memoirs analyzed in this book fit the requirement of being an "open statement", as the listener or reader did not lead the statement at the time of delivery.

The language used in an open statement is a "linguistic mirror" of reality. In other words, if we compare the language to the lens of a camera that takes a picture of reality, then the language of the text is the linguistic lens: how the person giving the statement perceives reality.

Another major concept of SCAN is the "unity" of the text, and the "unity" of the analysis. By this I mean that the analyst must maintain **consistency**. The analyst cannot explain one word in a certain way in one place, and give a different explanation of that same word in another place in the text. As the text is "sacred," so should be the analysis: unity for the text, and unity for the analysis.

This means that if one place in the statement contradicts the analyst's explanation, the explanation is wrong, and there is a need to either search for another explanation, or to fine-tune the original one. It is like a crossword or a sudoku puzzle. As the numbers in the sudoku puzzle need to fit up and down, left to right, and within the section, so it is with the analysis of the text. If a person finds a contradiction in their solution of a sudoku puzzle, the person needs to know that the solution is mistaken. The same applies in the analysis of a text. Although it involves words and not numbers, sentences and not squares, the concept is the same.

Change of Language

The Human Brain

It is very easy to underestimate the power of the human brain. It was once mentioned in the newspaper that scientists took several supercomputers and put them together, and they succeeded in simulating the brain of a cat. To emphasize it – the brain of one cat equals the power of several supercomputers combined together.

In the same piece of news it was stated that scientists do not see any time in the future to be able to simulate the power of a human brain. The reason is that there are not enough supercomputers on this globe, to put all of them together to be able to simulate the power of one human brain.

Fifty percent of the human brain is devoted to accommodating the ability to communicate. A well-known linguist in the US, Steven Pinker, says in his book "The Language Instinct" that there is enough evidence to conclude that grammar is found on the DNA. There is a gene that controls grammar. And if this gene is faulty, that person would never be able to communicate properly. The book gives the example of three generations of one family in the UK who couldn't talk English properly due to the fact that they inherited a faulty gene.

The human baby does not need to study grammar. The only thing the baby needs to learn is the sounds of the language. (For example, English has 26 letters but 40 distinct sounds.) During the second year, the baby puts the sounds together into words. By age 3 the baby talks in grammatically correct sentences, without anyone teaching the baby proper grammar.

The Brain and the "Open Statement"

Realizing the speed at which the brain is functioning to accommodate communication, we can now come to see the connection between the physiology of the brain and the delivery of information in an "open statement" (i.e. a statement given in reply to an open question such as "what happened?" with no other input by the interviewer).

When a person begins to give an "open statement", the person needs to go through two stages. In the first stage, the person needs to decide what is important, and what is not. Once the person decides that the information is important enough to enter the statement, the person would deliver that information, either by writing or by speaking.

This is the "editing process", which is an innocent process. Everyone does it upon giving an "open statement" (=free flow). This is a very quick process – so much so, that at the end of delivering the statement, the person will not be able to trace his/her own steps as to why they wrote something.

Upon deciding that something is important enough to enter the statement, the person needs to go through another stage before the information reaches the paper and/or the mouth. The person needs to phrase the information – to take something from memory and to transfer it into words. This is also a very quick process, and in this case as well, the person would not be able to explain, even to himself/herself, why they chose a certain way to phrase a sentence, and why they chose a certain word to describe something. In most cases, if the person would be asked after delivering the statement, why did you change your language (i.e. using two different words to refer to the same person or object) from point A in the statement, to point B, in almost all cases the person would say either "I don't know", or "I was told in school not be redundant." However, if the SCAN analyst would suggest to the person a reason for the change of language, based upon the content of the text, and mainly the location where the change of language took place, the person would be able to relate to what the SCAN analyst was saying and confirm the conclusion. (I do this all the time with the statements of students in my classes, and the students think I am a mind-reader.)

The Human Brain and Emotions

Again, going back to the human brain, it is important to know that the location where a person stores memory for long term is the center of emotions in the brain. This is the reason that people say that if a person wants to remember something for a long time, that person should attach an emotion to the information, and that would guarantee that the person would remember it forever.

Take for example the day of 9/11. No matter where the person was, even not in the US, it is quite likely that the person would be able to tell us what happened in his day from the time he got up till the time he went to sleep. Very accurately, and to the tiniest details.

In fact, we find out that most changes in language are due to emotions. People transmit emotions by changing their language. For example, "I **started** the laundry," and later on, "I **began** watching TV." The emotions are different during these two events.

Changes of language and detecting deception

In view of the high speed at which the brain functions, and knowing that most changes in language are due to emotions, we can now see how changes of language are the most accurate way to determine truth and/or deception.

The idea is that we expect a person to maintain consistency in his/her language. This means that people do not change language for no reason. In other words, we rule out the option of synonyms. If a person changes language, something in the past must have been different, before the language would change in the present. And as discussed, most changes of language are due to emotions.

For example, I had a student who changed his language while writing a statement about the Saturday before he came to the class. In the statement he said that he was going out on his motorbike to enjoy his time on the snow. However, throughout the statement he changed his language in the following way – three times he referred to the "motorbike", twice he called it "sled", once more he called it "motorbike", and then back to "sled".

I asked him my routine two questions: Did you know at the time of the writing that you changed your language? He answered in the negative. My second question was: do you know now (the time of discussion) why you changed your language? Again he answered in the negative.

I told him: I will tell you why you changed your language. While you were out on your "motorbike", the engine failed (so it turned into a sled = no engine), and you tried to fix it, and you believed that you fixed it (=back to "motorbike"). You went back on the "motorbike", only to find out that you still hadn't fixed it (=back to "sled").

He asked me, how did you know all of that? And I said, "I must have been there."

The main point is that at the time of writing the statement, the information was in his mind. However, later on, when we talked about his statement, the event was not there anymore, and he couldn't relate to it.

Please note that the problem with the engine was not mentioned anywhere in the **content** of the statement. It only entered the **language** of the statement.

In summary

There are two channels of communication. The first channel is the content – the sequence of events. The second channel is the language being used to describe the sequence of events.

We expect **consistency** between the language and the content. When a change of language is justified by the sequence of events, as it is described in the statement, then the conclusion is that the person is likely to be truthful. However, if we encounter **inconsistency** – a change of language that is not justified by the sequence of events – the conclusion is that the person is likely to be deceptive.

Change of language is the strongest signal by language to determine if a person is truthful or not. It has been found to be a reliable indicator by many investigators in many police and security organizations.

"I don't know / I don't remember" – Background Information

When we come to analyze a statement, whether of a witness or a suspect, we need to know whether the answer was given to a specific question, or if it is an answer to an "open question," making the answer an "open statement." For example, if we ask a person, "Do you know if such-and-such took place?" and the person answers, "I don't know," this might be a legitimate answer. When we direct the person's attention to a particular point and the person says, "I don't know" (or "I don't remember") such an answer cannot bring us to conclude anything.

However, when we deal with an "open statement," for example, when we ask a person to tell us "what happened [on a particular day]," then in the person's mind "the editing process" starts to determine what should be included in the "open statement" and what should not be included. The person needs to bring the event to the front of his mind and to ask one question all the time: "Is it important enough for me to include in my answer?" If the person answers in the affirmative, the person includes it in the open statement. However, if the person answers in the negative, the person does not include it in the open statement.

We should note two major points in regard to this "editing process." One, it is a very innocent process. The truthful person does it as well. Two, it is **a very quick** process in the person's mind, to the point that after giving the statement, if the person is asked about a certain point in the text, the person is not able to reconstruct the thoughts that were present in his/her mind at the time of delivering the statement. This quick pace of the mind brings the feeling that the process is subconscious, but actually it is not subconscious. If the SCAN analyst would bring the information derived from the text to the knowledge of the person, the person would confirm it.

The "editing process" means that any information a person includes in an "open statement" is labeled "important enough to enter the statement." This also means that the sentence "I don't know" or "I don't remember" is **illegitimate** when it is found in an "open statement." If a person does not know something, the person does not include it in an "open statement." However, if a person knows that he/she doesn't know, it should be considered a signal of concealing information.

"Concealing information" is not the same as deception. Both a truthful and deceptive person will conceal information. The information is simply something that the person didn't want us to know.

Sources

Intelligence Chiefs

JC   James R. Clapper with Trey Brown *Facts and Fears, Hard Truths from Life in Intelligence* (New York, Viking, 2018)

MH1   Michael V. Hayden, Playing to the Edge, American Intelligence in the Age of Terror, (New York, Penguin Press, 2016)

MH2   Michael V. Hayden, The Assault on Intelligence, American National Security in an Age of Lies, (New York, Penguin Press, 2018)

JB   Nomination of John O. Brennan to be Director of CIA, Hearing before the Select Committee on Intelligence of the US Senate, 2013

RH   Richard Helmes, A Look Over my Shoulder, A Life in the Central Intelligence Agency,(New York, Ballantine Books, 2003)

GT   George Tenet, *At the Center of the Storm, My Years at the CIA,* (New York, Harper Collins Publishers, 2007)

LP   Leon Panetta, *Worthy Fights,* (New York, Penguin Press, 2014)

CO   James Comey, A Higher Loyalty: Truth, Lies, and Leadership, (Flatiron Books, 2018)

Other books in English

The 9/11 Commission Report, Final Report of the National Commission on Terrorist Attacks upon the United States

Intelligence Matters, The CIA, the FBI, Saudi Arabia, and the Failure of America's War on Terror, Random House, New York

The NSA Report, Liberty and Security in a Changing World, The President's Review Group on Intelligence and Communications technologies, Princeton University Press, 2014

John McCain and Mark Salter, The Restless Wave, Good Times, Just Causes, Great Fights, and Other Appreciations, (New York, Simon & Schuster, 2018)

Hillary Clinton, *What happened*, (New York, Simon & Schuster, 2017)

The Snowden Files: The Inside story of the Word's Most Wanted Man", (Random House, 2016)

Zbigniew Brzeszinski, Power and Principle, Memoirs of the National Security Adviser 1977-1981, (Farrar Strauss Giroux, 1983)

Kenneth W. Bilby, *New Star in the Near East*, (New York, The Country Life Press, 1951)

Tuvia Tenenbom, *The Lie They Tell*, (New Jersey, Gefen Publishing House)

Oliver Stone, The Putin Interviews, Oliver Stone Interviews Putin, (New York, Hot Books, 2017)

Who is Trump?

AOD   Donald Trump, *The Art of the Deal*, (New York, Ballantine Books, 1987)

LTBT Corey R. Lewandowski and David N. Bossie, *Let Trump be Trump*, (New York, Center Street, 2017)

TR   Stephen Moore, and Arthur B. Laffer, *Trumponomics*, (New York, St. Martin's Press, 2018)

Books in Israel (Hebrew)

Prime Minister - Ehud Olmert, *In First Person*, (Rishon LeZion, Yedioth Ahronoth, 2018)

Defense Minister - Moshe Arens, *In Defense of Israel*, (Rishon LeZion, Yedioth Ahronoth, 2018)

IDF Chief of Staff - Dan Haloutz, *Straightforward*, (Miskal Yedioth Ahronoth Books and Hemed Books, 2010)

Member of the IDF High Command – Giora Eiland, *Do Not Sleep at Night – autobiography*, (Yedioth Aharonot, 2018)

Chiefs of Mossad

Meir Amit, *Head On*, (Or Yehuda, Israel, Hed Arzi Publishing House, 1999)

Ephrain Halevy, Man in the Shadows, Inside the Middle East Crisis with a Man Who Led the Mossad, (New York, St. Martin's Press, 2006)

Danny Yatom, *The Confidant: From Sayeret Matkal to the Mossad*, (Tel Aviv, Yedioth Ahronoth, Israel, 2009)

Nachik Navoth, *One Man's Mossad*, (Or Yehuda, Kinneret, Zomra-Bitan, 2015)

Shabtai Shavit, *Head of Mossad*, (Rishon Lezion, Yedioth Ahronoth, 2018)

Chiefs of Military Intelligence

Zvi Zamir & Efrat Mass, *With Open Eyes*, (Or Yehuda, Israel, Kineret, Zmora-Bitan, Divir, 2011)

Aharon Zeevi Farkash and Dov Tamari, *To the Best of Our Knowledge*, (Tel Aviv, Israel, Yedioth Ahronoth, 2011)

Amos Gilboa, *Mr. Intelligence – Ahrale Yariv*, (Tel Aviv, Yedioth Ahronoth, 2013)

Shlomo Gazit, *At Key Points of Time*, (Rishon Lezion, Yedioth Ahronoth, 2016)

Chiefs of General Security Service

Carmi Gilon, *Shin-Beth between the Schisms*, (Tel Aviv, Israel Yedioth Ahronoth, 2000)

Dror Moreh, *The Gatekeepers*, (Miskal – Yedioth Ahronoth Books and Hemed Books, 2014)

Israel Military

Giora Eiland, *Do Not Sleep at Night – Autobiography*, (Yediot Aharonot, 2018)

US document printed in Hebrew in Israel

"Central Intelligence Agency, Israel: Foreign Intelligence and Security Services Survey", Translated from English to Hebrew by Yossi Mellman, published in Israel in 1982

Endnotes

[1] The term "Palestinians" is in quotation marks for the simple reason that before the establishment of the state of Israel, the term "Palestinians" referred only to the Jews, and the Arabs were "Arabs". After Israel was established, the Jews became "Israelis", and the Arabs began to call themselves "Palestinians". In other words, the idea of a group of people calling themselves "Palestinians" is just a political ploy to portray Israel as Goliath against a "Palestinian" David. In fact, the opposite is true. Israel is "David" and the 22 Arab countries are "Goliath".

[2] As a matter of fact, Arafat's predecessor, Haj Amin Alhusseini, during the Second World War fled the British Palestine to Germany, and broadcasted over Nazi radio to all Moslems to rebel against the British and to kill the Jews. Moreover, he recruited a Moslem Brigade in the Balkans, and this brigade fought alongside the Nazi forces and participated in killing Jews.

[3] "The Gatekeepers," Dror Moreh, Miskal – Yedioth Ahronoth Books and Hemed Books, 2014

[4] Moshe Dayan was a Defense Minister from a rival party to the Prime Minister's party. He was imposed on the Prime Minister in the days leading to the 1967 war.

[5] Head On, Meir Amit, Hed Arzi Publishing House, Or Yehuda, Israel 1999

[6] The Putin Interviews, Oliver Stone Interviews Putin, Hot Books, New York, 2017

[7] Dare to Win: A Security Policy for Israel, Ofer Shelah, Yediot Ahronoth, Tel Aviv 2015

[8] Do Not Sleep at Night – autobiography, Giora Eiland, Yediot Aharonot, 2018

[9] Envoy to the Middle World, Adventures in Diplomacy, Ambassador George McGhee, Harper & Row Publishers, New York, 1969

[10] "Hasbara" is the Israeli term for national public relations or public diplomacy. The word in Hebrew means "explanation".

[11] "The Snowden Files: The Inside story of the Word's Most Wanted Man", Random House, 2016

[12] New York, Scribner, 2015

[13] By Greg Mortenson and David Oliver, Penguin, 2007

[14] John Russell Young, Around the World with General Grant, (The John Hopkins University Press, 2002)

[15] William H. Seward, Travels Around the World,, edited by Olive Risley Seward (Seward's wife), (New York, D. Appleton and Company, 1873)